KU-747-411

ICONS

Ed. Julius Wiedemann

TASCHEN

KÖLN LONDON LOS ANGELES MADRID PARIS TOKYO

CONTENTS

INTRO

The Best Portfolios are online

As an editor, I am always looking for references for all the publications I have been doing, and after some years I came to the conclusion that there is just one place to look for all I need: the web. And you got to know how to look for things, not to waste your precious hours to find the references you need. This book is just about that. You want the best in terms of navigation, graphics, programming, etc. This is the compact reference you need to use as a buyer of services, reference for clients, inspiration and challenge. We have collected 200 portfolios from more than 30 countries, to give you a broad view of what is available out there. But the book and the fun don't stop here, since you can go through many of the great pages linked to these ones, including the designers and offices that designed them.

You will see that this book focus on creative areas and there is logic for that. First of all are areas where people indeed use the term portfolio, which is the showcase of a production, intending to advertise or amuse potential clients, and other visitors. Secondly, creative areas such as photography, illustration, graphic design, etc, demand many times (or are desired to have as a differential) specific solutions to empower the work shown. Third, there is much more freedom for them to create without thinking about a corporate image or links with specific standards. That allow them to experiment more and discover many times new ways of navigate, display (and play with) works, and finally reach viewers` attention in ways that would be in principle unimaginable.

Doing this book I came to the conclusion the photographers are taking the step forward and creating (and paying for it) exhilarating online showcases. So if you are in this area and are not online, run, and fast. It is understandable in my view why graphic designers have great sites, as they are the ones directly interested in showcasing their work as its best. And they are mostly capable of doing it themselves. There are even ones that just use their site to show their creative capability. Finally, there are all those who believe that the Internet is the medium of the present, and not the future. To believe that the web is the door for capturing people's attention is to believe in the importance and the difference that this medium can make in these professional's lives.

One thing to pay attention to in this book is not just the portfolio, but also the people who did it. Just remembering that the best thing today is that there is basically no distances any more between producer and buyer. It is online and it is all Software. A visit to the sites producers' will prove to be an inspiring trip, as much as the one navigating through this book. What you also get in this book, is a set of parameters that are rarely seen somewhere. Including the costs in hours. Moreover, you get the designers' contacts, and the credits for the programmers. These last ones, rarely mentioned in publications are co-responsible for this revolution, and are seldom recognized for that. They know what is a challenge when a new idea has to be put in practice.

The selection process for a book like this is not easy at all. First of all because the amount of material you have available to see is in certain aspect infinite, as people not just upload new sites daily, but redesign them as well. Secondly, we do not work with submissions or payment. That makes the book much richer, as the reader gets a first class selection, and not just a group of people that could afford to be there. But that makes it much more challenging as well. And we do it tirelessly. We have also looked for ones that have been awarded, but that was not the main focus. You will see that most of them are done with Flash, and I feel that this is something to be seen as natural. One may argue about the time you will need to see the page. But patience is a virtue many times on the net. And connections are always getting better. I go online in many different countries due to my trips, and I know the difference that exists between countries and the services available. In the end, the important thing is the quality of the material selected.

You may ask yourself (and myself as well) why it is necessary to have this printed. Well, we could have this online as well, but here we give you a mobile and instant reference that you can take with you. With wireless connection becoming more popular, it is becoming increasingly easy to go online wherever you are. But a printed reference is still a very good one. We encourage everyone to go online and experience the sites online. And when you do it, you will do it already with your selection criteria. Go for it!

Julius Wiedemann

INTRO

Les meilleurs portfolios sont en ligne

En tant qu'éditeur, j'ai toujours cherché des références pour toutes mes publications et après plusieurs années d'expérience j'en suis venu à la conclusion qu'il n'y a qu'un seul endroit pour tout ce que je cherche : Internet. Mais il faut savoir comment chercher, afin de ne pas perdre de précieuses heures pour trouver les références dont on a besoin. Ce livre sert justement à cela. Vous voulez ce qu'il y a de mieux en termes de navigation, de graphisme, de programmation, etc. Ce livre est la référence compacte qu'il vous faut en tant qu'acheteur de services, de références pour clients, d'inspiration et de défi. Nous avons rassemblé 200 portfolios issus de plus de 30 pays et ce afin de vous offrir un large éventail de ce qu'il est possible de faire de nos jours. Mais ce n'est pas tout puisque vous pourrez aussi ouvrir de nombreuses pages extraordinaires liées à celles présentées ici, dont celles des designers et bureaux qui les ont conçues.

Vous verrez que ce livre est consacré aux domaines créatifs. Il y a plusieurs raisons à cela. Premièrement parce que dans ces domaines, les gens utilisent effectivement le terme portfolio, qui désigne la vitrine d'une production, et que leur intention est de se vendre ou d'amuser des clients potentiels ou d'autres visiteurs. Deuxièmement parce que les domaines créatifs tels que la photographie, l'illustration, le graphisme, etc. exigent bien souvent des solutions spécifiques pour mettre en valeur le travail présenté. Troisièmement parce que dans ces domaines, la liberté de créer sans penser à une identité d'entreprise ou à des liens est bien plus grande. Cela autorise beaucoup plus d'expérimentation et permet très souvent la découverte de nouvelles façons de naviguer, de présenter les œuvres et de jouer avec elles, et en fin de compte d'attirer l'attention des visiteurs de façon presque inimaginable.

Pendant la préparation de ce livre, j'ai constaté que les photographes sont en train de prendre l'ascendant en créant (et payant pour cela) des vitrines en ligne tout simplement époustouflantes. Si vous travaillez dans ce milieu et que vous n'êtes pas en ligne, foncez, et vite. De mon point de vue, il est compréhensible que les designer graphiques aient de formidables sites, puisqu'ils ont tout intérêt à présenter leur travail de la meilleure façon possible. Et la plupart d'entre eux sont capables d'accomplir cette tâche eux-mêmes. Il y en a même qui n'utilisent leur site que pour montrer leurs capacités créatrices. Ce sont finalement tous ceux qui croient qu'Internet est le média d'aujourd'hui et non celui du futur. Croire qu'Internet est une porte pour capturer l'attention des gens, c'est croire en l'importance de ce média et en la différence qu'il peut faire dans la vie de ces professionnels.

Dans ce livre, les portfolios ne sont pas tout. En effet, leurs auteurs méritent également qu'on s'y attarde. En se souvenant que l'avantage aujourd'hui est qu'il n'y fondamentalement plus aucune distance entre producteur et acheteur. Tout est en ligne et tout n'est plus qu'une question de logiciels. Une visite aux créateurs des sites sera un voyage plein d'inspirations, au même titre que de parcourir ce livre. Ce dernier offre également un ensemble de paramètres que l'on retrouve rarement ailleurs. Les coûts horaires par exemple. Figurent aussi les coordonnées des designers et les crédits des programmateurs. Rarement mentionnés dans les publications, ces derniers sont co-responsables de cette révolution et sont rarement reconnus à ce titre. Ils savent le défi que constitue la mise en pratique d'une nouvelle idée.

Le processus de sélection à opérer pour préparer un livre de ce genre n'est guère aisé. D'une part du fait que la quantité de matière disponible est dans une certaine mesure infinie parce que de nouveaux sites sont mis sur le Net chaque jour mais aussi parce que ces derniers sont redesignés. D'autre part parce que nous travaillons sans subventions ni commissions. Cela rend le livre plus riche, puisque la sélection est de première classe et qu'elle ne réunit pas les sites des seules personnes pouvant se permettre d'être mentionnées. Mais cela rend le défi encore plus grand. Et nous y travaillons inlassablement. Nous avons également cherché des sites qui avaient été récompensés mais les distinctions n'étaient pas la priorité. Vous constaterez que la plupart des sites ont été créés avec Flash, ce qui est tout à fait naturel il me semble. Certains pourront se montrer mécontents du temps qu'il faut pour consulter les pages. Mais la patience est bien souvent une vertu sur le Net. Et les connexions font des progrès constants. Lors de mes voyages dans de nombreux pays différents, je suis amené à me connecter à Internet et sais donc quelles différences existent entre les services proposés de par le monde. En fin de compte, l'important est la qualité de la matière sélectionnée.

Vous pourriez vous demander (et me demander par la même occasion) à quoi sert que ce travail soit imprimé. Nous aurions pu le mettre en ligne mais grâce au support papier, vous disposez d'une référence mobile et instantanée que vous pouvez emporter avec vous. Avec la popularisation des connexions sans fil, il est de plus en plus facile de se connecter à Internet où que l'on soit. Mais une référence imprimée reste toujours aussi précieuse. Nous recommandons à tous nos lecteurs de visiter en ligne les sites présentés. Et lorsqu'ils le feront, ils le feront déjà avec leur critères de sélection. Il n'y a plus de temps à perdre, connectez-vous !

Julius Wiedemann

INTRO

Die besten Portfolios findet man online

Als Herausgeber bin ich stets an Referenzen zu meinen Veröffentlichungen interessiert und nach einigen Jahren Erfahrung bin ich zu dem Ergebnis gekommen, dass es nur einen Ort gibt, an dem ich alles finden kann, was ich brauche: das Web. Man hat gelernt, unter minimalem Zeitaufwand die nötigen Referenzen zu finden. Und genau darum geht es in diesem Buch. Sie erwarten höchstes Niveau in Bereichen Navigation, Grafik, Programmierung etc. Dieses komplette Nachschlagewerk ist Inspiration und Herausforderung zugleich, es dient Ihnen zum Einkauf von Internetservice sowie als Kundenreferenz. Wir haben für Sie aus über 30 Ländern 200 Portfolios zusammengestellt, um Ihnen den bestmöglichen Überblick zu verschaffen. Aber weder endet das Buch hier noch hört der Spass schon auf, im Gegenteil, Sie können nun alle diese hervorragend gestalteten Webseiten besuchen – mit zusätzlichem Link zum Designer oder den Studios, die für die Kreation dieser Seiten verantwortlich sind. Wie Sie selbst feststellen werden, behandelt dieses Buch - einer ganz bestimmten Logik folgend - verschiedene kreative Bereiche. Zum Einen gibt es die Bereiche, für welche man den Begriff "Portfolio" benutzt. Dabei handelt es sich um die Darstellung einer Produktion mit der Absicht, Werbung zu machen oder ganz einfach potentielle Kunden sowie anderweitig interessierte Besucher zu unterhalten. Zum Anderen gibt es die kreativen Bereiche wie Fotografie, Illustration, Grafikdesign, etc., die oft ganz spezielle Lösungen zur Funktionalität einer dargestellten Arbeit voraussetzen. Sind die Designer nicht an das Erscheinungsbild eines Unternehmens oder vorgegebene Konzepte gebunden, können sie sich wesentlich mehr künstlerische Freiheit herausnehmen. Dies verschafft ihnen einen grösseren Spielraum zum Experimentieren, sowie die Möglichkeit, neue Wege in der Navigation und dem Display von Arbeiten zu entdecken. Somit wird wiederum die Aufmerksamkeit des Kunden oder Besuchers mit Hilfe von Mitteln gewonnen, die vorher undenkbar gewesen wären.

Während ich an diesem Buch arbeitete, bin ich zu der Erkenntnis gekommen, dass es die Fotografen sind, welche die ganz besonders beeindruckenden Präsentationen online kreieren und dafür auch zahlen. Falls Sie auf diesem Gebiet tätig sein sollten, und noch nicht online sind, dann müssen Sie jetzt handeln, aber ganz schnell. Meiner Meinung nach ist es einleuchtend, dass Grafikdesigner geniale Webseiten vorweisen können, schliesslich haben sie ein ganz besonderes Interesse an der optimalen Darstellung ihrer Arbeiten. Zudem verfügen Sie über die Kenntnisse, ihre Webseite selbst zu gestalten. Es gibt sogar Grafiker, die die Webseite lediglich zur Demonstration ihrer kreativen Fähigkeiten nutzen. Und schliesslich gibt es all diejenigen, die an das Internet als Medium der Gegenwart, aber nicht der Zukunft, glauben. Wenn ich davon überzeugt bin, dass das Web mir Türen zu neuen Kunden öffnet und ich dadurch deren Aufmerksamkeit erreichen kann, dann steht für mich auch fest, welch wichtigen Unterschied dies in der Laufbahn eines jeden Professionellen macht.

In diesem Buch sollte man nicht nur besondere Aufmerksamkeit den einzelnen Portfolios schenken, sondern auch dessen Herstellern. Das Geniale heutzutage ist ja die Tatsache, dass es kaum noch eine Distanz zwischen Hersteller und Käufer gibt. Alles ist online und alles ist Software. Ein Besuch der Webseiten der Designerstudios sowie die Navigation durch dieses Buch wird ganz sicher ein inspirierendes Erlebnis für Sie. Ausserdem bietet Ihnen dieses Werk eine Reihe von Parametern, die Sie kaum woanders finden werden: inklusive die Auflistung der Kosten pro Stunde. Desweiteren finden Sie Kontaktadressen zu den Designern sowie eine Stellungnahme zu den Programmierern. Auch wenn die Programmierer selten erwähnt werden und nur wenig Anerkennung für ihre Arbeit bekommen, sind sie doch im hohen Masse mitverantwortlich für diese Revolution. Sie kennen die Herausforderung, neue Ideen in die Tat umzusetzen.

Die Selektion für ein Buch dieser Art zu treffen, ist keinesfalls einfach. Zum einen ist die Auswahl an Material unbegrenzt, da täglich neue Webseiten erscheinen und diese auch ständig neu gestaltet werden. Zum anderen berechnen wir keine Aufnahmegebühren. Das steigert den Wert des Buches für unseren Leser, der hier eine erstklassige Auswahl vorfindet und nicht nur eine Selektion derjenigen Studios, die es sich leisten können, in unserem Werk vertreten zu sein. Andererseits bedeutet dies natürlich eine grössere Herausforderung für uns und wir stellen uns dieser Herausforderung gerne. Wir haben auch Unternehmen mit Auszeichnungen berücksichtigt, doch dies war in keinem Fall ein ausschlaggebendes Kriterium. Sie werden feststellen, dass die meisten Arbeiten mit Flash erstellt sind – ein natürlicher Umstand, wie ich finde. Sicherlich könnte man sich hierbei über die Zeit streiten, die man benötigt, eine Seite zu öffnen. Doch im Netz erweist sich Geduld oft als eine Tugend. Ausserdem werden die Verbindungen von mal zu mal besser. Da ich viel reise, gehe ich in verschiedenen Ländern online und bin mir der unterschiedlichen Serviceangebote, die in den einzelnen Staaten zur Verfügung stehen, durchaus bewusst. Letztendlich zählt jedoch die Qualität des Angebotes.

Sie mögen sich die Frage stellen (und ich mir auch), welchen Sinn es eigentlich hat, all dies niederzuschreiben. Natürlich könnten wir diese Fülle an Informationen ebenfalls online bringen, aber in Buchform geben wir Ihnen die Möglichkeit, stets eine Referenz zur Hand zu haben, die Sie überall mithinnehmen können. Durch die ständige Zunahme kabelloser Verbindungen wird es immer einfacher, online zu gehen, ganz gleich, wo Sie sich befinden. Trotz allem ist eine gedruckte Referenz nie verkehrt. Wir ermutigen Sie, online zu gehen und Ihre Erfahrung mit den ausgewählten Webseiten zu machen. Und wenn Sie dies tun, dann wissen Sie schon genau, worauf es ankommt und nach welchen Kriterien Sie Ihre Auswahl zu treffen haben. Also dann, los geht's!

Julius Wiedemann

3:AM DESIGN

CANADA

www.3am-design.com

2001

Concept

Caffeine is a harsh mistress. //// La caféine est une maîtresse sévère. //// Koffein ist eine widerspenstige Geliebte.

Infos

Design: 3:AM Design Inc. /// **Programming:** Jody Poole. /// **Awards:** the World Heavyweight Belt. /// **Tools:** html, Macromedia Flash, Quicktime, Adobe Affter Effects. /// **Cost:** 25 hours. /// **Maintenance:** 2 hours per month.

808INC.

USA

www.808inc.com

2004

Concept

Full-bodied, organic, intuitive presentation of variously formatted creative content. //// Présentation corsée, organique et intuitive de contenus créatifs de formats différents. //// Eine dichte, organische und intuitive Präsentation von kreativen Inhalten mit unterschiedlicher Formatierung.

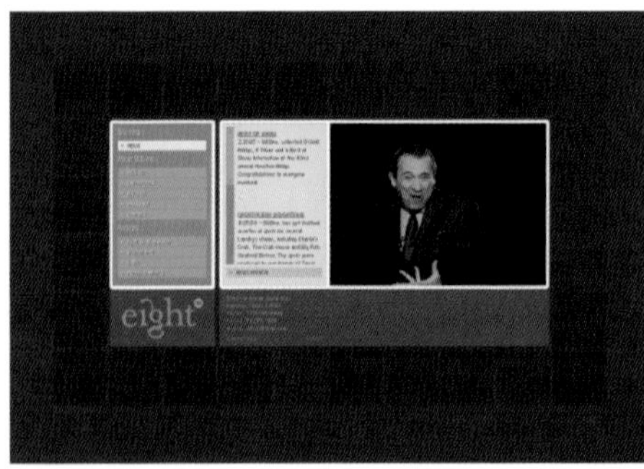

Infos

Design: Joshua Davis <www.joshuadavis.com> and The Department of Notation. /// **Programming:** Branden Hall (The Department of Notation). /// **Tools:** Macromedia Flash. /// **Cost:** $50K. /// **Maintenance:** 3 hours per month.

3RD EDGE COMMUNICATIONS

USA

www.3rdedge.com

2004

Concept

Our approach to design is revealed in the beautiful simplicity of this site. //// Notre approche du design se traduit par la belle simplicité de ce site. //// Unser Anspruch an Design spiegelt sich in der wunderschönen Einfachheit dieser Seite wieder.

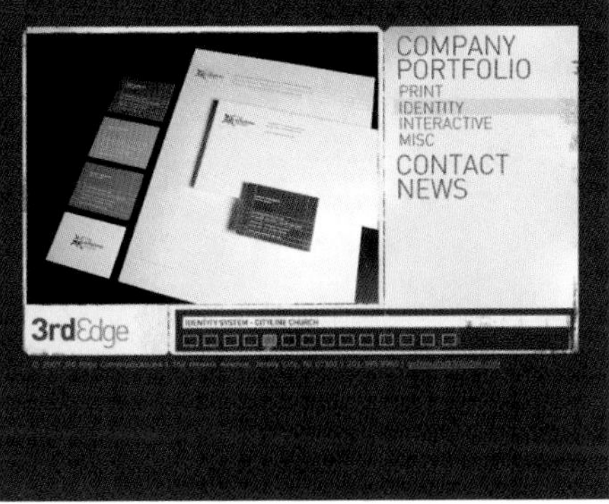

Infos

Design: 3rd Edge Communications. /// **Programming:** Manny Dilone. /// **Tools:** html, Macromedia Flash. /// **Cost:** 120-140 hours /// **Maintenance:** 4 hours per month.

417NORTH

USA

www.417north.com

2004

Concept

Simple and clean. Intuitive and personal. //// Simple et net. Intuitif et personnel. //// Einfach und übersichtlich. Intuitiv und persönlich.

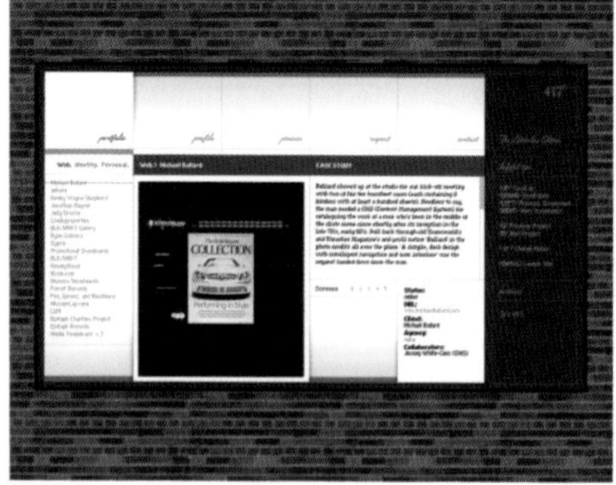

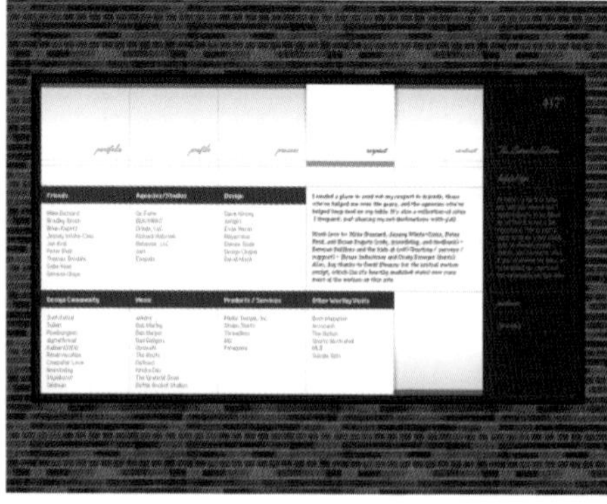

Infos

DESIGN AND PROGRAMMING: Greg Huntoon (Go Farm) <www.gofarm.la>. /// **AWARDS:** Reboot Winner, TINY (Site of the Month), FWA (Site of the Day). /// **TOOLS:** Macromedia Flash, xml. /// **COST:** 200 hours. /// **MAINTENANCE:** 5-10 hours per month.

777RUN

FRANCE

www.777run.com

2000

Concept

The blacker you have, the more hope you find. //// Tant qu'il y a du noir, il y a de l'espoir. //// Je dunkler die Nacht, desto mehr Hoffnung gibt es.

Infos

DESIGN: RUN (Semper Fi) <www.semperultimo.com>. /// **PROGRAMMING:** Bens and GUS (Semper Fi). /// **AWARDS:** Flash Forward, Flash Festival. /// **TOOLS:** Macromedia Flash. /// **COST:** 130 hours. /// **MAINTENANCE:** 1 hour per month.

AARON JASINSKI

USA

www.aaronjasinski.com

2004

Concept

An elegant and minimal presentation of a large body of work that doesn't distract from the focus of the site. //// Une présentation élégante et minimale qui n'éclipse pas le vaste ensemble des travaux mis en ligne. //// Eine elegante und minimalistische Präsentation eines umfassenden Portfolios, das jedoch keinesfalls vom Schwerpunkt der Seite ablenkt.

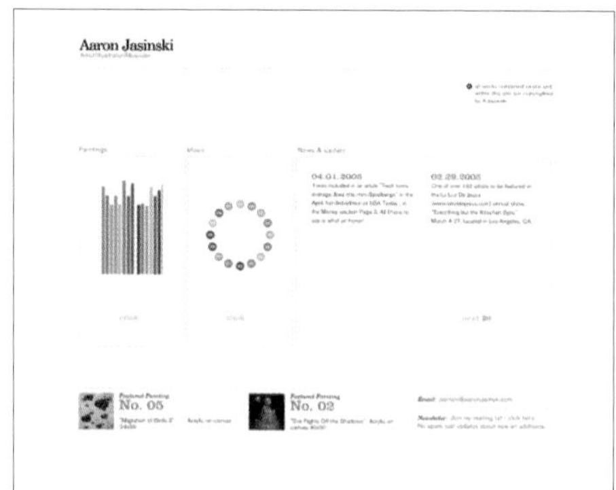

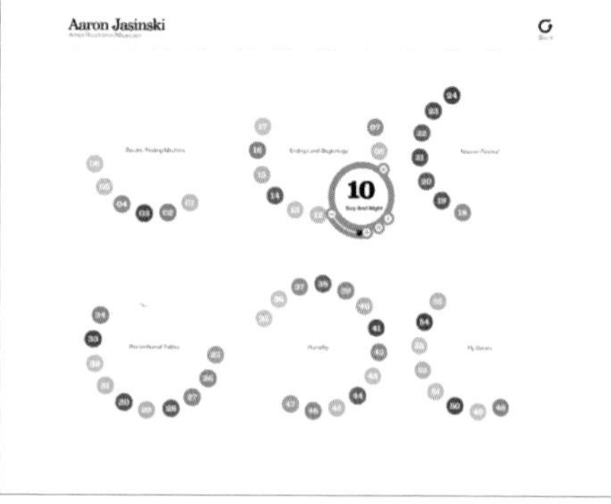

Infos

DESIGN: Craig Erickson (Section Seven) <www.sectionseven.com>. /// **PROGRAMMING:** Jason Keimig. /// **AWARDS:** TINY (Featured Site), FWA (Site Of The Day), TAXI (Site of the Day). /// **TOOLS:** Macromedia Flash. /// **COST:** 100 hours. /// **MAINTENANCE:** 0-5 hours per month.

ACHT FRANKFURT

GERMANY

www.acht-frankfurt.de

2004

Concept

The company website for the post production company 'Acht Frankfurt' combines the principle of movies with the interactivity of the Net. The current portfolio presents itself in form of a dynamic show reel. //// Le site de la société de post-production « Acht Frankfurt » associe le concept film avec l'interactivité du Net. Le portfolio présenté prend la forme d'une bande démo dynamique. //// Die Corporate Site der Postproduction "Acht Frankfurt" verbindet das Prinzip mit der Interaktivität des Netzes. Das Portfolio der Firma wird als dynamisches Showreel präsentiert.

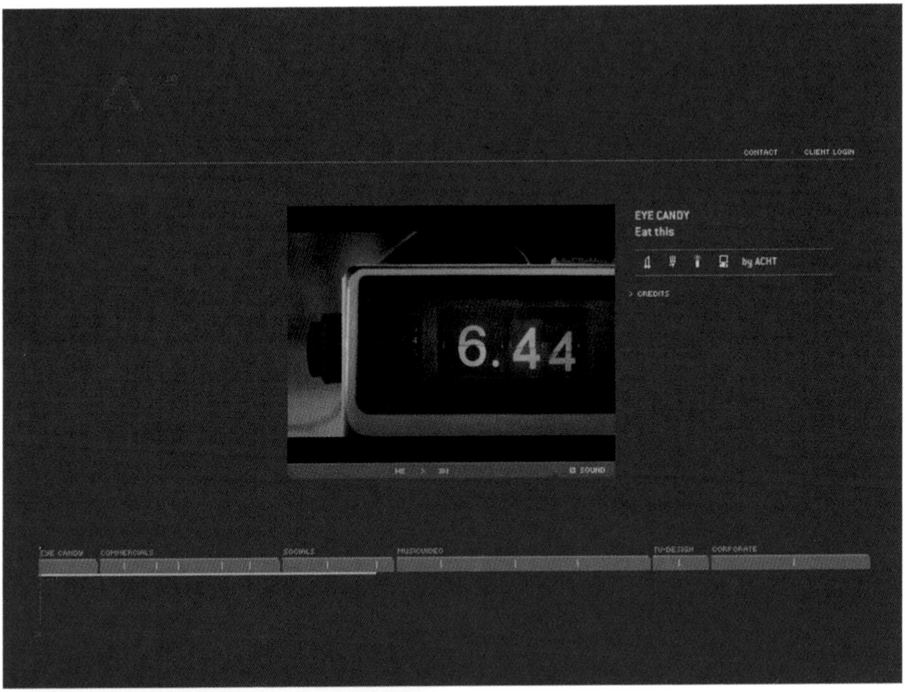

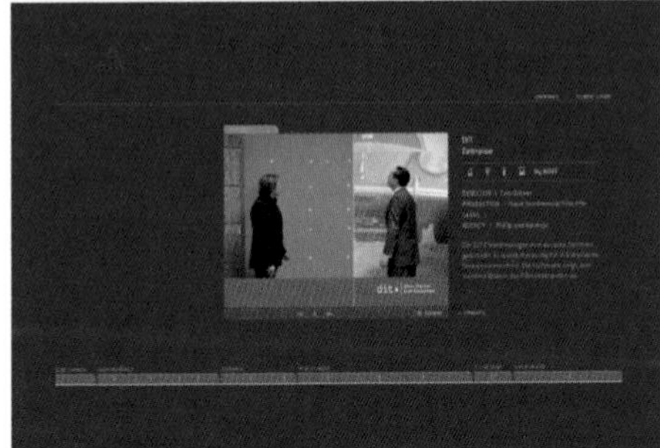

Infos

Design: Scholz & Volkmer <www.s-v.de>. /// **Programming:** Duc-Thuan Bui and Manfred Kraft. /// **Awards:** Art Directors Club Berlin, Best of Business-to-Business-Award (Bonn), Golden Awards (Montreux), Clio, One Show Interactive, Cannes Cyber Lion, iF Communication Design, I.D. Interactive Media Design Review, and more. /// **Tools:** html, Macromedia Flash, xml, music, film. /// **Cost:** n/a. /// **Maintenance:** n/a.

ACIDTWIST GALLERY

CANADA

www.acidtwist.com

2004

Concept

The concept was to take the phrase "image gallery" literally - it was inspired by photographs of art gallery walls. //// L'idée a été de prendre l'expression « galerie d'images » au sens littéral. Elle nous a été inspirée par des photos de murs de galeries d'art. //// Das Konzept bestand darin, eine "Bildergalerie" im direkten Wortsinn umzusetzen - inspiriert durch Fotografien einer Kunstgalerie.

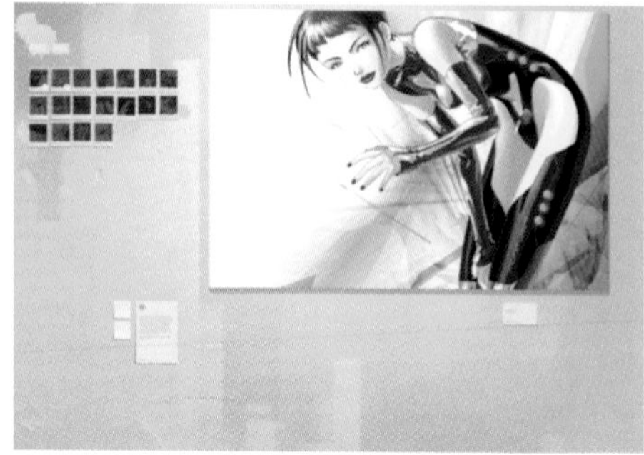

Infos

Design: Tavish (Acidtwist). /// **Tools:** Macromedia Flash, xml, html. /// **Cost:** 60 hours. /// **Maintenance:** 1-2 hours per month. New images are uploaded to a folder on the server, and their filenames are added to an xml file. The Flash front-end adapts automatically to the image dimensions.

AERIFORM VISCOM

UK

www.aeriform.co.uk

2003

Concept

The graphic maps coupled with bold and complimentary colours created a striking yet simple site with intuitive interface that delivers the work with minimum fuss. //// Le graphique des photos associé à des couleurs vives et flatteuses a été utilisé pour créer un site tout à la fois marquant, simple et doté d'une interface intuitive présentant les travaux de façon fluide. //// Die Kartensprache in Verbindung mit sowohl kraftvollen als auch Farben wurde dazu genutzt, eine beeindruckende Seite mit interaktivem Interface zu kreieren, die die Arbeiten unter möglichst wenig Aufwand präsentiert.

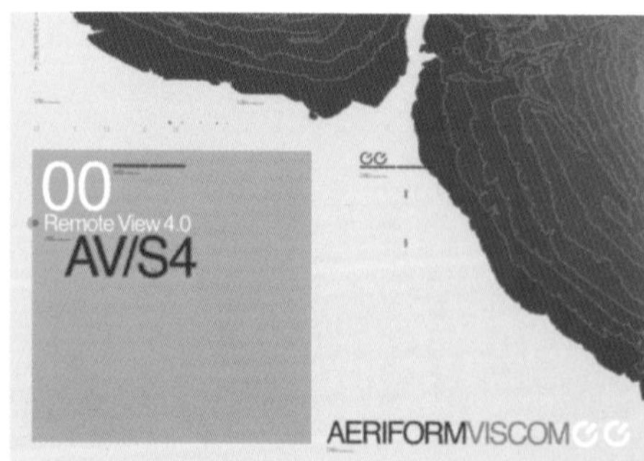

Infos

Design and Programming: Aeriform Viscom. /// **Tools:** html, Macromedia Flash. /// **Cost:** 48 hours per month.

ACTIVATE.RU

RUSSIA

www.activate.ru

2004

Concept

Something positive, straight and emotional... The main concept was to explain my vision of the contemporary design's mission. //// Quelque chose de positif, de net et d'émotionnel... L'idée principale était d'expliquer ma vision de la mission du design contemporain. //// Etwas Positives, Direktes und Emotionales... Das Hauptkonzept bestand darin, meine Vision in Bezug auf die aktuellen Tendenzen des Designs wiederzugeben.

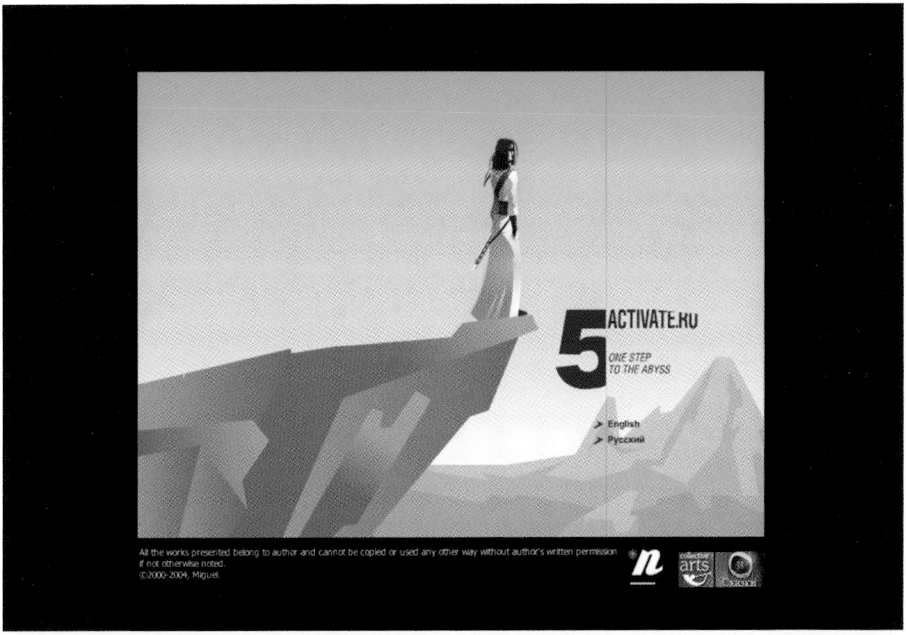

Infos

Design and Programming: Mikhail Ivanov. /// **Awards:** Netdiver Design Forte, ComputerSpace, and several minor awards. ///
Tools: html, Macromedia Flash. /// **Cost:** 50-60 hours. /// **Maintenance:** several hours per month to upload new images and update information.

MONSIEUR A

FRANCE

www.adenek.com

2004

Concept

A search to give a great importance to visual, making a visual immersive design. //// Une envie de donner une grande importance au visuel, en concevant un design immersif visuel. //// Der Versuch, besonderes Augenmerk dem visuellen Aspekt zu schenken, völlig eingetaucht in ein visuelles Design.

Infos

Design and Programming: Mathieu Zylberait (Monsieur A). /// **Awards:** Moluv's Picks, Plasticpilots, Netdiver, DOPE, NewWebPick. /// **Tools:** Macromedia Flash. /// **Cost:** 2 weeks. /// **Maintenance:** 2 hours per month.

AD PLANET

SINGAPORE

www.adplanet.com.sg

2002

Concept

The mood of the website is strong, inspirational and emotive, to reflect a client who is fiercely proud of their local (Singaporean) origins and their achievements. //// L'atmosphère du site est intense, inspirée et émotionnelle, elle est à l'image d'un client viscéralement fier de ses origines singapouriennes et de ses succès. //// Die Stimmung der Webseite ist stark, inspirierend und motivierend und reflektiert einen Kunden, der besonders stolz auf seine (singaporeanische) Herkunft und seine Erfolgserlebnisse ist.

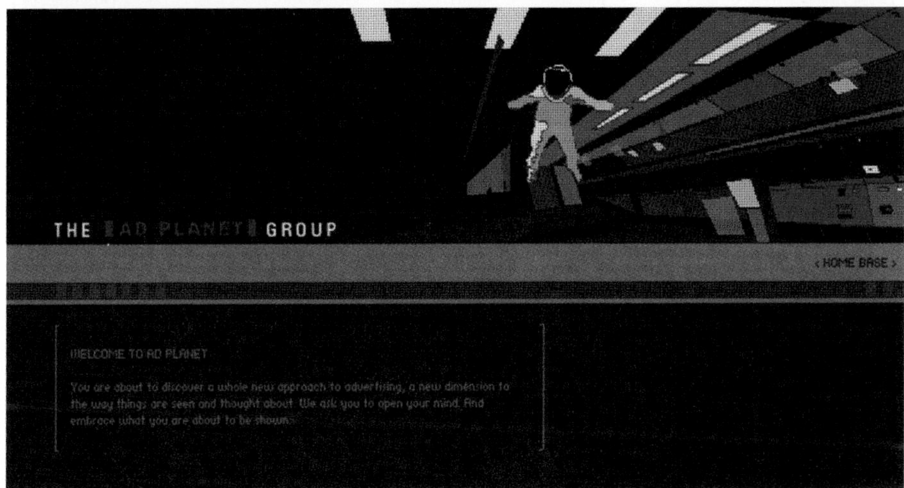

Infos

Design: Kinetic Interactive <www.kinetic.com.sg>. /// **Programming:** Sean Lam. /// **Awards:** One Show Interactive, New York Festival, Singapore Creative Circle, FWA. /// **Tools:** Macromedia Flash, Macromedia Dreamweaver, Adobe Photoshop, Soundedit. /// **Cost:** 70 hours. /// **Maintenance:** 1 hour per month.

ALBERT BOULLET

NORWAY

www.albert.st

2002

Concept

The site has been made as minimally as possible in order that the photographs are the main feature and are themselves the design. //// Le site est aussi minimal que possible afin que les photos en constituent le caractère principal et le design. //// **Die Seite wurde so minimalistisch wie möglich gestaltet, um der Fotografie volle Aufmerksamkeit zu schenken. Die Fotos sind das Design der Webseite.**

Infos

DESIGN: Screenplay <www.screenplay.no>, and Hei <www.hei.no>. /// **AWARDS:** Web by Visuel (Gold - Best Presentation). /// **TOOLS:** Macromedia Flash, xml. /// **COST:** no cost, exchanged jobs. /// **MAINTENANCE:** no cost, I maintain the site myself.

ALLEN VENABLES PHOTO

MALTA

www.allenvenables.com

2003

Concept

To showcase the portfolio of Allen Venables we had to somehow capture the dry sense of Allen's humor. //// Pour présenter le portfolio d'Allen Venables, nous avons dû capturer en quelque sorte l'aspect pince-sans-rire de son humour. //// **Um das Porfolio von Allen Venables präsentieren zu können, haben wir versucht, Allens trockenen Humor geltend zu machen.**

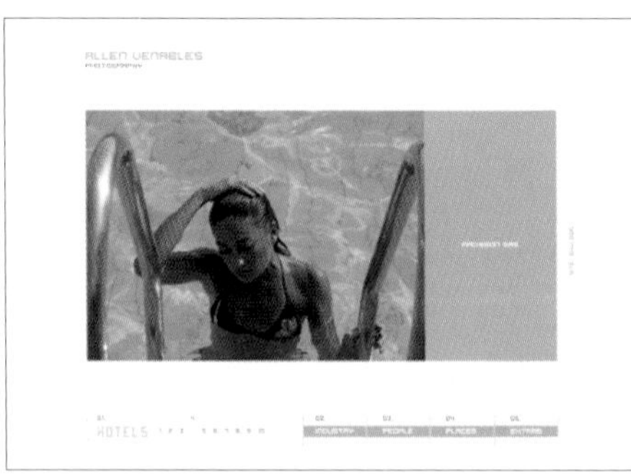

Infos

DESIGN: Ren Spiteri (Virtual Bulldog) <www.virtualbulldog.com>. /// **AWARDS:** Bombshock, FWA, Best Website Award, Worldwide Web Awards. /// **TOOLS:** Macromedia Flash. /// **COST:** 1 month.

MY EYES, YOUR WORLD

USA

www.amivitale.com

2001

Concept

A fast, clean portfolio where the images take precedence, and the navigation invites the user to explore. //// Un portfolio rapide et clair où les images prennent l'ascendant sur le reste et où la navigation invite l'utilisateur à l'exploration. //// Ein schnelles, klares Portfolio, bei denen wir den Bilder Vortritt lassen und mit unserem Navigationssystem den Besucher auf eine Erlebnissreise einladen.

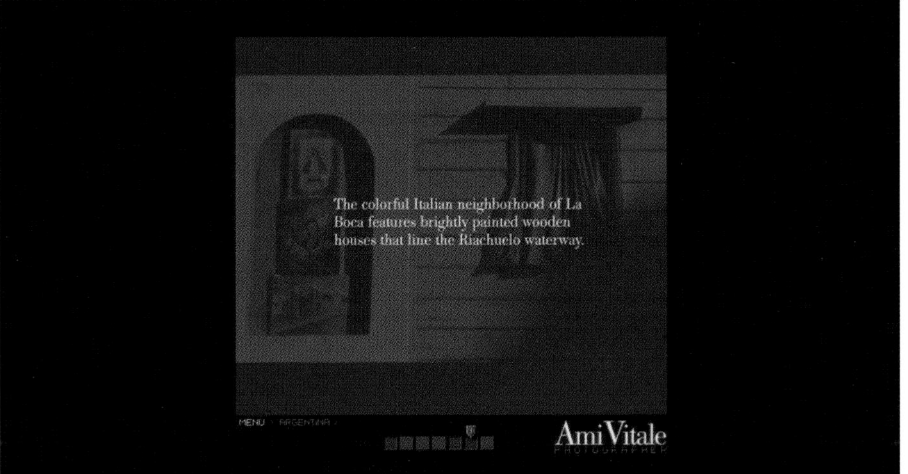

Infos

Design and Programming: Jayson Singe (Neon Sky Creative Media) <www.neonsky.com>. /// **Awards:** Photo District News "PIX" Digital Imaging Competition (Best Site), Flash Film Festival Amsterdam, Flash Forward. /// **Tools:** Macromedia Flash,html, Adobe Photoshop, Apple Final Cut Pro. /// **Cost:** 100 hours. /// **Maintenance:** 1 hour per month.

ANATOL KOTTE

GERMANY

www.anatolkotte.com

2004

Concept

The minimalist design and navigation of the site give a dynamism to the contents and adds a feeling of life to it. //// Le design et la navigation minimalistes du site confèrent du dynamisme au contenu et lui donnent un supplément d'âme. //// Durch sein reduziertes Design und das smarte Navigationskonzept lässt das Portfolio den Bildern den Vortritt, das dynamische Verhalten der Navigation addiert ein subtiles Gefühl von Lebendigkeit.

Infos

Design: Sven Loskill <www.slad.de> and Emjot <www.emjot.de>. // **Programming:** Emjot. /// **Tools:** Macromedia Flash, xml, php, MySQL. /// **Cost:** Design and Concept: 56 hours. Flash Development: 98 hours. Content Management System Development: 120 hours. /// **Maintenance:** since we have a customized backend solution to implement our pictures, it depends on the amount of new content to be put online. One new picture takes about a minute. That includes uploading, downsampling and positioning.

ANNA MOLLER PHOTOGRAPHY

USA

www.annamoller.net

2003

Concept

A sense of simplicity and intimacy, which compliments the mood of the photographs. //// Un sens de la simplicité et de l'intimité, qui vient en complément de l'atmosphère qui se dégage des photos. //// **Ein Sinn für Einfachheit und Intimität, als Ergänzung zur Stimmung der einzelnen Fotografien.**

Infos

DESIGN AND PROGRAMMING: Bela Spohrer (ProTrigga Design) <www.protrigga.com>. /// **TOOLS:** Macromedia Flash. /// **COST:** 40 hours. /// **MAINTENANCE:** 1 hour per month.

ANTON WATTS PHOTOGRAPHY UK

www.antonwatts.com 2004

Concept

Concise navigation and clean graphic feel. //// Une navigation concise et un sens net du graphisme. //// Präzise Navigation und ein eindeutiges Gefühl für Grafik.

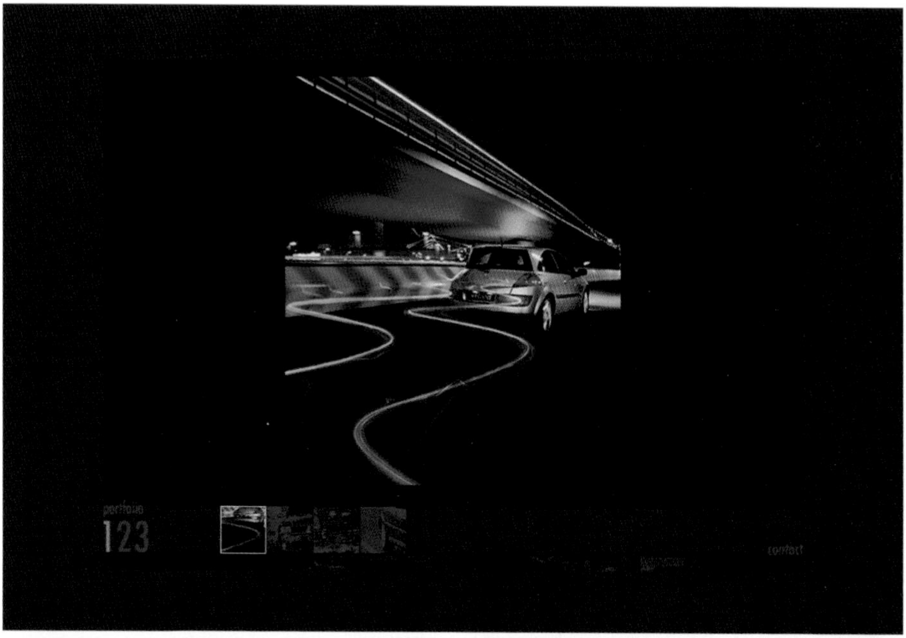

Infos

DESIGN: Chris Christodoulou (Saddington & Baynes) <www.sb-showcase.com>. /// **PROGRAMMING:** Duncan Hart. ///
TOOLS: Adobe Photoshop, Macromedia Flash. /// **COST:** £3,000.

ANTTI VIITALA PHOTO

FINLAND

www.anttiviitala.com

2004

Concept

We are giving the potential client a possibility to view the photographs easily and without any distractions. //// Nous donnons à nos clients potentiels la possibilité de voir les photos facilement et sans entrave. //// Wir geben unserem potentiellen Kunden die Möglichkeit, sich unsere Fotos auf einfachem Wege und ohne Störfaktoren ansehen zu können.

Infos

DESIGN: Saddington & Baynes <www.sb-showcase.com>. /// **TOOLS:** Macromedia Flash. /// **COST:** 1 month. /// **MAINTENANCE:** 1 hour per month.

BOOGIE PHOTOGRAPHER

USA

www.artcoup.com

2002

Concept

Presents both features and daily postings in an easy-to-use/navigate, fully-automated way. //// Présente des photos et des postages quotidiens dans un cadre facile à naviguer et complètement automatisé. //// Präsentation von sowohl bestehendem Material als auch täglichen Neuveröffentlichungen, leichte Anwendbarkeit und Navigation, alles vollautomatisch.

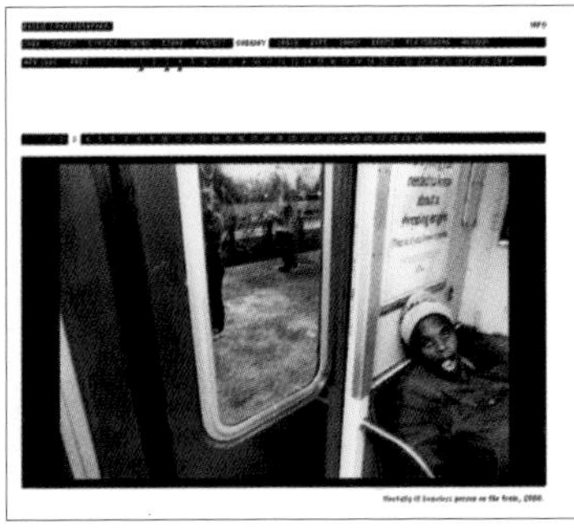

Infos

DESIGN: Dead By Design <www.deadbydesign.us>. /// **PROGRAMMING:** Rastko Samurovic <www.reakcija.com>. /// **TOOLS:** Macromedia Flash, xml, asp, database. /// **COST:** 150 hours. /// **MAINTENANCE:** 5 hours per month.

AR2DESIGN

MEXICO

www.ar2design.com

2004

Concept

The clean and simple of an image can make a better look of things. //// La précision et la simplicité d'une image peuvent donner un meilleur aspect aux choses. //// Klarheit und Einfachheit eines Bildes können ein besseres Erscheinungsbild bewirken.

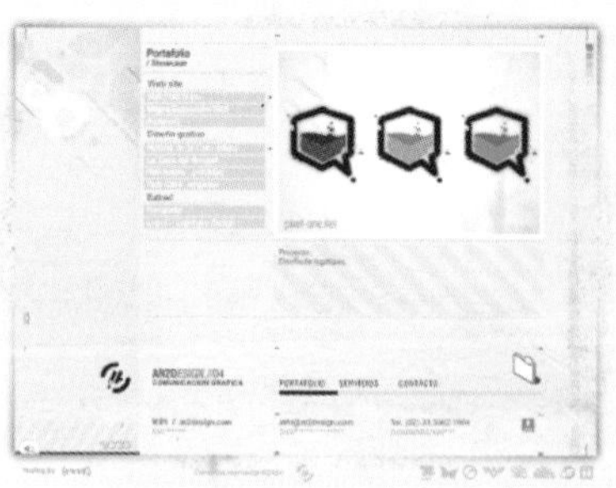

Infos

DESIGN: Arturo Esparza (AR2Design). /// **AWARDS:** TINY, e-Creative, DOPE. /// **TOOLS:** html, Action Script, Macromedia Flash, Adobe Photoshop. /// **CONTENT:** music from TYCHO (The Science of Patterns EP), and some images from my portfolio. /// **COST:** 60 hours. /// **MAINTENANCE:** 5 hours per month.

AREADESIGN

SWITZERLAND

www.areadesign.ch

2003

Concept

Drag and drop the head to activate robots... //// Glissez-déposez la tête pour activer les robots... //// Drag und Drop zur Aktivierung von Robotern.

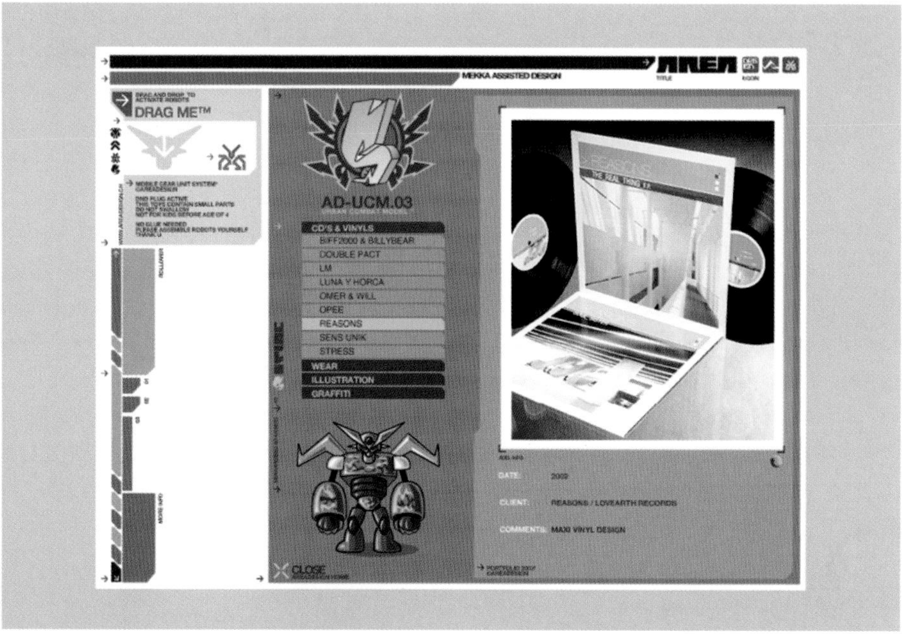

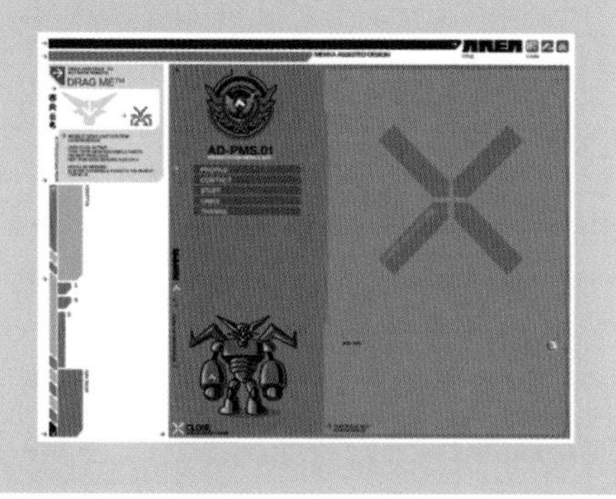

Infos

Design: Alberto Russo and Pascal Wicht (AREADESIGN). /// **Programming:** Luigi Iannitelli. /// **Awards:** FWA, Moluv's Picks, Bombshock, Golden Web Award. /// **Tools:** action script, html, Macromedia Flash, music. /// **Cost:** 1 month.

ARJAN VERSCHOOR

THE NETHERLANDS

www.arjanverschoor.nl

2004

Concept

A spatial and custom-build website which has to deal with many images and which is easy to manage. //// Un site Web spatial sur mesure contenant de nombreuses images et facile à utiliser. //// Eine räumlich strukturierte und kundenspezifisch aufgebaute Webseite mit viel Bildmaterial. Einfach anzuwenden.

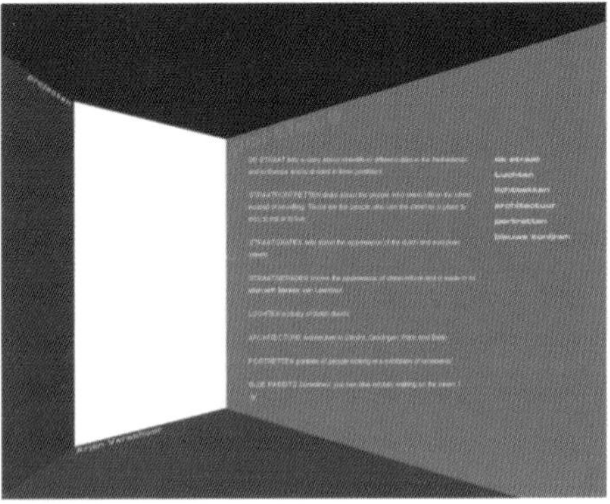

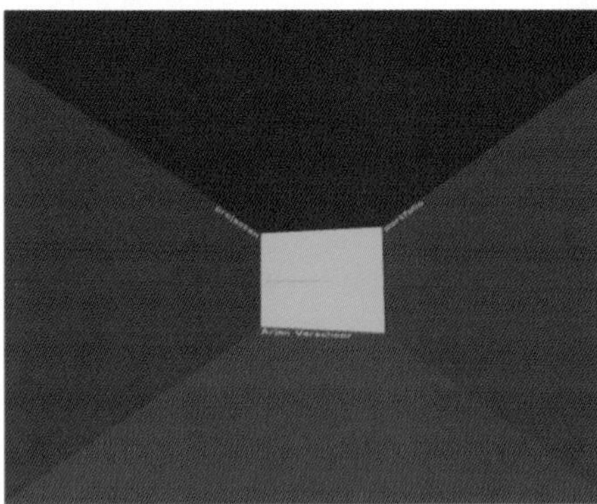

Infos

Design: Gruppen Grafische Vormgeving <www.henkgruppen.nl>. /// **Programming:** Henk Gruppen. /// **Tools:** Macromedia Flash. ///
Cost: 30 hours. /// **Maintenance:** 2 hours per month.

ARNE & CARLOS

NORWAY

www.arne-carlos.com

2004

Concept

Looking at fashion with color. //// La mode côté couleur. //// Mode unter dem Aspekt der Farbe betrachtet.

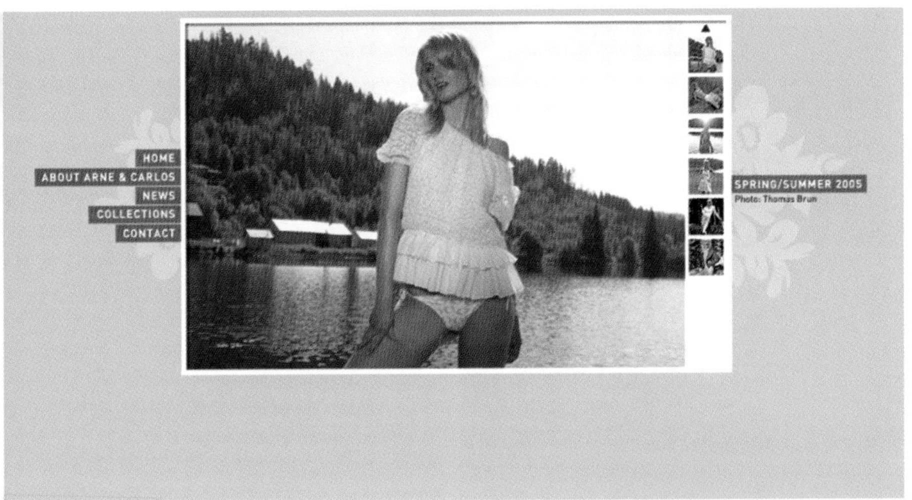

Infos

Design and Programming: Are Bu Vindenes <www.arervindenes.com>. /// **Tools:** Macromedia Flash, html. ///
Cost: 50 hours. /// **Maintenance:** 1 hour per month.

ASMALLPERCENT

USA

www.asmallpercent.com

2001

Concept

Ease of use - utilitarian simplicity. //// Simplicité d'utilisation, simplicité fonctionnelle. //// Problemlos anzuwenden - nutzerfreundliche Einfachheit.

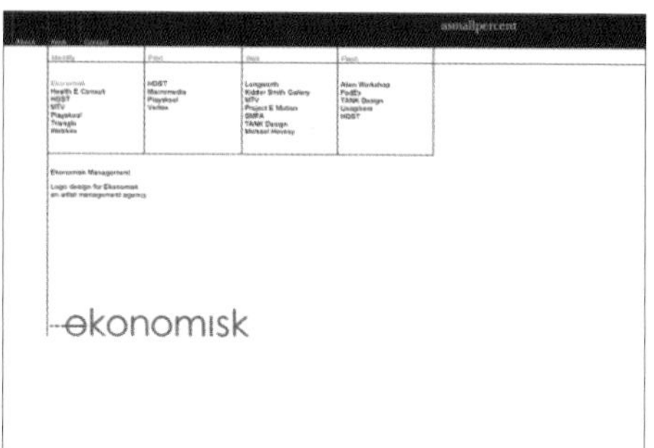

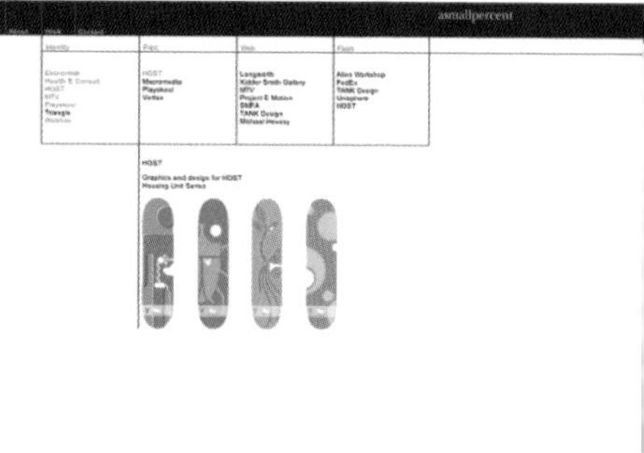

Infos

Design and Programming: Tim Ferguson Sauder (Asmallpercent). /// **Tools:** html, Macromedia Flash. /// **Cost:** 20 hours. /// **Maintenance:** 1 hour per month.

BEPOSITIVE DESIGN

THAILAND/USA

www.bepositivedesign.com

2001

Concept

The website acts as an empty plate to be filled with a colorful food. //// Ce site Web est comme une assiette vide qu'il faut remplir avec de la nourriture colorée. //// Die Webseite steht für einen leeren Teller, der mit farbigem Essen gefüllt werden möchte.

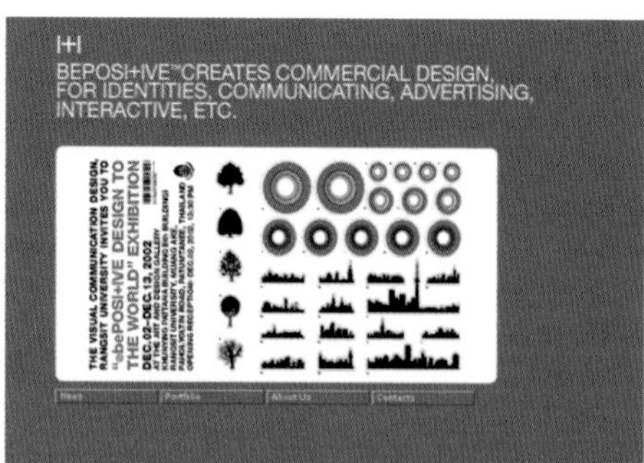

Infos

Design: Tnop and Bepositive Design. /// **Programming:** Akwit Vongsa-ngiam and Tnop Wangsillapakun. /// **Tools:** html, Macromedia Flash, dhtml. /// **Cost:** 200 hours. /// **Maintenance:** 0-5 hours per month.

ATTILA HARTWIG

GERMANY

www.attilahartwig.com

2003

Concept

A typical client - photographer situation. //// Un client typique - le cas d'un photographe. //// Eine typische Situation zwischen Kunde und Fotograf.

Infos

Design: 52NORD Designbuero <www.52nord.de>. /// **Programming:** Sven Stüber. /// **Awards:** FWA, e-Creative. /// **Tools:** html, Macromedia Flash, music, screenfonts. /// **Cost:** 40 hours. /// **Maintenance:** 8 hours every 6 months.

BLUEMAN

BRAZIL

www.blueman.com.br

2004

Concept

Modern, following the brand's visual identity. //// Moderne, à l'image de l'identité visuelle de la marque. //// **Modern, der visuellen Identität von Markenprodukten folgend.**

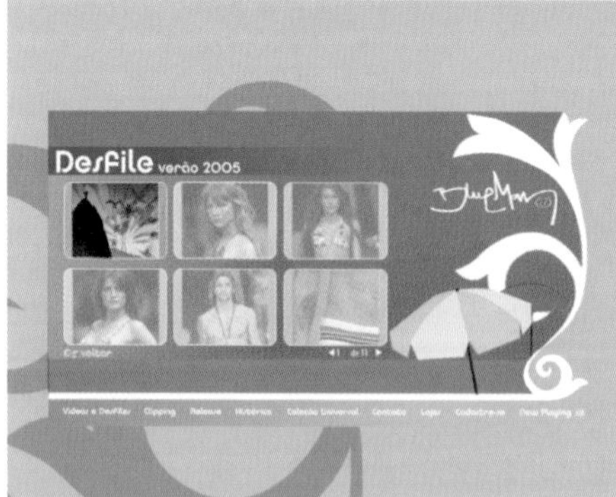

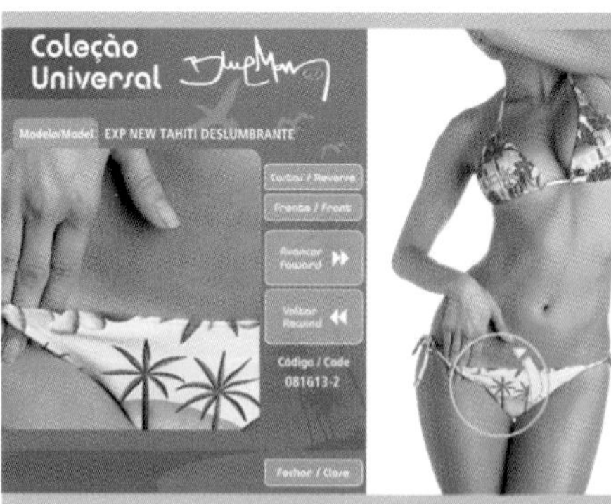

Infos

DESIGN: ZonaInternet <www.zonainternet.com>. /// **PROGRAMMING:** André Tenenbaum (ZonaInternet). /// **TOOLS:** html, Macromedia Flash, action-script, xml, asp, music, film. /// **COST:** 45 days. /// **MAINTENANCE:** 10 hours per month.

BORIS POLJICANIN PHOTO

CROATIA

www.borispoljicanin.com

2003

Concept

The concept is to present the eternal photographers' obsessions: light vs. dark and sharp vs. blurry by implementing its elements into the site's contents and navigation. //// L'idée est de présenter les obsessions éternelles des photographes : luminosité contre obscurité et net contre flou, en mettant en œuvre ces éléments dans le contenu et la navigation du site. //// Die wohlbekannte Besessenheit der Fotografen bestimmt das Konzept dieser Seite: Licht und Dunkelheit, Schärfe und Unschärfe. Sie sind elementäre Bestandteile der Seite und ihrer Navigation.

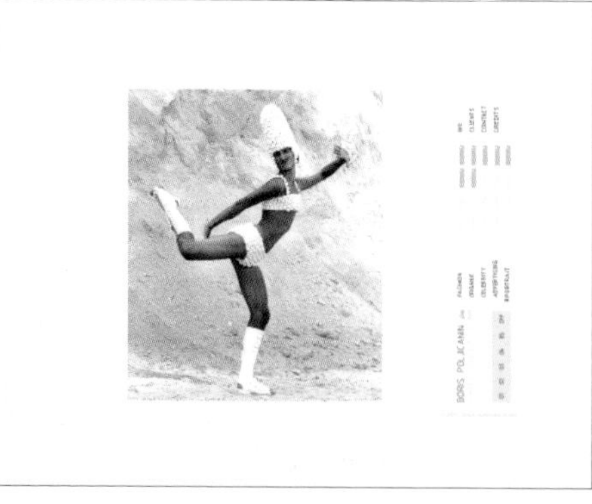

Infos

DESIGN AND PROGRAMMING: Igor Skunca (Invent: Multimedia Studio) <www.invent.hr>. /// **AWARDS:** Croatian Advertising Festival, Magdalena International Advertising Festival of Creative Communications. /// **TOOLS:** Macromedia Flash, Macromedia Dreamweaver, Adobe Photoshop. /// **COST:** 100 hours. /// **MAINTENANCE:** 4 hours per month.

BOXER

UK

www.boxer.uk.com

2004

Concept

Designed primarily to reflect our personality and identity. All imagery shows everyday situations with quirky twists. //// Conçu à l'origine pour révéler notre personnalité et notre identité. Toutes les images illustrent des situations quotidiennes agrémentées de pirouettes excentriques. //// In erster Linie zur Demonstration unserer Persönlichkeit und Identität designed. Das Bildmaterial reflektiert alltägliche Situationen mit verrückten Wendungen.

Infos

DESIGN: Boxer in conjunction with EngageStudio <www.engagestudio.com>. /// **PROGRAMMING:** James Stone (EngageStudio). /// **TOOLS:** Macromedia Flash, html. /// **COST:** £10-15k. /// **MAINTENANCE:** 2-3 days per month.

BEN WITTNER

GERMANY

www.bwausg.de

2004

Concept

Minimalist, clear, user-friendly website as engaging tool with the purpose of spotlighting the photography and graphic design work. //// Un site minimaliste, clair et convivial ayant pour but d'attirer l'attention sur des travaux de photographie et de graphisme. //// **Minimalistische, klare und benutzerfreundliche Webseite, die auf überzeugende Art und Weise Fotografie und Grafikdesign ins Rampenlicht rückt.**

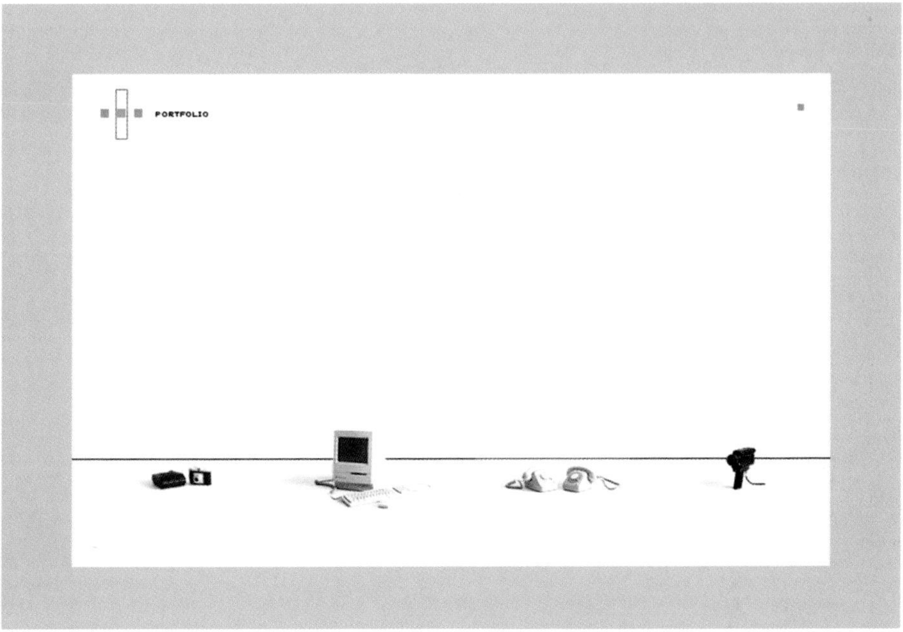

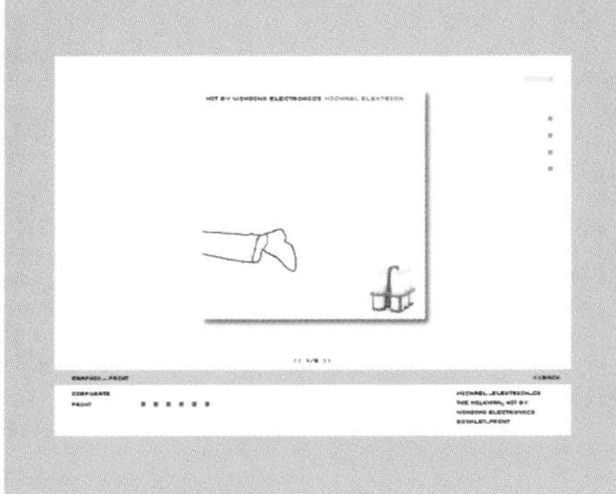

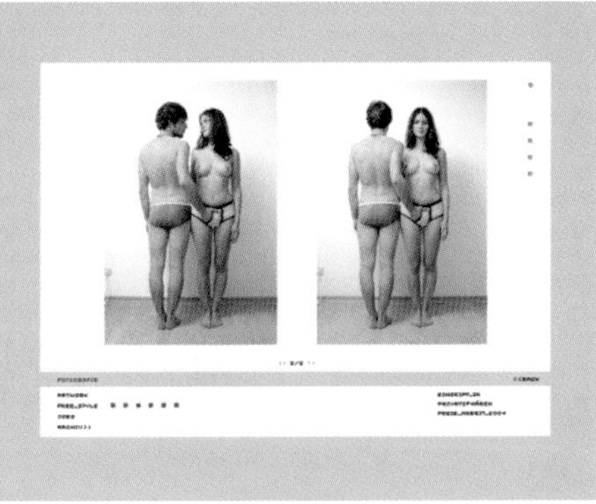

Infos

DESIGN AND PROGRAMMING: Ben Wittner. /// TOOLS: Macromedia Flash, html, Quicktime. /// COST: uncounted number of hours. /// MAINTENANCE: depending on the works to update.

CALIBREPICS

SINGAPORE

www.calibrepics.com

2004

Concept

The idea was transforming your ideas into reality. Hence, a drawing approach was used for the navigation where users mark where they wish to go. //// Le concept de ce portfolio est de faire de vos idées une réalité. C'est ainsi que la navigation s'inspire du dessin, les utilisateurs devant utiliser un marqueur pour indiquer où ils souhaitent se rendre. //// Das Portfolio zielt darauf ab, die Ideen seiner Webseiten-Besucher in die Realität umzusetzen. Eine Zeichnung ermöglicht es dem Besucher genau dort zu markieren, wohin er sich innerhalb des Navigationssystems bewegen möchte.

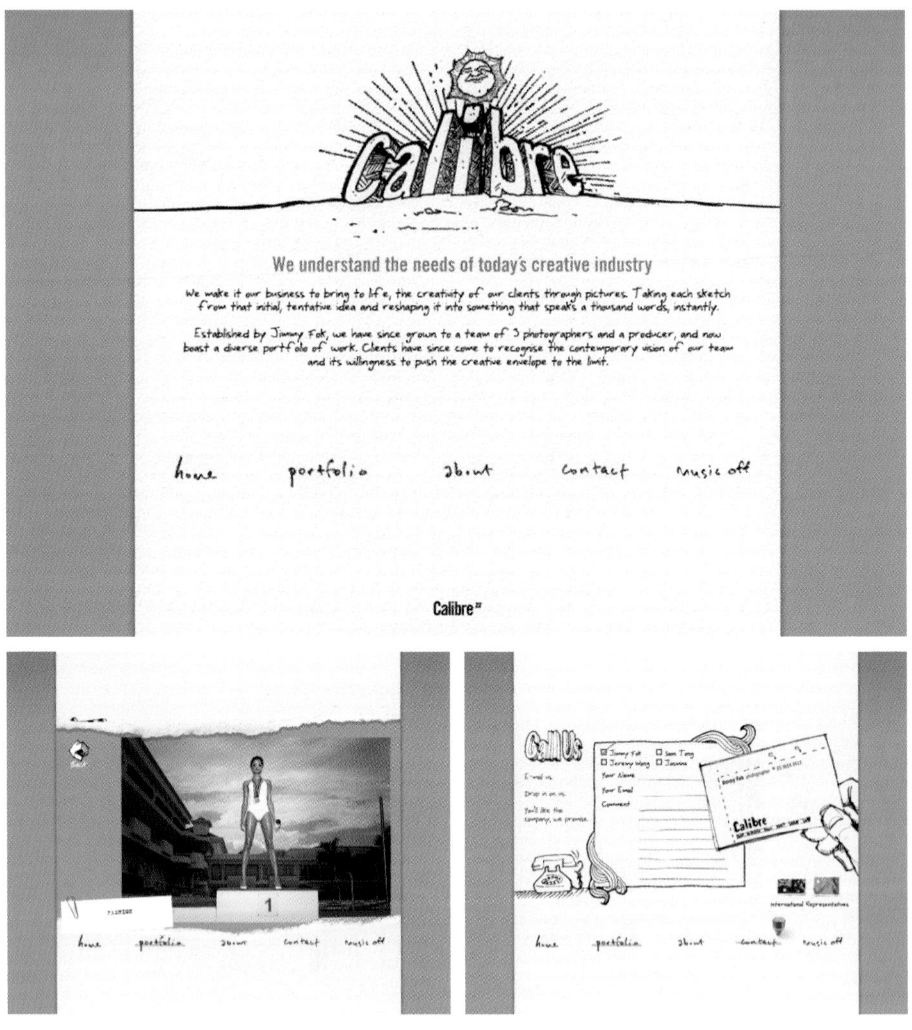

Infos

Design: Kinetic Interactive <www.kinetic.com.sg>. /// **Programming:** Benjy Choo. /// **Tools:** html, Macromedia Flash, php. /// **Cost:** 80 hours. /// **Maintenance:** 8 hours a week.

CARL DE KEYZER PHOTO BELGIUM

www.carldekeyzer.com 2004

Concept

The projects listed in the menu pages scroll behind a magnifying panel that displays a preview and short description of each project. //// Les projets des pages de menu défilent derrière un panneau grossissant contenant une prévisualisation et une brève description. //// Die auf der Menüseite gelisteten Projekte erscheinen hinter einer Vergrösserungsscheibe, die eine Vorschau sowie eine kurze Beschreibung eines jeden Projektes liefert.

Infos

Design and Programming: group94 <www.group94.com>. /// **Awards:** Bombshock, BestFlashAnimationSite.com, FWA (Site of the Day/Site of the Month), Netdiver Design Forte, Flash Kit (Site of the Week). /// **Tools:** Macromedia Flash, php, MySQL. /// **Cost:** 7 weeks.

CAROL ACORD PHOTOGRAPHY USA

www.carolacord.com 2003

Concept

After looking at Carol's body of work, we knew immediately that the photography itself should have the loudest voice. //// En observant les travaux de Carol, nous avons immédiatement su que la photographie devrait avoir la part belle. //// Beim Aufbau der Webseite für Carols Werke, war uns sofort klar, dass das Schwergewicht auf der Fotografie liegen sollte.

Infos

Design: Struck Design <www.struckdesign.com>. /// **Programming:** Ryan Goodwin. /// **Awards:** FWA, TINY (Site of the Week), HOW Magazine Interactive Annual, AIGA 100. /// **Tools:** Macromedia Flash, html, Adobe AffterEffects. /// **Cost:** 35 hours. /// **Maintenance:** very few.

COLIN GORDON

UK

www.chimpchum.freeserve.co.uk

2003

Concept

The site was designed to be simple and easy to navigate, quickly to load and without distracting pop-ups. //// Ce site a été conçu pour être facile à naviguer, rapide à charger et dépourvu de pop-ups encombrantes. //// Die Seite wurde sowohl zur einfachen Navigation als auch zum schnellen Laden und ohne störende Pop-Ups designed.

Infos

DESIGN AND PROGRAMMING: Colin Gordon. /// **TOOLS:** Adobe Illustrator, Macromedia Dreamweaver. /// **COST:** 25 hours. /// **MAINTENANCE:** 2 hours per month.

CLARK STUDIOS

USA

www.clark-studios.com

2004

Concept

The vintage record label home page and 'CD' portfolio navigation was the perfect way to 'marry' our passion for music and design. //// L'étiquette de disque vintage de la page d'accueil et la navigation sous forme de CD dans le portfolio constituent la meilleure façon de marier notre passion pour la musique et le design. //// Unsere Homepage als klassisches Plattenlabel und das Navigationssystem des 'CD'-Portfolios diente uns als perfekte Lösung, unsere Passion für Musik und Design zu verbinden.

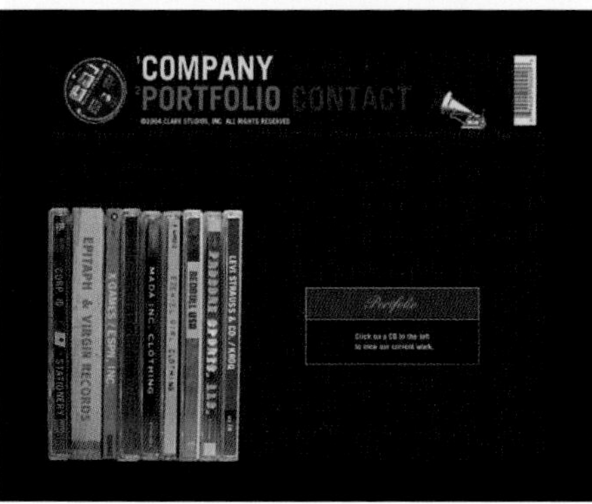

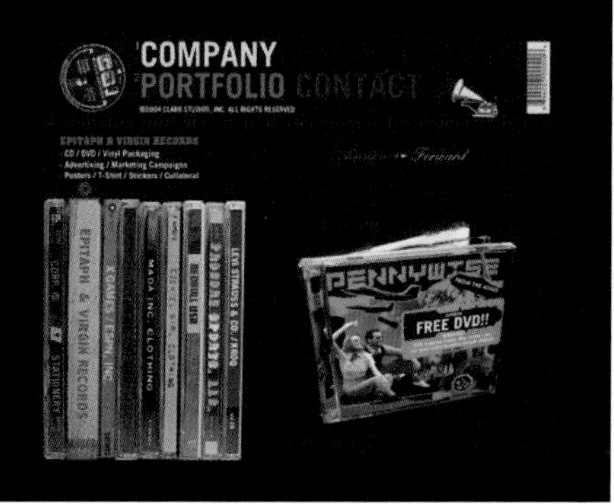

Infos

Design and Programming: Justin Clark (Clark Studios). /// **Tools:** html, Macromedia Flash, digital camera. Sound mixed by Rick Truhls. ///
Cost: 60 hours. /// **Maintenance:** 4 hours per month.

COLOPLAY STUDIO

HUNGARY

www.coloplay.hu

2004

Concept

The concept was to be wordless, we let the works speak for themselves. //// L'idée était de s'affranchir de tout texte, de laisser les travaux parler d'eux-mêmes. //// Unserer Konzept bestand darin, wortlos zu sein, wir lassen die Arbeiten für sich selbst sprechen.

Infos

DESIGN: Gábor Balogh (ColoPLAY). /// **PROGRAMMING:** Péter Nehoda (ColoPLAY). /// **AWARDS:** Hungarian Webdesign (Site of the Week). /// **TOOLS:** Macromedia Flash, php, Adobe Photoshop, Adobe Illustrator. /// **COST:** 90 hours. /// **MAINTENANCE:** 5-8 hours per month.

DANYBOY.COM

FRANCE

www.danyboy.com

2003

Concept

Personal graffiti website, let break the Dino egg to know! //// Site Web personnel de graffitis. Ouvrez l'œuf de dinosaure pour en savoir plus ! //// Persönliche Graffiti-Webseite: Zerbrechen wir das Ei des Dinosauriers und lassen es alle wissen!

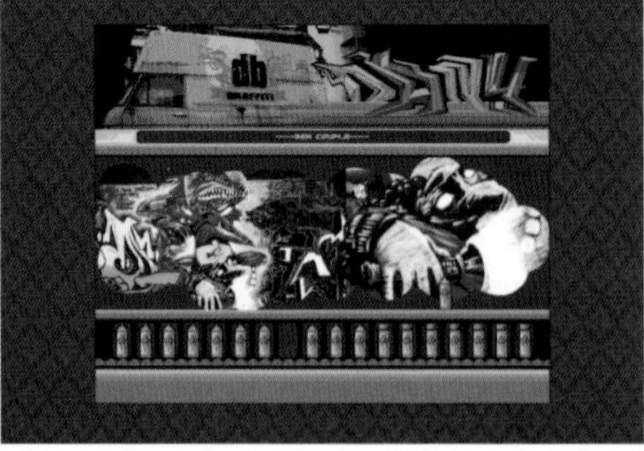

Infos

DESIGN: Danyboy <www.danyboy.com>; <www.semperultimo.com>. /// **PROGRAMMING:** 16ar <www.16argarden.com>; Gus <www.semperultimo.com>. /// **AWARDS:** FWA. /// **TOOLS:** Macromedia Flash, D'n'B music. /// **COST:** 300 hours. /// **MAINTENANCE:** every month.

D5IVE

USA

www.d5ive.com

2003

Concept

This version took a deeper more internal concept, with the dark color palette, distressed typography and the audio. //// Cette version repose sur un concept plus profond et interne, avec une palette de couleurs sombres, une typographie dépouillée et des sons. //// Das Konzept meiner Version ist sehr intim, mit seiner dunklen Farbpalette, nervösen Schrifttypen und dem Sound.

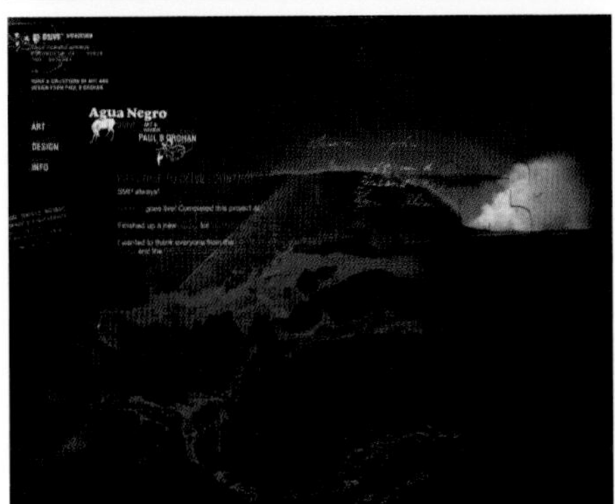

Infos

Design: D5ive. /// **Programming:** Paul B. Drohan and Chris Andrade. /// **Awards:** Flash Forward & Film Festival, STEP Inside magazine. /// **Tools:** Macromedia Flash, Adobe Photoshop, Macromedia Freehand. /// **Cost:** 40 -50 hours.

DELCASTO.DE

GERMANY

www.delcasto.de

2004

Concept

The main-page is built out of a scanned artwork made of plastic, silicon, grey spray-paint, and others for its simple design. //// La page principale est donc créée à partir d'un travail scanné créé avec du plastique, de la silicone, de la peinture grise en bombe et des matières fondues, un travail choisi pour son design simple. //// Die Hauptseite ist aus eingescanntem Plastik, Silikon, grauen Sprühfarbe-Arbeiten, usw. Alles Kunstwerke mit klarem und einfachem Design.

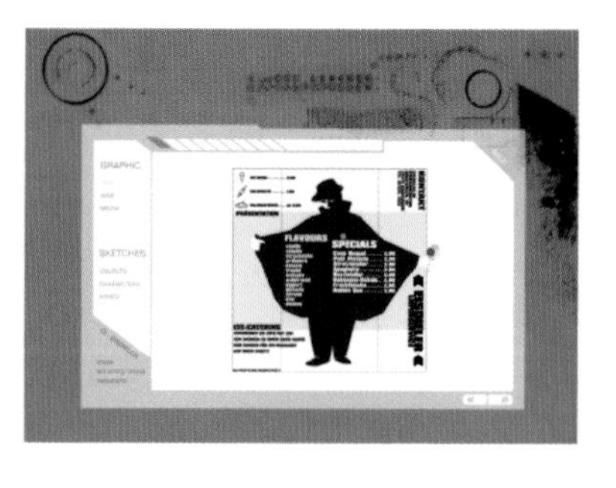

Infos

DESIGN AND PROGRAMMING: Sascha Thoma (Delcasto.de). /// TOOLS: Macromedia Flash, html, Quicktime. /// COST: 5 months. /// MAINTENANCE: depends on the freetime.

DETREMMERIE

BELGIUM
2004

www.detremmerie.be

Concept

The website navigates fast and without any "wait while loading" as all images are preloaded and therefore accessible only when they are actually loaded. //// On navigue rapidement dans ce site Web, sans temps d'attente puisque toutes les images sont préchargées et donc immédiatement accessibles. //// Die Navigation dieser Webseite ist schnell und ohne "Wartezeit während des Ladeprozesses", da alle Bilder schon vorgespeichert und daher sofort zugänglich sind.

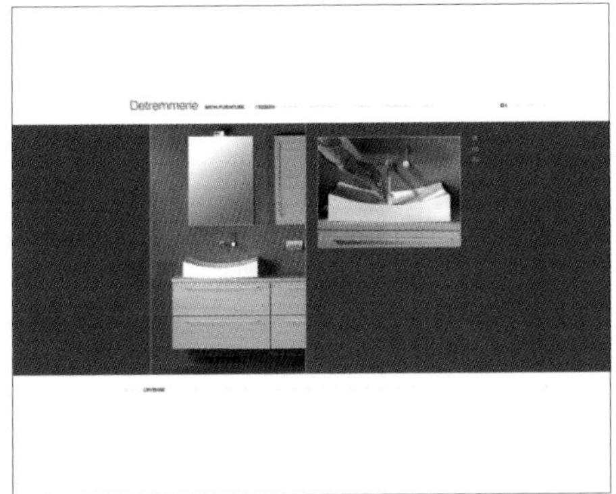

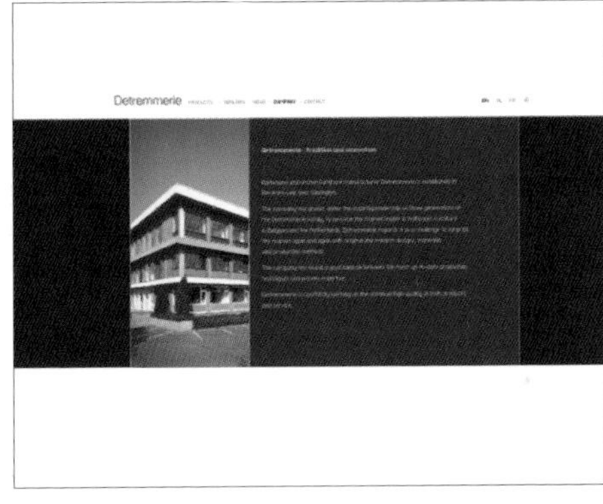

Infos

Design and Programming: group94 <www.group94.com>. /// **Awards:** FWA (Site of the Day). /// **Tools:** Macromedia Flash, php, MySQL. /// **Cost:** 5 weeks. /// **Maintenance:** 1-2 days every 6 months.

DHM DESIGN

THE NETHERLANDS

www.dhmdesign.nl

2001

Concept

You actually visit my hard-drive, where my work is stored. //// Vous visitez en fait mon disque dur, où j'ai stocké mon travail. //// Sie besuchen direkt meinen Harddrive, auf dem alle meine Arbeiten gespeichert sind.

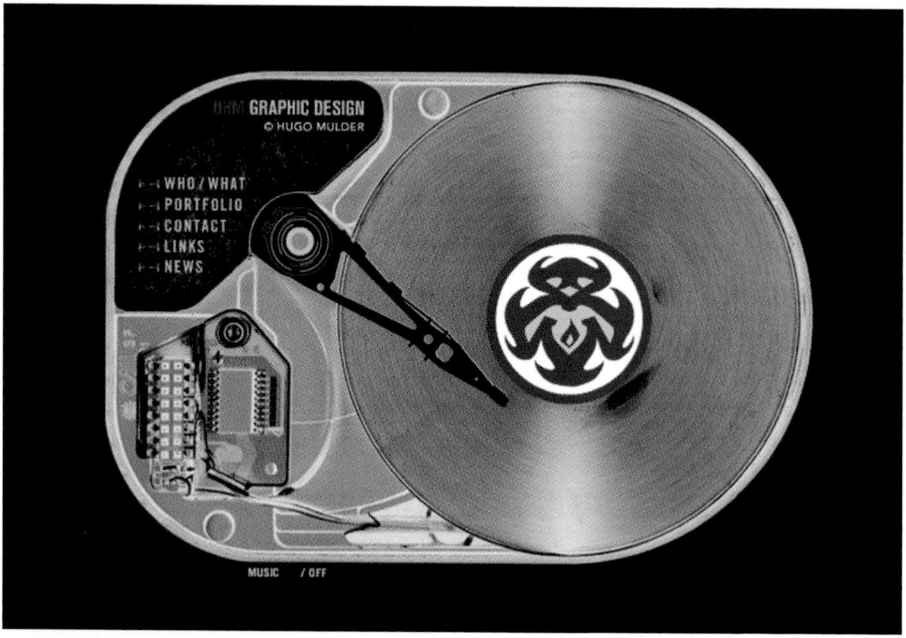

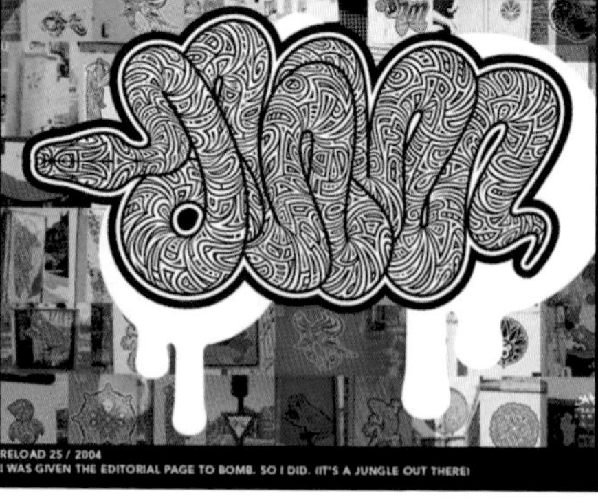

RELOAD 25 / 2004
I WAS GIVEN THE EDITORIAL PAGE TO BOMB. SO I DID. (IT'S A JUNGLE OUT THERE)

Infos

DESIGN: Hugo Mulder (DHM). /// **PROGRAMMING:** Rogier Mulder. /// **TOOLS:** Macromedia Flash, music. /// **COST:** too much, I can't remenber. /// **MAINTENANCE:** 10 hours per month.

DHP ARCHITECTEN

BELGIUM

www.dhp-architecten.be

2004

Concept

Simple, clean, dynamic, surprising, explore... //// Simple, net, dynamique, surprenant, curieux... //// Einfach, klar, dynamisch, überraschend, entdecke es selbst...

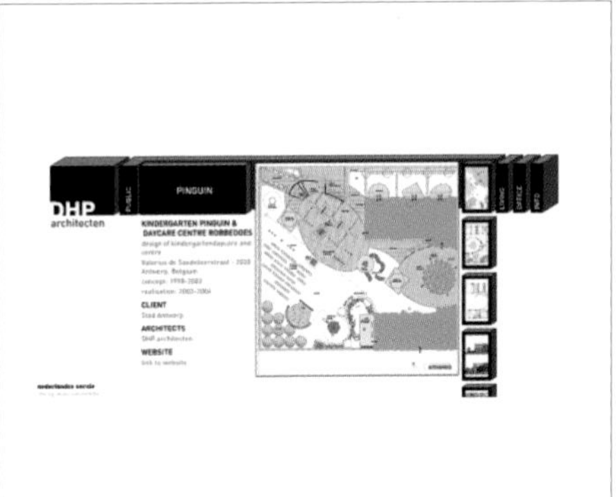

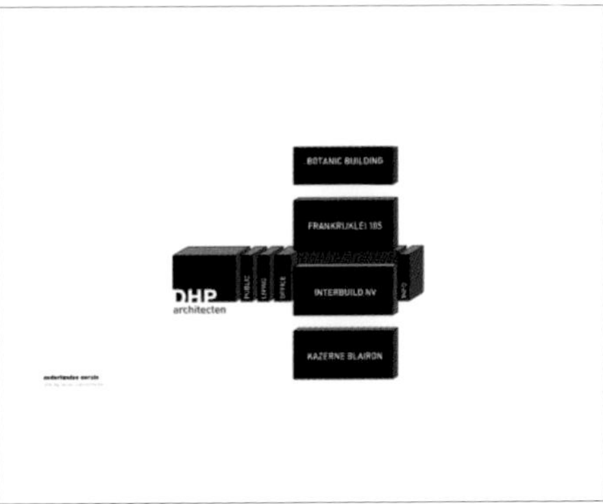

Infos

DESIGN: pieter Lesage and Ann Bruyns (Concrete) <www.concrete.be>. /// **PROGRAMMING:** Onno Baudouin (Concrete). /// **AWARDS:** Netdiver, flashmxpro.com, DOPE, Moluv's Picks, crossmind.net, netinspiration.com, digitalthread.com, thedreamer.com.br, nicewebsite.co.uk, etc. /// **TOOLS:** Macromedia Flash, xml. /// **COST:** 150 hours. /// **MAINTENANCE:** a few hours per month.

DIRK HOFFMANN

GERMANY

www.dirkhoffmann.net

2004

Concept

Unusual drawings in a minimalist interface. //// Des dessins inhabituels dans une interface minimaliste. //// **Ungewöhnliche Zeichungen auf minimalistischem Interface.**

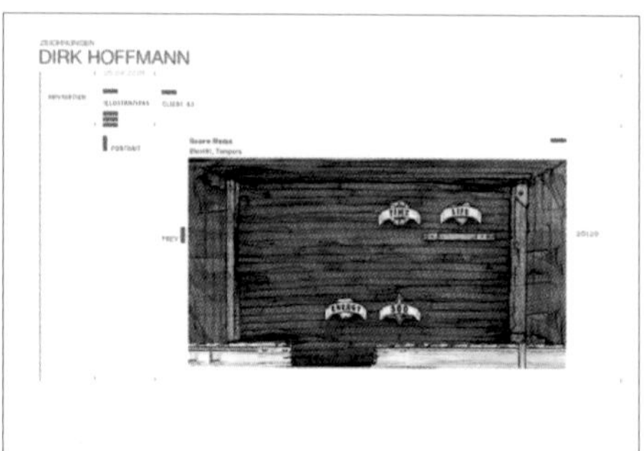

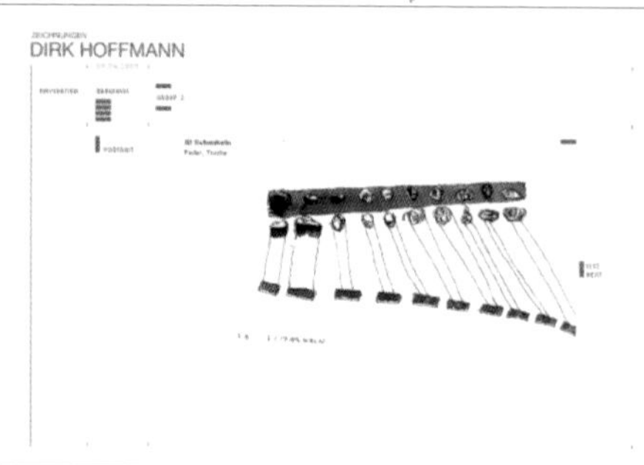

Infos

DESIGN: Dirk Hoffmann and Patrik de Jong <www.punktx.com>. /// **PROGRAMMING:** Patrik de Jong. /// **AWARDS:** TINY [featured site - Categorie Art]. /// **TOOLS:** Macromedia Flash. /// **COST:** 260 hours. /// **MAINTENANCE:** 4 hours per month.

DIRK LAMBRECHTS PHOTO

BELGIUM

www.dirklambrechts.com

2003

Concept

The concept was to create a technical 'lightbox-ish' atmosphere with a very intuitive navigation system: click to open, click to enlarge, click to reduce. //// L'idée était de créer une atmosphère de type table lumineuse avec un système de navigation très intuitif. cliquez pour ouvrir, cliquez pour agrandir, cliquez pour réduire. //// **Das Konzept bestand darin, eine technische, „leuchtkastenähnliche" Atmosphäre mit intuitivem Navigationssystem zu schaffen: anklicken zum Öffnen, anklicken zum Vergrössern, anklicken zum Verkleinern.**

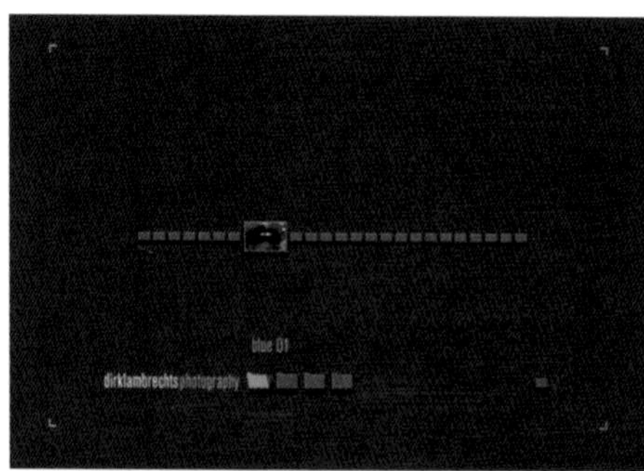

Infos

DESIGN AND PROGRAMMING: Group94 <www.group94.com> /// **AWARDS:** FWA [Site of the Day]. /// **TOOLS:** Macromedia Flash. /// **COST:** 4 weeks. /// **MAINTENANCE:** 1 day every 6 months.

STEVE DOUBLE PHOTOGRAPHY

USA

www.double-whammy.com

1999

Concept

A subdued design to allow the focus to rest on the photographs, with a playful navigation interface to engage the user. //// Un design sobre pour que les photographies aient la vedette, avec une interface de navigation ludique pour séduire l'utilisateur. //// Ein Design, das es erlaubt, die volle Konzentration der Fotografie zu schenken und den Besucher mit einem spielerisch zu navigierenden Interface fesselt.

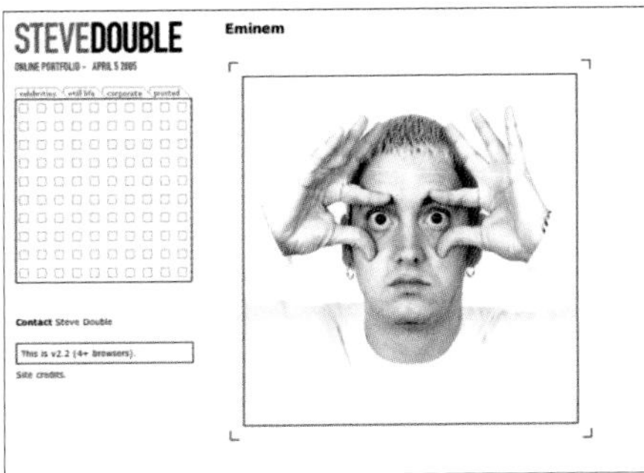

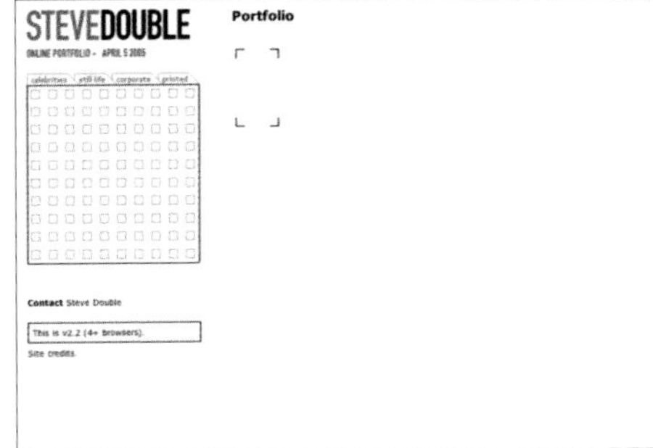

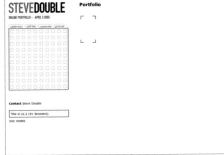

Infos

DESIGN AND PROGRAMMING: Angus Keith <www.adaadat.com>. /// **AWARDS:** Net Design (Best Site), Max Hits: Building and Promoting Successful Websites. /// **TOOLS:** dhtml, Javascript, Textpad, Adobe Photoshop, Adobe Illustrator, asp, MySQL. /// **COST:** 120 hours. /// **MAINTENANCE:** 5 hours per month.

DREAM INTERACTIVE

HUNGARY

www.dream.hu

2005

Concept

The current site was created temporary with the aim of briefly presenting some of our latest works and dedication to professional design. //// Le site qu'on peut visiter aujourd'hui a été créé à l'origine pour être temporaire et avait pour objectif de présenter quelques-uns de nos derniers travaux et notre prédilection pour le design professionnel. //// Die aktuelle Seite demonstriert temporär und in Kurzfassung einige unsere neuesten Arbeiten sowie unsere Hingabe zu professionellem Design.

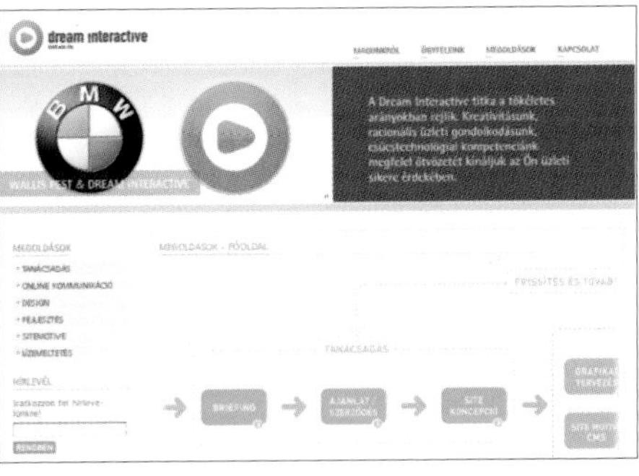

Infos

DESIGN: Gábor Tuba, Zsolt Vajda (Dream Interactive) <www.dream.hu>. /// **PROGRAMMING:** Tamás Turcsányi, Gábor Nagy (Dream Interactive) /// **TOOLS:** html, CSS, Macromedia Flash, xml, php, Smarty. /// **COST:** 25-30 hours. /// **MAINTENANCE:** 6-8 hours per month.

DOUGLAS FISHER PHOTOGRAPHY UK

www.douglasfisher.co.uk 2004

Concept

Website with fluid navigation system. The type of imagery asked for minimalist and "simple" graphic elements to focus as much as possible on the images themselves. //// Site portfolio doté d'un système de navigation fluide. Le genre des images exigeait des éléments graphiques minimalistes et « simples » afin de diriger l'attention au maximum sur les images elles-mêmes. //// Webseite mit fliessendem Navigationssystem. Die Art des Bildmaterials erfordert minimalistische und "einfache" grafische Elemente, um so den Bildern so viel Aufmerksamkeit wie möglich schenken zu können.

Infos

DESIGN AND PROGRAMMING: Group94 <www.group94.com> /// TOOLS: Macromedia Flash, php. /// COST: 6 weeks.

DSLAB

BRAZIL

www.dslab.art.br

2004

Concept

DeSign is a infinity evolution looping! //// DeSign est une mise en boucle évolutive infinie ! //// **DeSign ist eine endlose Evolutionsschleife!**

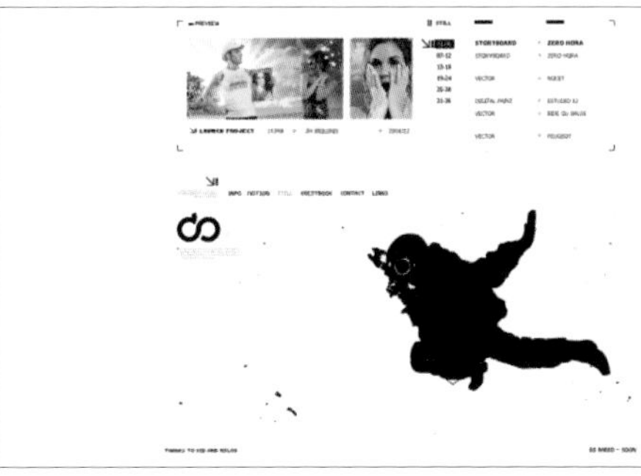

Infos

DESIGN: Everson Nazari (DSLAB). /// **PROGRAMMING:** Fábio Oliveira. /// **TOOLS:** html, Macromedia Flash, asp, movie, illustration, web, identity. /// **COST:** 40-60 hours. /// **MAINTENANCE:** 20 hours per month.

EL GRANDO BEAUTY SALON

ESTONIA

www.elgrando.ee

2004

Concept

Impressive, but very informative, glamourous. //// Tout à la fois impressionnant, pleins d'informations et glamour. //// **Beeindruckend, dennoch informativ und einfach glamourös.**

Infos

DESIGN: Vladimir Morozov (Lime Creative) <www.lime.ee>. /// **PROGRAMMING:** Sander Sellin, Vladimir Morozov. /// **AWARDS:** FWA (Site of the day). /// **TOOLS:** Macromedia Flash, html, php. /// **COST:** 250 hours. /// **MAINTENANCE:** 5 hours per month.

FRANCE

www.dunun.com

2004

Concept Dunun is a consistent world just like ours. You will see (quite as at your window and at the same moments) the time changing its sound environment and its navigation landscape. //// Dunun est un monde cohérent tout comme l'est le nôtre. Vous verrez comment son environnement sonore et son paysage de navigation évolue avec le temps (presque en temps réel). //// Dunun ist eine real existierende Welt, genau, wie die unsrige. Als ob Sie in diesem Augenblick aus Ihrem Fenster schauten, können Sie beobachten, wie die Zeit ihre Umgebung und die Landschaft der Navigation verändert.

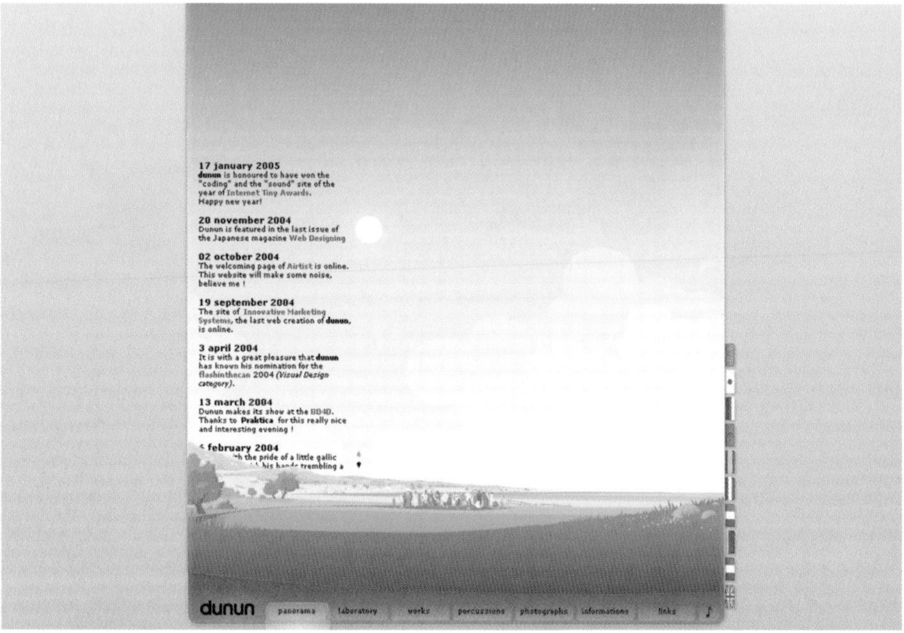

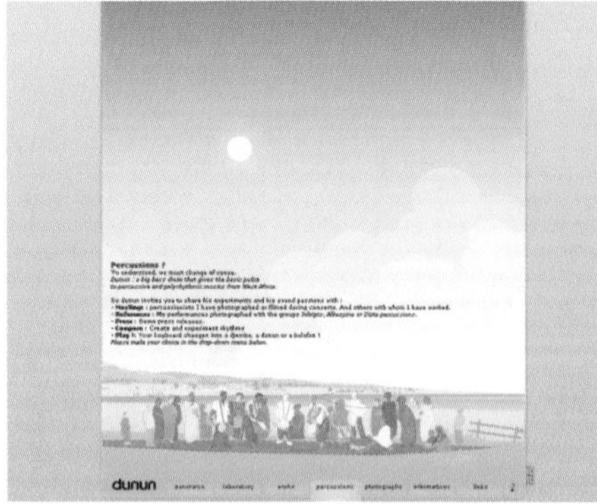

Infos DESIGN: Dunun. /// PROGRAMMING: Micael Reynaud. /// AWARDS: FWA, Bombshock, TINY, fcukstar.com, wellvetted.com, Plasticpilots, Flash Forward, Flashxpress, Designfirms.org, Flash In The Can.com. /// TOOLS: Macromedia Flash, xml, php, html, JavaScript. /// CONTENT: interactive music, photo, video. /// COST: 500 hours. /// MAINTENANCE: 50 hours per month.

SACHA DEAN BIYAN

USA

www.eccentris.com

2002

Concept

Fusing fashion photography, web design, music and motion to create a unique sensory experience. Sacha Biyan envisioned his site to be "high-end" in every aspect. //// Faire fusionner des photos de mode d'avant-garde, du design Web, de la musique et des animations pour créer un environnement sensoriel unique. Sacha Biyan a souhaité un site haute-gamme à tout point de vue. //// **Überzeugend Modefotografie, Webdesign, Musik sowie Bewegungsabläufe, um eine ganz besondere Sinneserfahrung zu machen. Sacha Biyan hatte die Vision einer hochwertigen Seite in jedem Detail.**

Infos

DESIGN: Rita Lidji (Firstborn) <www.firstbornmultimedia.com>. /// **PROGRAMMING:** Josh Ott. /// **AWARDS:** Communication Arts, Flash In The Can, FWA. /// **TOOLS:** Macromedia Flash, SoundForge, Adobe AfterEffects, Adobe Premiere. /// **COST:** 400 hours.

MONICA CALVO

SPAIN

www.eendar.com

2003

Concept

Based on the colors of an old Japanese painting. I wanted something very simple and nice to watch, with a very easy navigation. //// Eendar.com s'inspire des couleurs d'une ancienne peinture japonaise. Je voulais quelque chose de très simple et de très joli à regarder, avec une navigation vraiment facile. //// Die Kreation von Eendar.com basiert auf den Farben eines alten, japanischen Gemäldes. Ich suchte etwas Einfaches, schön Anzusehendes und mit leicht anwendbarer Navigation.

Infos

DESIGN: Monica Calvo. /// PROGRAMMING: Monica Calvo and Carlos Rincon. /// TOOLS: Adobe Photoshop, html, Macromedia Flash. ///
COST: 32 hours. /// MAINTENANCE: 2 hours per month.

ESAO.NET

USA

www.esao.net

2001

Concept

An interactive website showcasing the artists paintings and other artwork with the actual design being an extension of his art rather than just presenting it. //// Site Web interactif présentant les peintures d'artistes ainsi que d'autres œuvres d'art, avec un design qui constitue une extension des œuvres présentées plutôt qu'ayant la seule finalité de les présenter. //// Eine interaktive Webseite, die Gemälde sowie andere Kunstwerke des Künstlers darstellt, wobei das Design als ein Zusatz zu seiner Kunst angesehen werden muss und nicht etwa nur als Präsentationstechnik.

Infos

Design and Programming: Esao Andrews. /// **Tools:** Macromedia Flash. /// **Cost:** worked on during spare time. /// **Maintenance:** $15.00 per month via <www.crystaltech.com>.

FARUK AKIN PROJECT

TURKEY

www.farukakin.com

2002

Concept

The design concept something like a shooting game is a park . The interactive page displays both 2D and 3D works just by scrowlling to the right or left. //// Le design de ce site repose sur un concept de jeu de tir. La page interactive montre des travaux en 2D et en 3D que l'on peut faire défiler vers la droite ou la gauche. //// Das Konzept des Designs ist vergleichbar mit einem Park von Schiessfiguren. Die interaktive Seite weist sowohl 2D- als auch 3D-Arbeiten auf, die durch einfaches Ziehen der Maus nach links oder rechts betrachtet werden können.

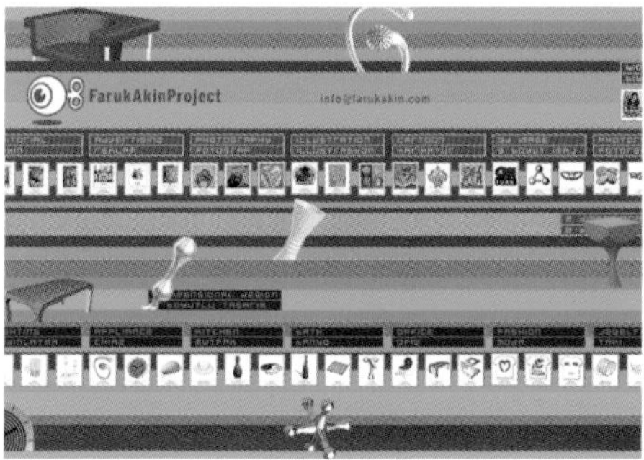

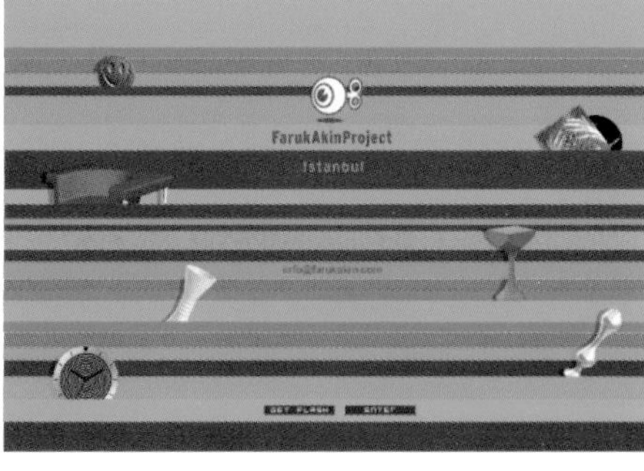

Infos

Design: Faruk Akin Project <www.farukakin.com>. /// **Programming:** Guven Dinneden. /// **Tools:** Macromedia Flash.

EMMANUELLE BERNARD

BRAZIL

www.emmanuellebernard.com

2004

Concept

Clean and feminine. The photos are the main priority of the website. //// Clair et féminin. Les photos sont la priorité de ce site. //// **Klar und feminin. Die Fotografie bildet den Schwerpunkt der Webseite.**

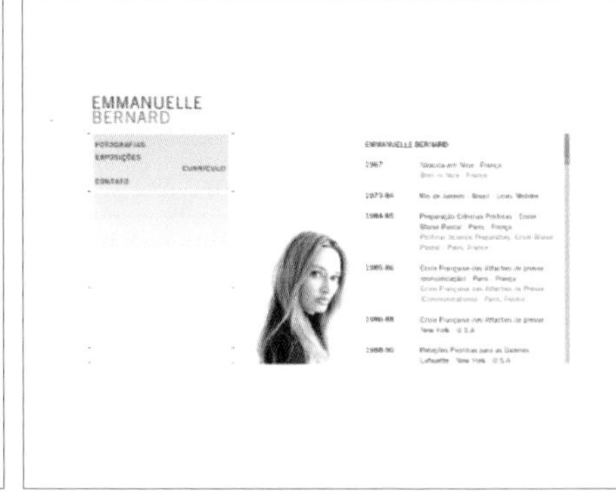

Infos

DESIGN: Bruno Fraga (6D estúdio) <www.6d.com.br>. /// **PROGRAMMING:** Gabriel Marques (6D estúdio). /// **TOOLS:** Macromedia Flash. /// **COST:** 320 hours. /// **MAINTENANCE:** 8 hours per month.

ERIK OTTEN – SEVEN

THE NETHERLANDS

www.erikotten.nl

2004

Concept

We tried to highlight the work the best way possible while displaying it in a technical high standing and eye catching Flash website. //// Nous avons essayé de mettre en valeur les travaux du mieux possible tout en les présentant dans un site Web Flash techniquement très bien conçu et attirant l'œil. //// Ziel ist, durch eine technisch perfekte und optisch beeindruckende Flash-Webseite unsere Arbeiten besonders hervorzuheben.

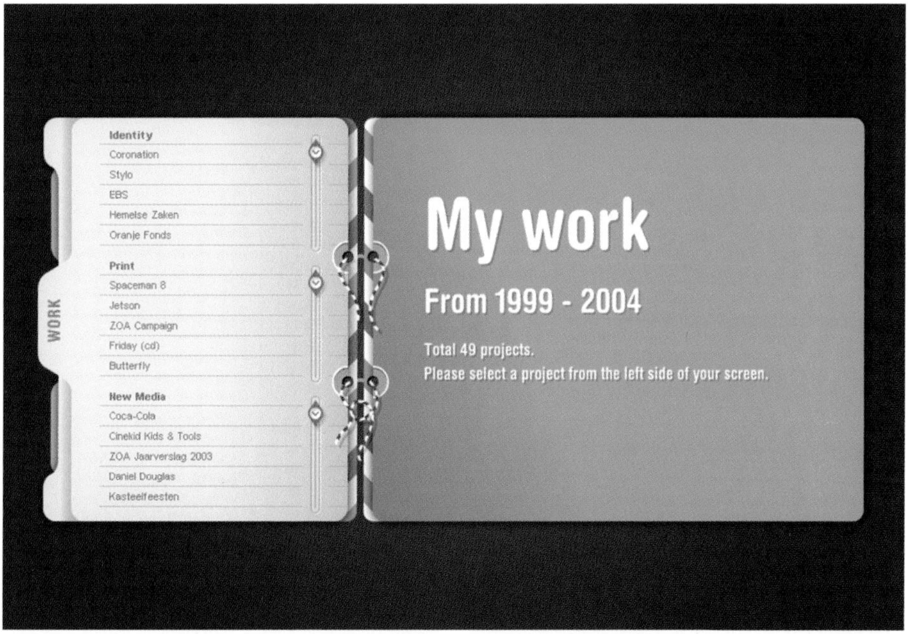

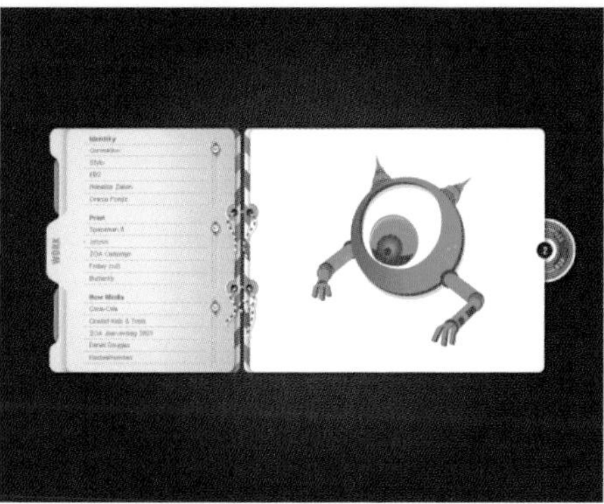

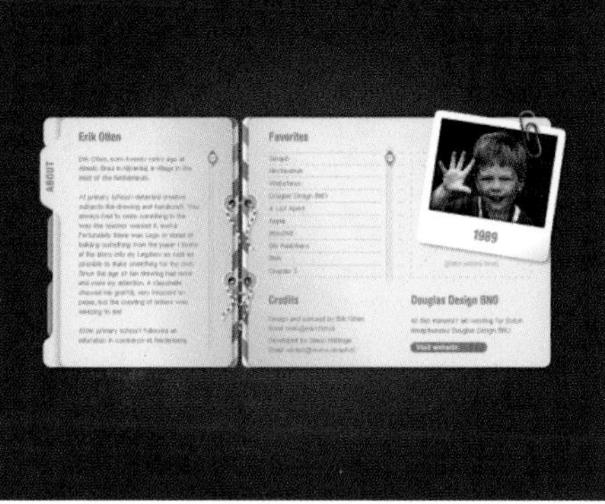

Infos

DESIGN: Erik Otten. /// **PROGRAMMING:** Seraph (www.seraph.nl). /// **AWARDS:** FWA, TINY (Site of the Month), Netdiver, fcukstar.com, Kirupa. /// **TOOLS:** Macromedia Fireworks, Adobe Illustrator, Macromedia Flash. /// **COST:** 200 hours. /// **MAINTENANCE:** 1 hour per month.

ESTHER FRANKLIN

UK

www.estherfranklin.co.uk

2004

Concept

Site influences: nighttime moods to slick, sexy elegance. //// Influences du site : ambiances nocturnes lisses, élégance sexy. //// Webseiten beeinflussen: nächtliche Stimmung hin zu schicker, sexy Eleganz.

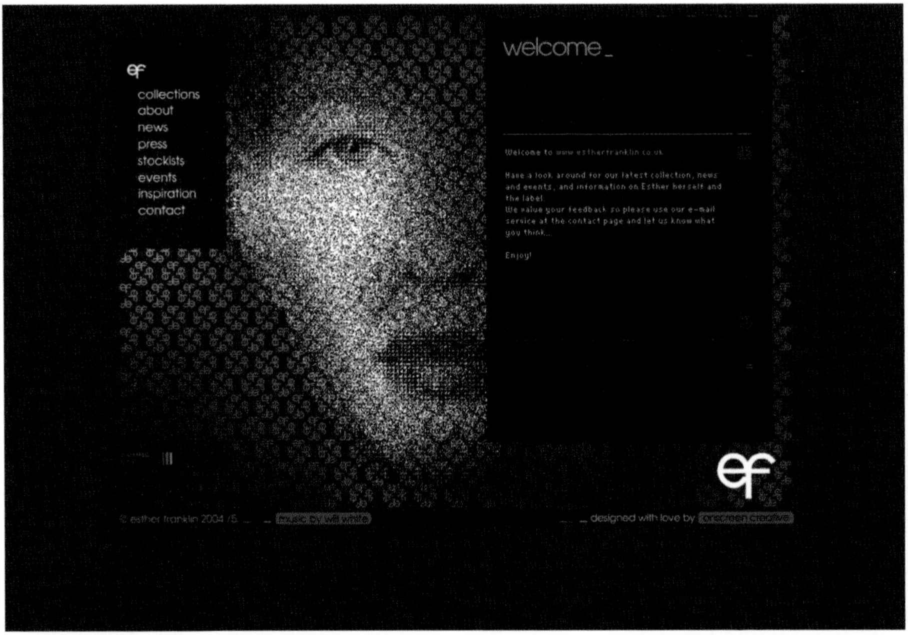

Infos

Design: Onscreen Creative <www.onscreencreative.com>. /// **Programming:** Rob and Zulma. /// **Music:** Will White. /// **Tools:** Adobe Photoshop, Adobe Illustrator, Macromedia Flash, Macromedia Dreamweaver, php. /// **Cost:** 6-8 weeks.

THE NETHERLANDS

www.exactitudes.com

2002

concept

Visualizes the complex relationship between the individuality and the collectivity: the apparent contradiction of wanting to stand out from the others and be unique by assuming a group identity. //// Visualise la relation complexe entre l'individualité et la collectivité : l'apparente contradiction qui consiste à vouloir sortir du lot et être unique en prenant une identité de groupe. //// Es strebt eine Verbindung zwischen Individualität und Kollektivität an: der offensichtliche Widerspruch, einerseits herausstechen zu wollen und andererseits einzigartige Teamarbeit zu leisten.

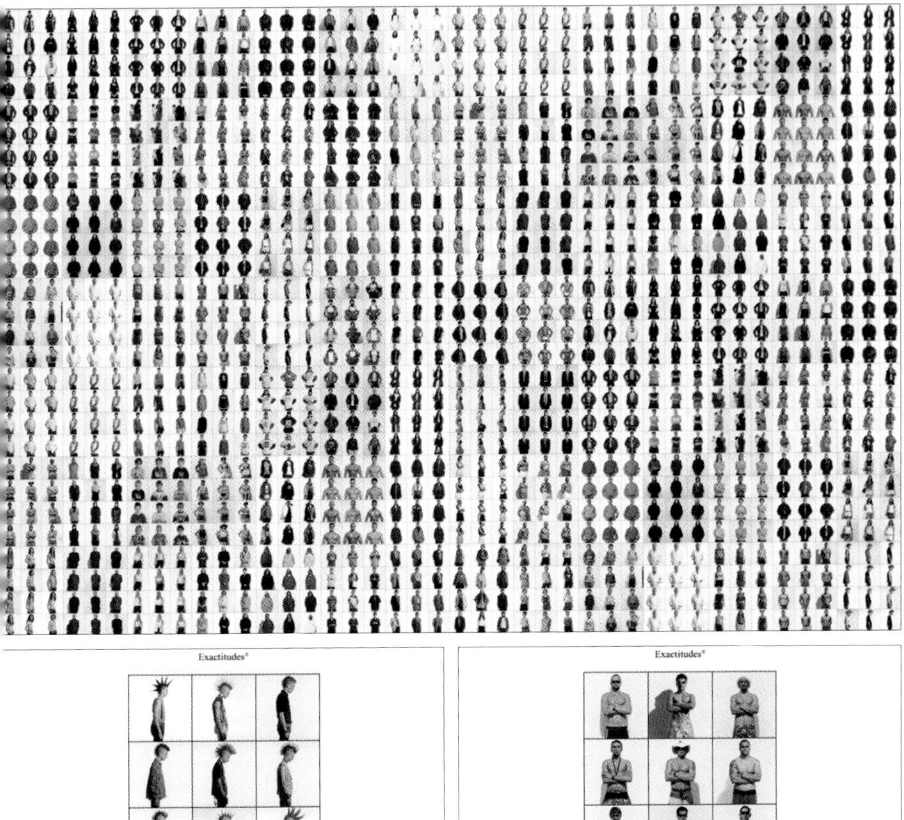

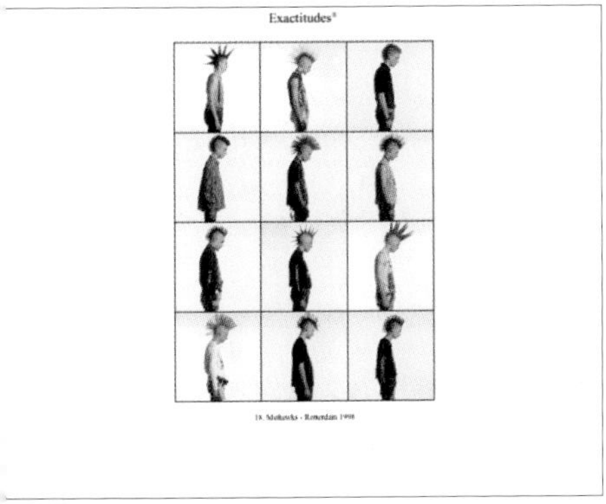

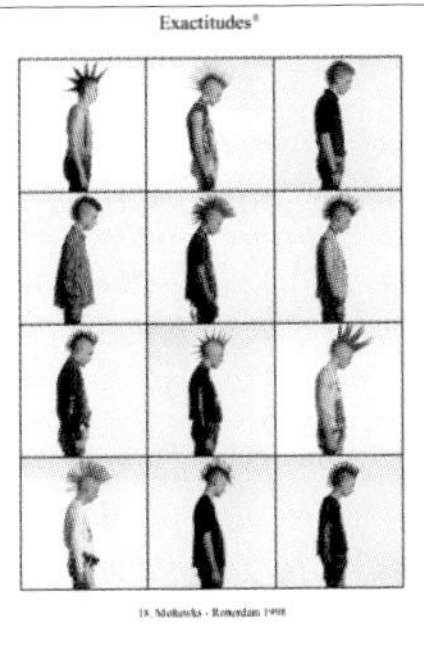

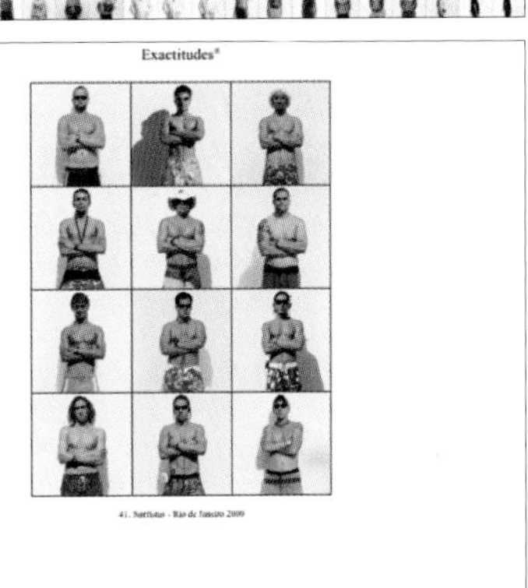

infos

Design: Ari Versluis, Ellie Uyttenbroek and Joost Burger <www.i-b-o-o.com>. /// **Programming:** Joost Burger. /// **Tools:** php, html. /// **Cost:** 4 days. /// **Maintenance:** 3 hours per month.

FABIAAN VAN SEVEREN

BELGIUM

www.fabiaanvanseveren.com

2004

Concept

A smart loading minimalistic portfolio for a Belgian design studio in which content can be pulled out and pushed away, like a cupboard drawer you open and close. //// Un portfolio minimaliste à chargement malin dont l'auteur est un studio de design belge de premier plan et dont le contenu peut être tiré et poussé, comme un tiroir que l'on ouvre et que l'on ferme. //// **Minimalistisches Portfolio eines belgischen Designstudios, mit intelligenter Download-Technik, bei der man Information herausziehen und wieder ablegen kann, geradezu wie in der Schublade eines Möbelstückes.**

FabiaanVanSeveren | MAY 17

01 CHAIRS
02 TABLES
03 CUPBOARDS
04 LIGHTING
05 BEDS
06 BAGS
07 SPECIALS

PDF CATALOGUE

NEWS | CREW | PROJECTS | SHOWROOM | CONTACT

FabiaanVanSeveren | MAY 17

FabiaanVanSeveren | MAY 17

Infos

DESIGN AND PROGRAMMING: MMM [Multimediamadness] <www.multimediamadness.be>. /// **AWARDS:** FWA. /// **TOOLS:** html, xml, Macromedia Flash, php, MySQL. /// **COST:** 150 hours. /// **MAINTENANCE:** 1/2 hour per month. Thanks to an excellent CMS.

FLATLINER

UK

ww.flatlineronline.com

2001

Designed to be similar in style to the actual illustrations showcased, simple flat and graphic. The navigation represents a simple approach to that of portfolio sleeves of a printed portfolio. //// Le site a été conçu avec l'idée qu'il ait un style similaire aux illustrations qu'il présente : simple, rapide et graphique. La navigation et l'affichage reflètent une approche simple propre aux pochettes d'un portfolio imprimé. //// **Die Seite beabsichtigt, ihren Stil an die Illustration anzugleichen, einfach und graphisch. Navigation ist eine Annäherung an die übliche Präsentationsform eines Portfolios auf Papier.**

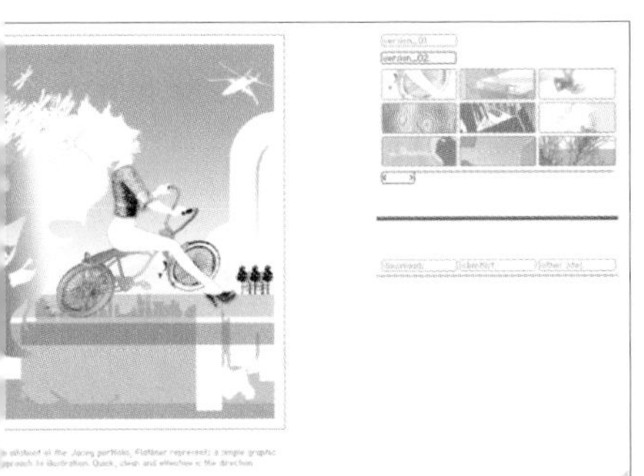

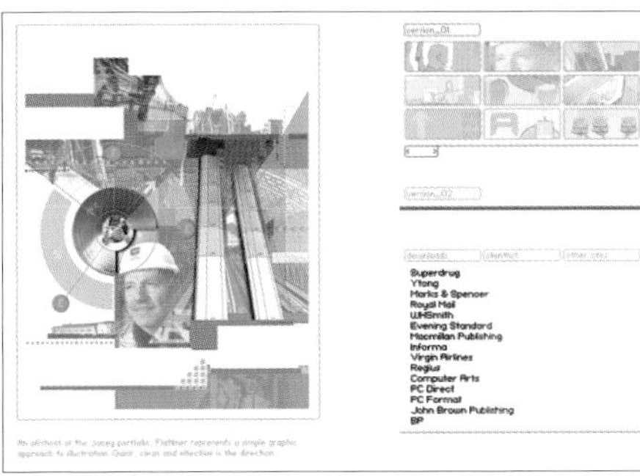

DESIGN AND PROGRAMMING: Jason Cook <www.jasoncook.co.uk>. /// **TOOLS:** Macromedia Flash, html. /// **COST:** 12 hours. /// **MAINTENANCE:** updated once every 3 months.

FOSOD STUDIOS

USA

ww.fosod.com

2001

We tirelessly pushed for three ideals: simplicity, ease-of-use and elegance. //// Nous avons voulu que trois idéaux soient représentés : la simplicité, la facilité d'utilisation et l'élégance. //// **Wir haben uns unermüdlich für drei Ideale eingesetzt: Einfach, leicht zu gebrauchen und elegant.**

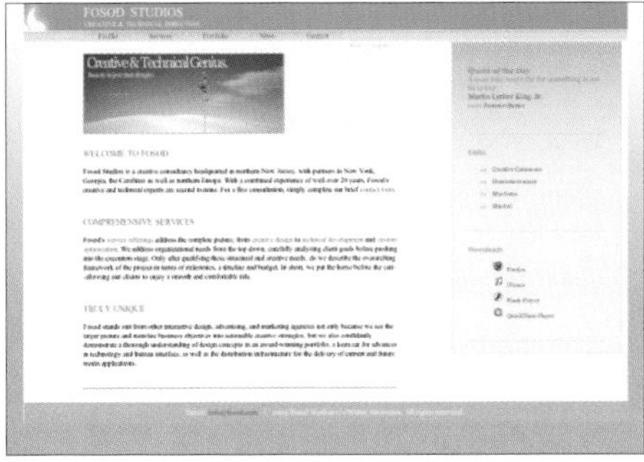

DESIGN AND PROGRAMMING: Walter T. Stevenson (Fosod Studios). /// **AWARDS:** Aljapaco, Biomutation, VIPE, CreativePublic (Site of the Month), Design Inspiration, NewWebPick (Very Cool Site), CoolestDesigns, Plasticpilots (One Star) /// **TOOLS:** xhtml, CSS, Macromedia Flash, xml, MIDI, Mp3, audio editing applications, Mpeg, video editing applications. /// **COST:** 2 months. /// **MAINTENANCE:** 5 hours per month maintenance, redesigned annually.

FINGER INDUSTRIES

UK

www.fingerindustries.co.uk

200

Concept

We developed the cityscape with the main menu being a signpost and each area being located within a different building. //// Nous avons développ un paysage urbain où un poteau indicateur fait figure de menu principal et des bâtiments différents représentent chacune des zones. //// Wir haben ein Stadtbild entwickelt, mit einem Hauptmenü in Form von Schildern, die als Wegweiser dienen. Jeder Themenbereich ist in einem unterschiedlichen Gebäude untergebracht.

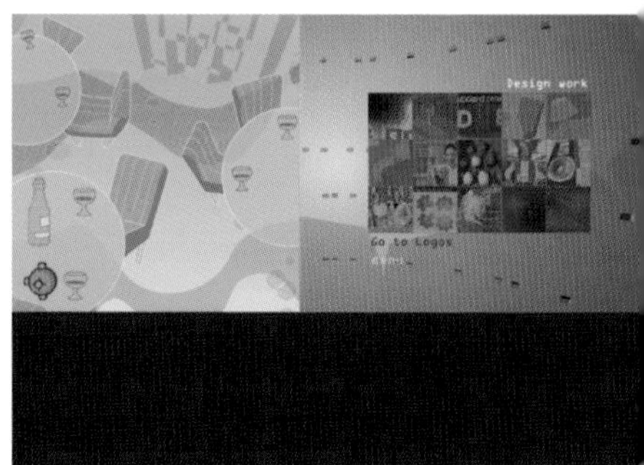

Infos

Design and Programming: Marcus Kenyon and Jonny Ford (Finger Industries). /// **Awards:** Netdiver Design Forte, American Design Award (Gold), TAXI (Site of the day), NewWebPick. /// **Tools:** Macromedia Flash, Discreet Plasma. /// **Cost:** 6 weeks over 3 months. /// **Maintenance:** 5 hours per month.

FLORIAN LOHMANN PHOTO

GERMAN

www.florianlohmann.de

200

Concept

Passionate photography portfolio presented by sexy "chica". //// Un portfolio de photos passionné présenté par une chica très sexy. //// Portfolio mit leidenschaftlicher Fotografie, die von einer sexy "chica" präsentiert wird.

Infos

Design: Slick <www.slickdesign.de>. /// **Programming:** Johannes Auffermann. /// **Tools:** Macromedia Flash, video (blue box), xml, html. /// **Cost:** 250 hours. /// **Maintenance:** 4 hours per month.

THE NETHERLANDS

www.fluid.nl

2001

The site's navigation connects with the way Fluid deals with the high-tension zone between playfulness and functionality. //// La navigation du site est en rapport avec la manière dont Fluid appréhende la zone de haute tension entre le jeu et la fonctionnalité. //// Das Navigationssystem dieser Seite verbindet auf unsere Art die kritische Spanne zwischen Verspieltheit und Funktionalität.

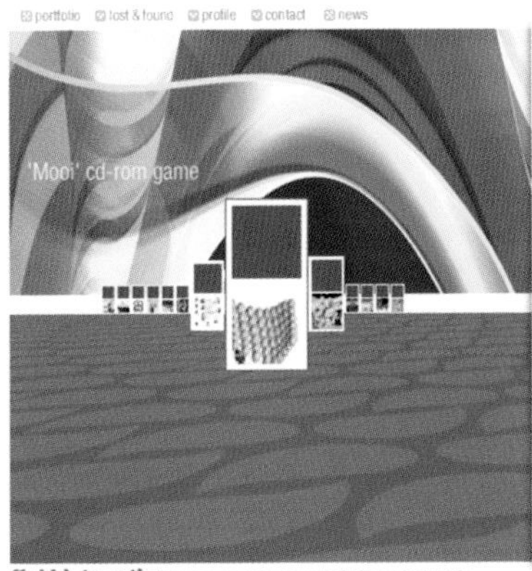

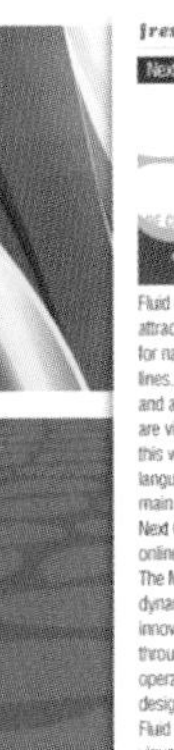

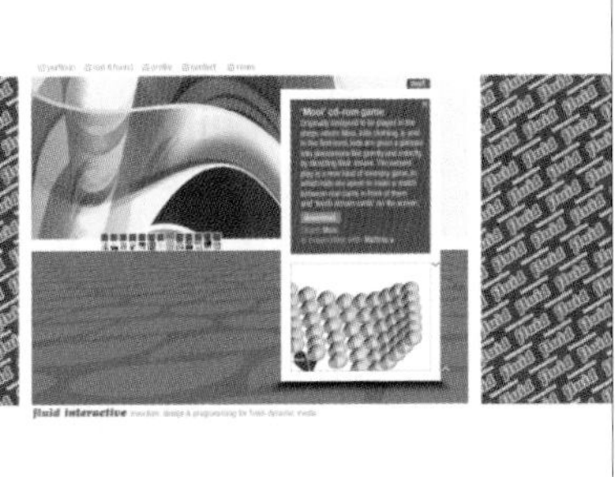

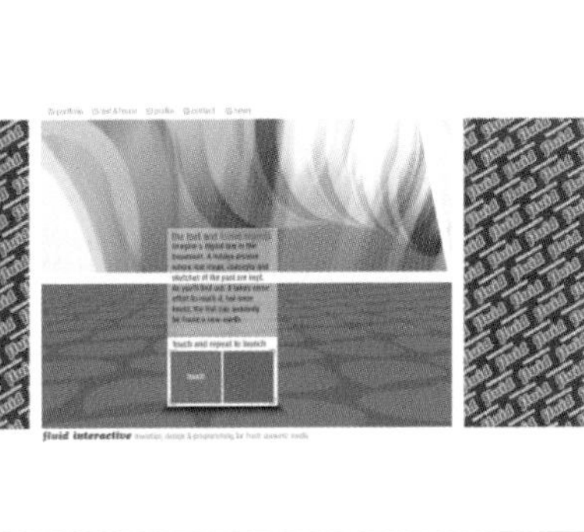

DESIGN AND PROGRAMMING: Remon Tijssen (Fluid). /// **AWARDS:** FWA. /// **TOOLS:** Macromedia Director, Macromedia Flash, html, interactivity, behaviors, animation, video, audio, text. /// **COST:** 2-3 months. /// **MAINTENANCE:** 4 hours per month.

FOR OFFICE USE ONLY

US
200

www.forofficeuseonly.com

Concept

Concept: create an interface that was update-able, and make the aesthetic consistent with the overall style and ideas of the studio. //// Le concept du site : créer une interface qu'il soit possible de mettre à jour et qui permette de présenter des design intermédiaires en plus des design finaux, et rendre l'esthétique du site cohérentes avec le style et les idées générales du studio. //// Konzept: ein Interface kreieren, sowohl das Design im Arbeitsprozes als auch das fertige Design zu präsentieren, und dabei Ästhetik der Seite in Einklang mit dem Stil und den Ideen des Studios zu bringen.

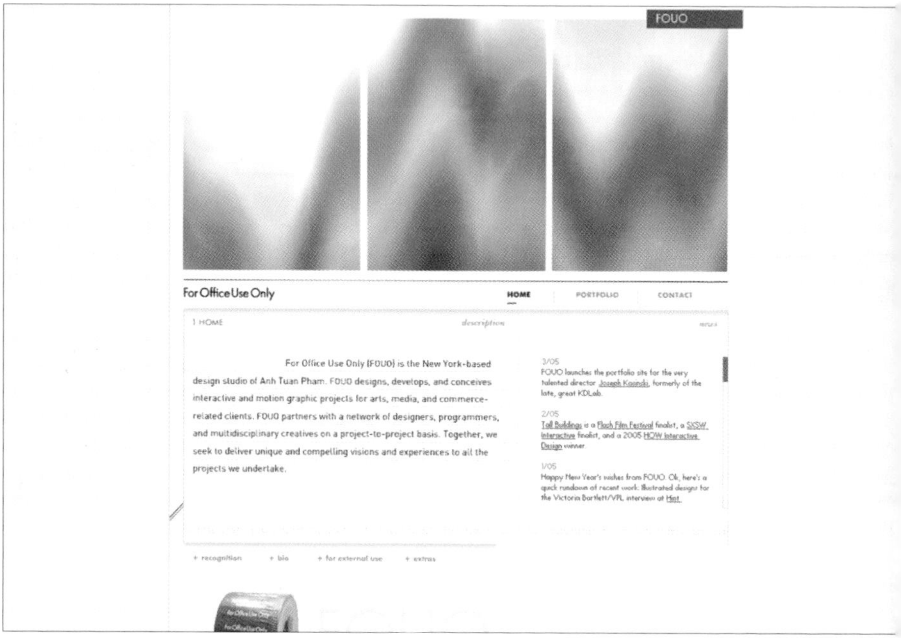

FOUO

For Office Use Only

HOME PORTFOLIO CONTACT

1 HOME description

For Office Use Only (FOUO) is the New York-based design studio of Anh Tuan Pham. FOUO designs, develops, and conceives interactive and motion graphic projects for arts, media, and commerce-related clients. FOUO partners with a network of designers, programmers, and multidisciplinary creatives on a project-to-project basis. Together, we seek to deliver unique and compelling visions and experiences to all the projects we undertake.

3/05
FOUO launches the portfolio site for the very talented director Joseph Kosinski, formerly of the late, great KDLab.

2/05
Tall Buildings is a Flash Film Festival finalist, a SXSW Interactive finalist, and a 2005 HOW Interactive Design winner.

1/05
Happy New Year's wishes from FOUO. Ok, here's a quick rundown of recent work: illustrated designs for the Victoria Bartlett/VPL interview at Hint.

+ recognition + bio + for external use + extras

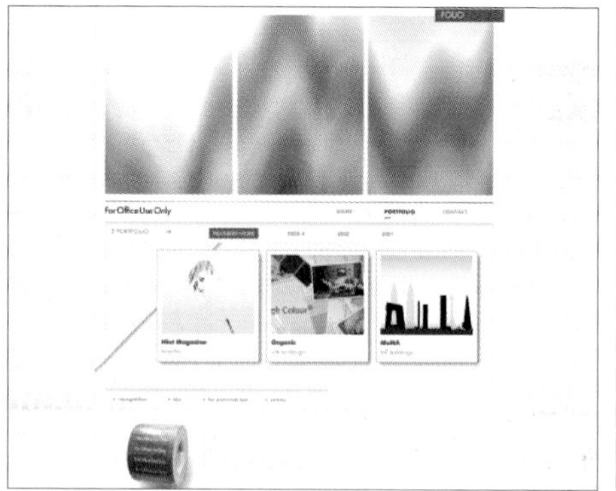

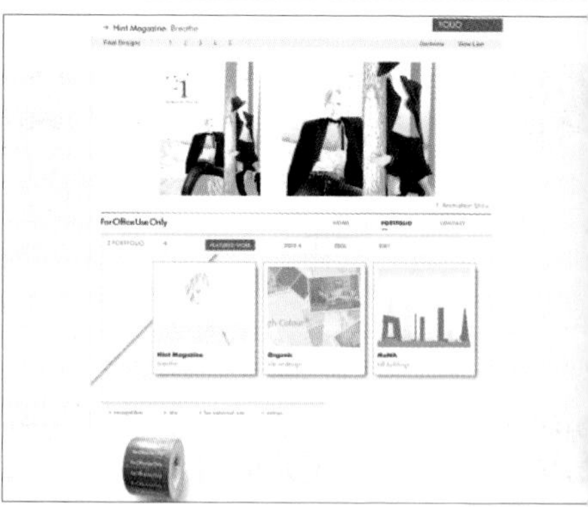

Infos

DESIGN AND PROGRAMMING: For Office Use Only. /// TOOLS: Macromedia Flash, Adobe Photoshop, Adobe Illustrator, SoundEdit.

FU-DESIGN.COM

TAIWAN

www.fu-design.com

2003

Fu-design.com is a creative and happy place with Chu Keng Fu 's artworks, music and animations. //// Fu-design.com est une vitrine créative et joyeuse des œuvres d'art, de la musique et des animations de Chu Keng Fu. //// Fu-design.com ist ein kreativer und fröhlicher Ort mit Chu Keng Fus Kunstwerken, Musik und Animation.

Design and Programming: Chu Keng Fu (FU-Design). /// **Awards:** Netdiver (BOTY), FWA (Site Of The Day), Plasticpilots (Two Star), TINY, Graphics.com Team, Coolhomepage.com, Coolstop's Portal Cool Zone, Noteworthy Cool Site, Upwardlink. /// **Tools:** Macromedia Flash, Adobe Photoshop, Macromedia Dreamweaver. /// **Cost:** 1 month. /// **Maintenance:** 1 hour a day.

GIOSIMI

BRAZIL

www.giosimi.com

2004

You are finished, when you repeat yourself. //// Quand vous vous répétez, vous êtes fini. //// Sie sind dann fertig, wenn Sie sich selbst wiederholen.

Design: Giosimi. /// **Programming:** Giosimi and Zoltan. /// **Tools:** Macromedia Flash, Adobe Illustrator, Lightwave 3D , html. /// **Cost:** 20 hours. /// **Maintenance:** 4-6 hours per month.

FREAKY FACETS

www.freakyfacets.com

20

Concept

Simple easily navigation, to showcase some personal illustration work that makes people sit up and say 'who is this nutter'? //// Une navigati
simple pour un site présentant des travaux d'illustration personnels qui font dire aux gens : « Mais c'est qui ce dingue ? » //// Einfache und klare Na
tion, um persönliche Illustrationen zu präsentieren und Neugierde zu erwecken. Damit man sich die Frage stellt, wer wohl diese Verrückten s

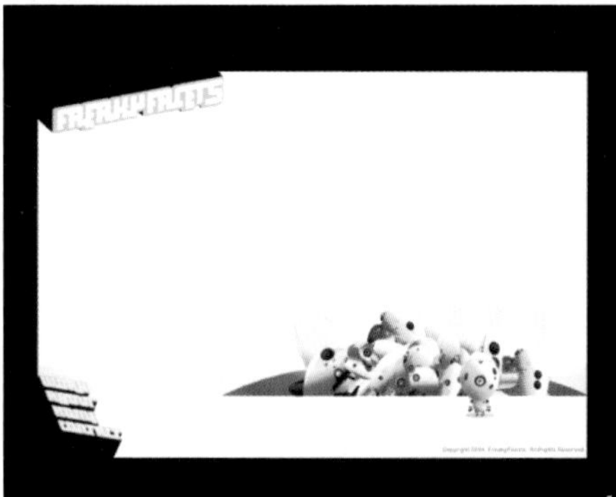

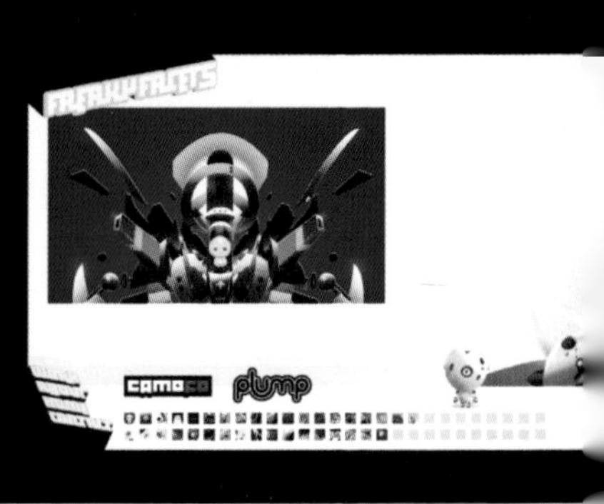

Infos

Design and Programming: John Taylor (Freaky Facets). /// **Tools:** html, Macromedia Flash, Adobe Illustrator, Adobe Photoshop. ///
Cost: 2 months. /// **Maintenance:** minimal hours per month.

GALLAGHER & ASSOCIATES USA

www.gallagherdesign.com 2004

Concept

This 4 level deep portfolio consists of a system of floating and folding panels displaying the structure in an intuitive and visual way. ////
Ce portfolio en 4 niveaux consiste en un système de panneaux flottants et pliants qui affichent la structure de manière intuitive et visuelle. ////
Dieses auf 4 Ebenen aufgebaute Portfolio besitzt ein System, das mit fliessenden und faltbaren Panelen funktioniert und eine intuitive und visuelle Struktur aufweist.

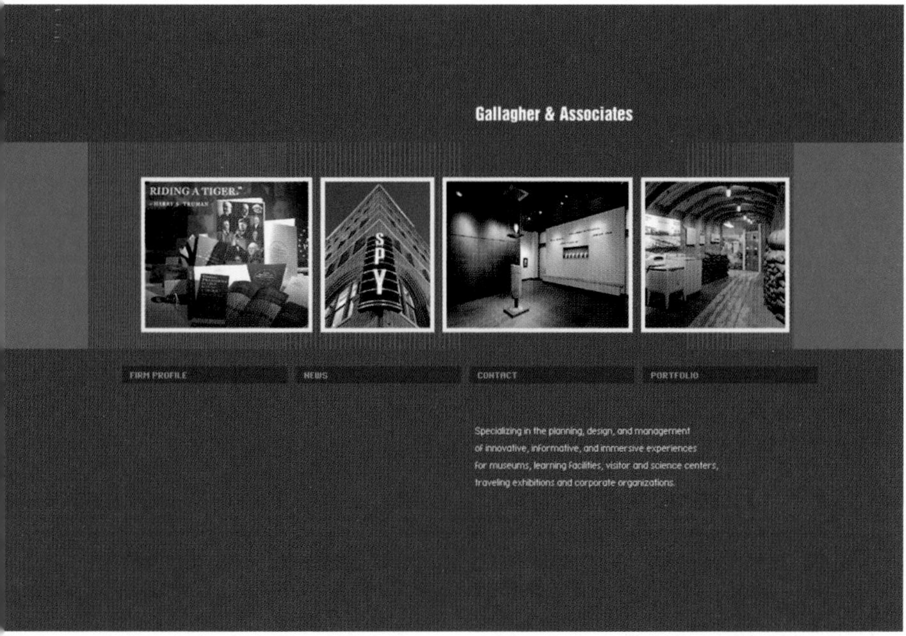

Gallagher & Associates
RIDING A TIGER.
SPY
FIRM PROFILE
NEWS
CONTACT
PORTFOLIO
Specializing in the planning, design, and management
of innovative, informative, and immersive experiences
for museums, learning facilities, visitor and science centers,
traveling exhibitions and corporate organizations.

Gallagher & Associates
PORTFOLIO
Master Planning and Exhibition Design
Environmental Graphics and Wayfinding
Graphic Design

Gallagher & Associates
PORTFOLIO

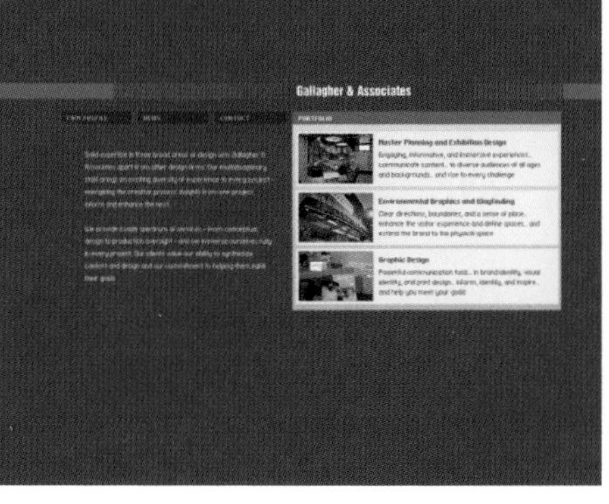

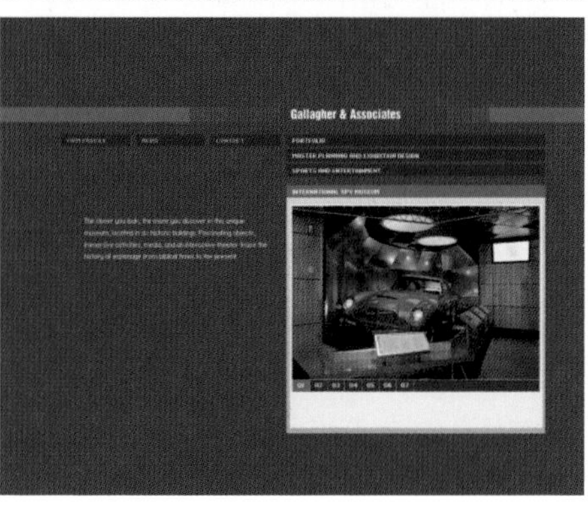

infos

Design and Programming: group94 <www.group94.com>. /// **Tools:** Macromedia Flash, php, MySQL. /// **Cost:** 5 weeks.

GIGUE FASHION

BELGIUM

www.gigue.com

2001

Concept

Although the site contains mostly images, there is no need to 'wait while loading', since each button is generated, and thus clickable, at the moment that the desired image is loaded. ////Bien que le site contienne principalement des images, nul n'est besoin d'attendre leur chargement car chaque bouton est généré et donc cliquable, dès le moment que l'image souhaitée est chargée. //// Auch wenn die Seite haupsächlich Bilder beinhaltet, gibt es keine Wartezeiten, da die Tastatur funktionsfähig bleibt, auch wenn ein Bild geladen wird.

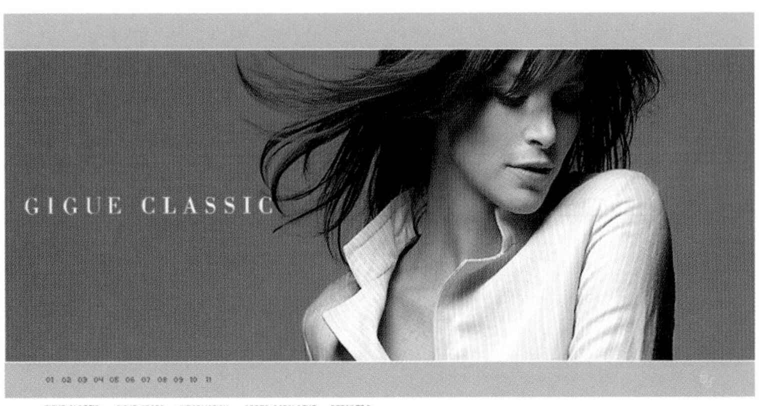

Infos

Design and Programming: Group94 <www.group94.com> /// **Tools:** Macromedia Flash, php. /// **Cost:** 4 weeks. /// **Maintenance:** 2 days every 6 months.

I AM SIA

SWEDEN

www.iamsia.com

2003

Concept

Real old, yet not. //// Attention jeune talent. //// Wirklich alt und wiederum gar nicht alt.

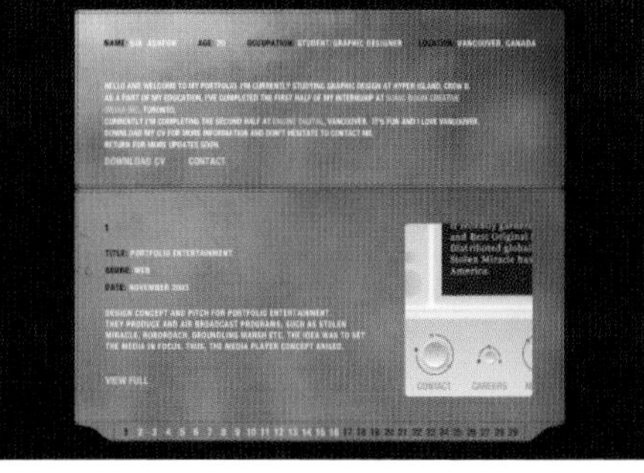

Infos

DESIGN: Sia Ashegh (I Am Sia) <www.iamsia.com>. /// **PROGRAMMING:** Emmanuel Adams. /// **TOOLS:** Macromedia Flash, html. /// **COST:** 8-10 hours /// **MAINTENANCE:** almost nothing.

GRUPPEN DESIGN

THE NETHERLANDS

www.henkgruppen.nl

2002

Concept

The site reflects the (web) design principles of GGV: clear, consistent and sober designs. Not to be confused with simple. Keeping a design clear, consistent and sober isn't all that simple... //// Le site reflète les principes de design (Web) de GGV : des designs nets, cohérents et sobres. Mais pas simples pour autant. Un design net, cohérent et sobre ne peut en effet être simple. //// Diese Seite spiegelt die (Web)-Design-Grundregeln wieder: klar, konsequent und nüchtern. Nicht zu verwecheln mit einfach. Denn ein Design klar, konsequent und nüchtern zu halten, ist keinesfalls einfach...

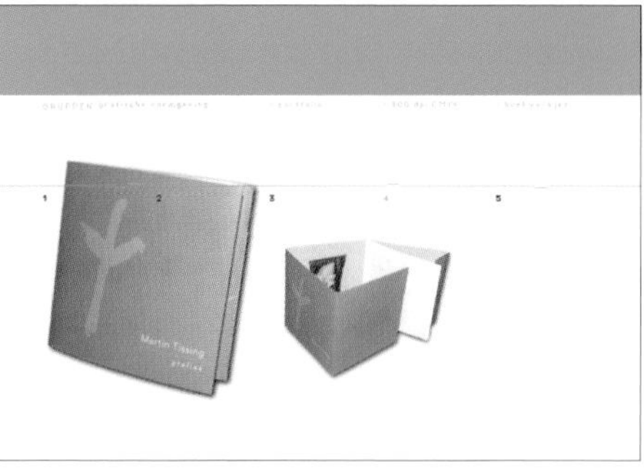

Infos

DESIGN AND PROGRAMMING: Gruppen Grafische Vormgeving. /// **TOOLS:** Macromedia Flash. /// **COST:** 20 hours. /// **MAINTENANCE:** 1 hour per month.

H4CHE

MEXICO/USA

www.h4che.com

2004

Concept

A year ago I moved from Mexico City to the USA, I rediscover my roots. Missing the flavors, the taste of color, and sound of my Country. //// Il y a un an, j'ai quitté la ville de Mexico pour m'installer aux Etats-Unis. J'ai alors redécouvert mes racines. Mon site exprime ma nostalgie des senteurs, des goûts, des couleurs et des bruits de mon pays. //// Vor einem Jahr zog ich von Mexiko Stadt in die USA, ich verfiel in eine Nostalgie, bei der ich meine Vergangenheit wieder neuentdeckte. Ich vermisste die Gerüche, den Geschmack der Farben, die Klänge und Töne meines Landes.

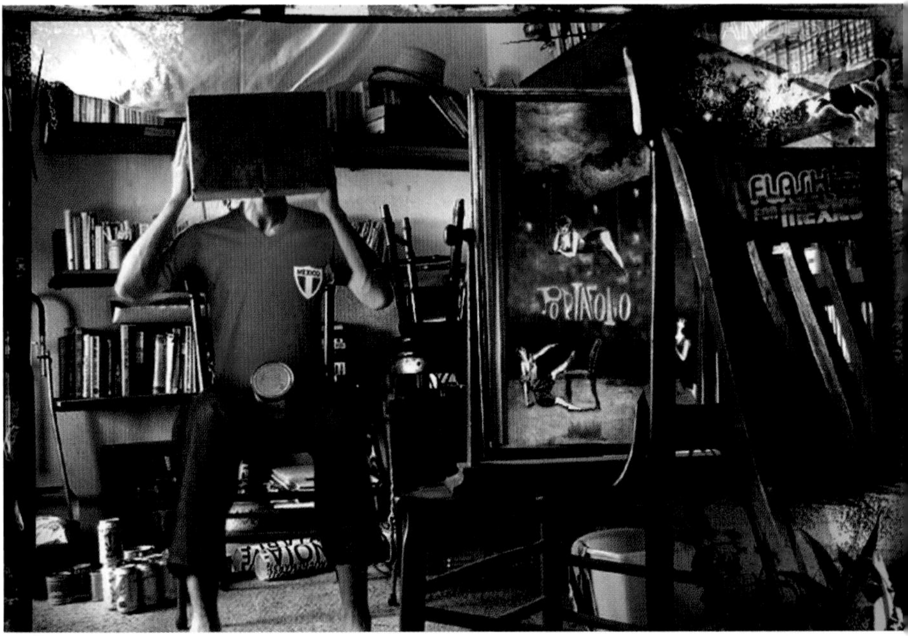

Infos

Design and Programming: Jorge Calleja (H4CHE) <www.h4che.com>; <www.l3che.com>. /// **Awards:** TAXI, e-Creative, Newstoday, Uialab, Gold Addy, Best in Show. /// **Tools:** digital camera, Adobe Photoshop, Macromedia Flash. /// **Cost:** 3 months. /// **Maintenance:** 2 hours per month.

HEIMO PHOTOGRAPHY

USA

www.heimophotography.com

2002

Concept

An interface to display Heimo's photography, in a fun way, without detracting from the work itself. //// Une interface qui présente la photographie de Heimo, de façon amusante mais sans que ses travaux n'en soient éclipsés. //// Ein Interface zum Display von Heimos Fotografie, witzig dargestellt, ohne von der Wichtigkeit der eigentlichen Arbeit abzulenken.

Infos

Design and Programming: Andreas Tagger, Butler, Shine, Stern and Partners <www.projectangora.com>, <www.bsands.com>. /// **Awards:** One Show (Silver Pencil). /// **Tools:** Adobe Photoshop, Adobe Illustrator, Macromedia Flash, BBEdit. /// **Cost:** 100 hours. /// **Maintenance:** 1 hour per month.

HELLO DESIGN

USA

www.hellodesign.com

2004

Concept

We believe in building systems that are useful, usable, and desirable. //// Nous croyons en la création de systèmes utiles, utilisables et désirables. //// Wir sind von Systemstrukturen überzeugt, die brauchbar, funktionsfähig und wünschenswert sind.

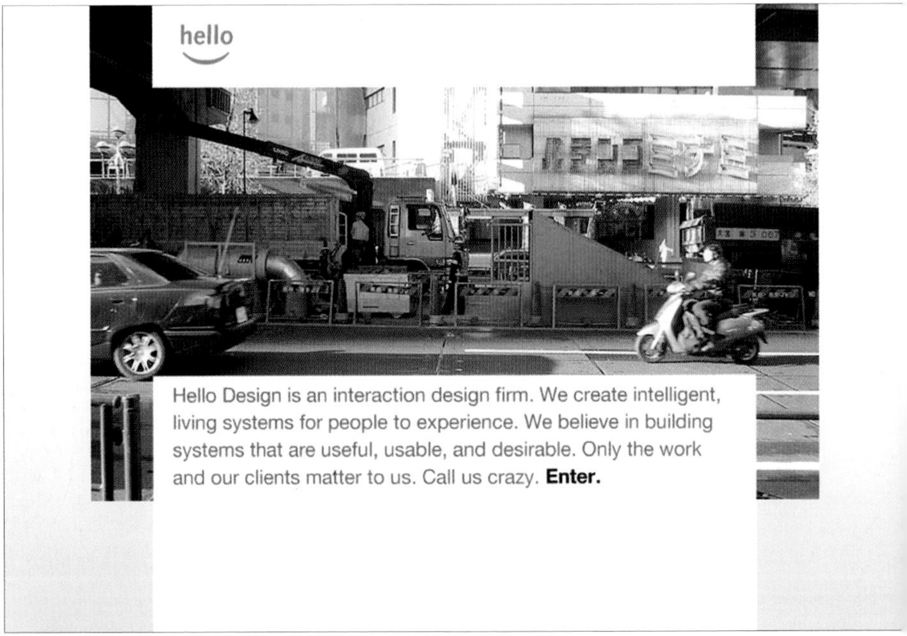

hello

Hello Design is an interaction design firm. We create intelligent, living systems for people to experience. We believe in building systems that are useful, usable, and desirable. Only the work and our clients matter to us. Call us crazy. **Enter.**

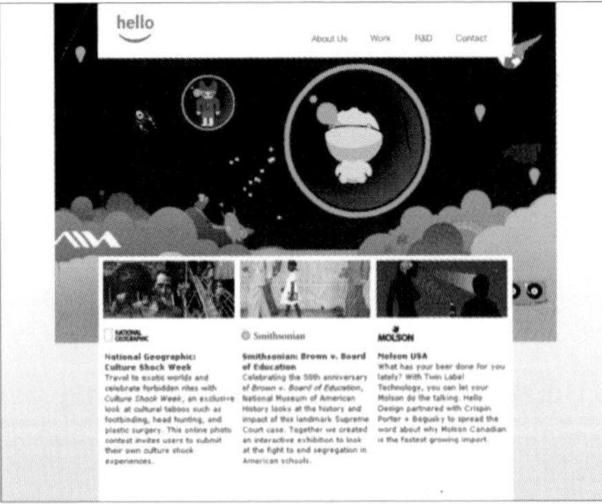

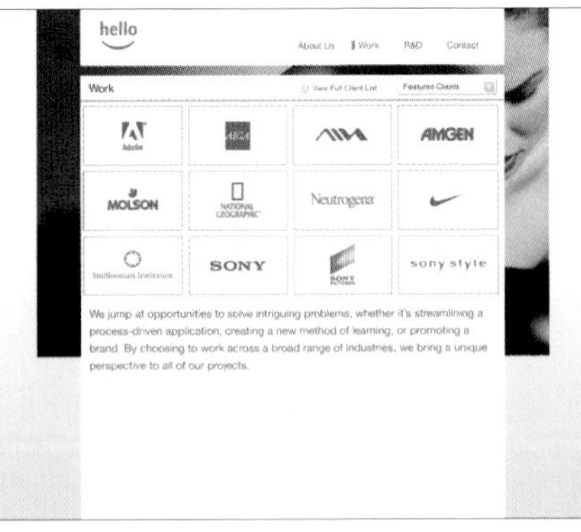

Infos

DESIGN: David Lai, Hiro Niwa, Christel Leung, Szu Ann Chen and George Lee (Hello Design). /// **PROGRAMMING:** Dan Phiffer. /// **TOOLS:** Macromedia Flash, html, xml, MySQL. /// **COST:** 3 months.

HIDDEN BROOK STUDIO

USA

www.hiddenbrookstudio.com

2004

Concept

Our goal was to illustrate the environment in which the photographer lives and works, the sounds of nature and animals, the seasonal weather, the atmosphere. //// Notre objectif était d'illustrer l'environnement dans lequel le photographe vit et travaille, les sons de la nature et des animaux, le temps, l'atmosphère. //// Unser Ziel war es, die Umgebung, in der ein Fotograf lebt und arbeitet, darzustellen: Natur- und Tiergeräusche, das ständig wechselnde Wetter, die Atmosphäre.

PORTFOLIO 1 2 3
ABOUT
CONTACT
SHOPPING CART
LOUISE W FIELD

Infos

DESIGN: Giorgio Baravalle (de.MO) <www.de-mo.org>. /// **PROGRAMMING:** Arnaud Icard. /// **TOOLS:** Macromedia Flash, php, MySQL, film, natural sound effects. /// **COST:** 120 hours. /// **MAINTENANCE:** 1 hour per month.

HIPATRIP

BELGIUM

www.hipatrip.com

2002

Concept

The colours in the navigation represent the diversity of projects ordered by discipline. Each square shows a different project. The minimal design brings out the content. //// Les couleurs du système de navigation reflètent la diversité des projets, classés par discipline. Chaque carré représente un projet différent. Le design minimal fait ressortir le contenu. //// **Bei dieser Navigation repräsentieren die Farben die Vielfalt der Projekte, nach Kategorien geordnet. Jedes Feld zeigt ein anderes Projekt. Das minimalistische Design hebt den Inhalt hervor.**

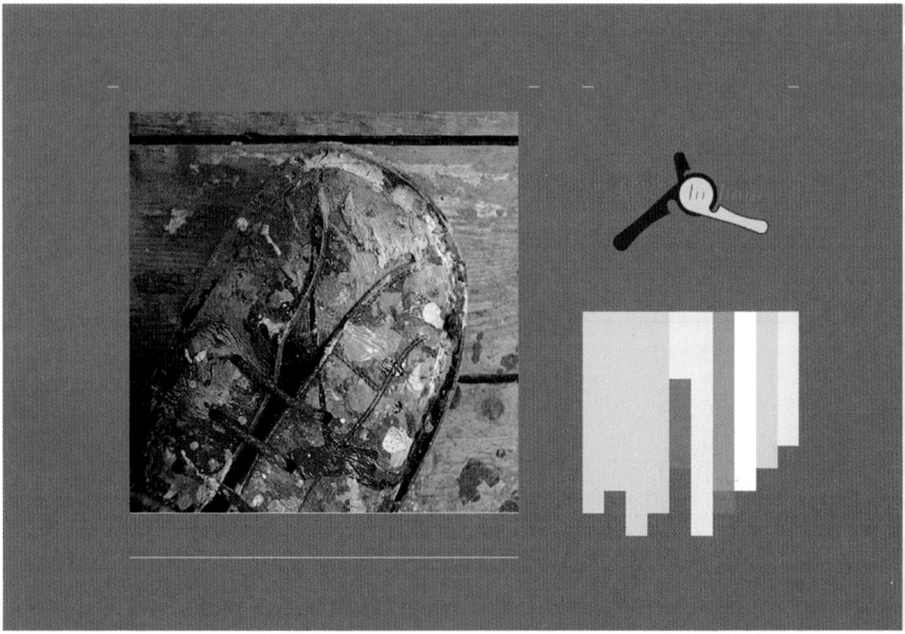

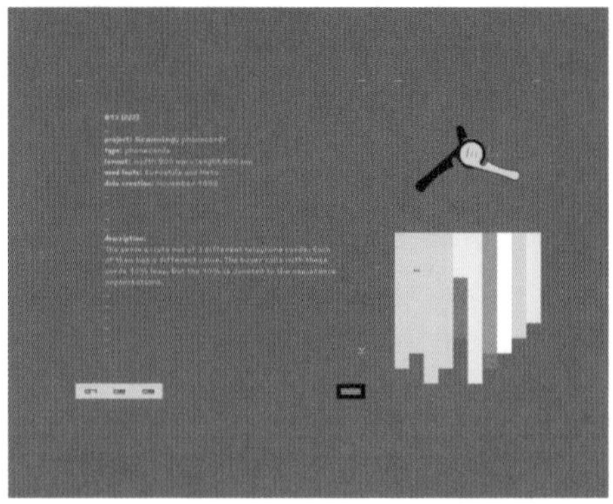

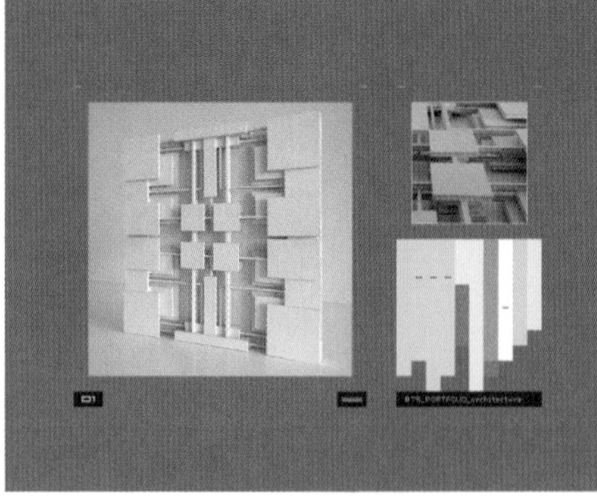

Infos

Design and Programming: Jurgen Vanbrabant (Hipatrip). /// **Awards:** Wow-Factor SOTW, Topten flash-es.net. /// **Tools:** Macromedia Flash, Action-script. /// **Cost:** a lot of freetime. /// **Maintenance:** 4 hours per month.

HUIDI LAUHOFF

GERMANY

www.huidi-lauhoff.de

2004

Concept

Reduced and focused on the essential - this is how Scholz & Volkmer presents the new autumn/winter collection from the Wiesbaden-based fashion designer Huidi Lauhoff on the web. //// Minimaliste et centrée sur l'essentiel, c'est ainsi que Scholz & Volkmer présente sur le Web la nouvelle collection automne/hiver de la designer Huidi Lauhoff, basée à Wiesbaden. //// Reduziert und auf das Wesentliche fokussiert - so präsentiert Scholz & Volkmer die neue Herbst- und Winter-Damenkollektion der Wiesbadener Modedesignerin Huidi Lauhoff im Netz.

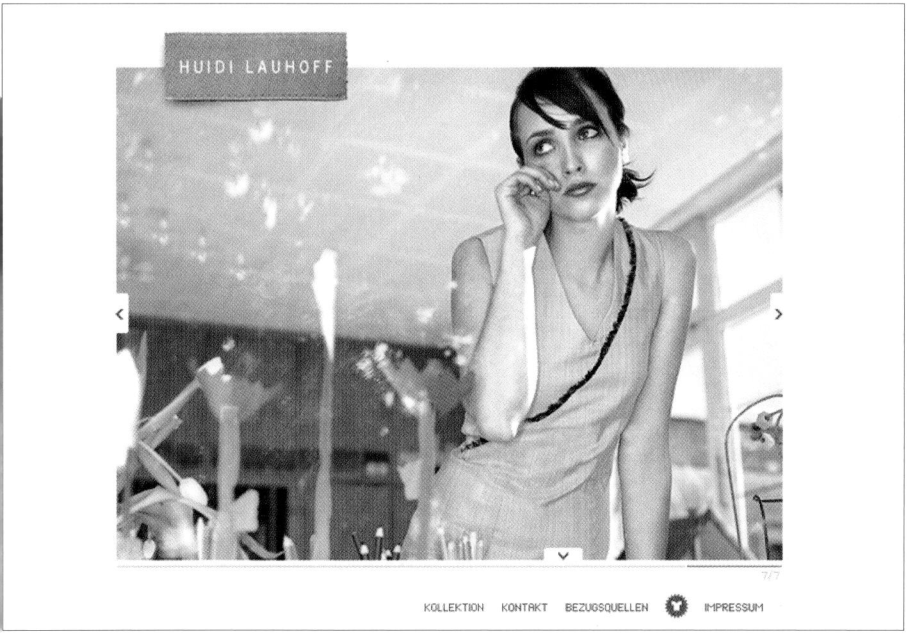

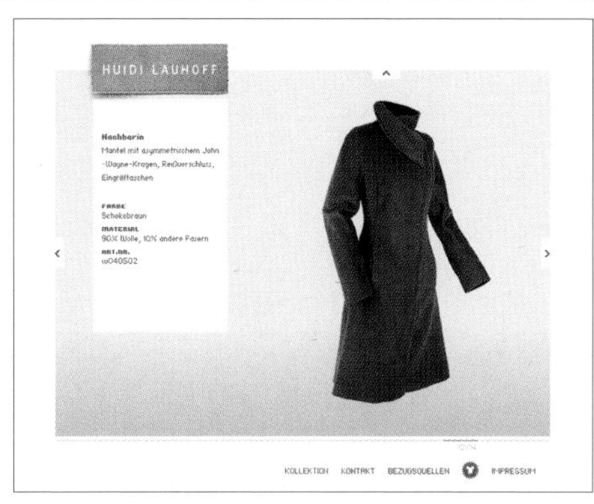

Infos

DESIGN: Scholz & Volkmer. /// **PROGRAMMING:** Flash Programming: Oliver Hinrichs; Technical Direction: Thorsten Kraus. /// **AWARDS:** Annual Multimedia Award, Communication networked Award of the German Designer Club (Silver). /// **TOOLS:** html, Macromedia Flash, xml. /// **COST:** 45 days.

HUT SACHS STUDIO

USA

www.hutsachs.com

2003

Concept

Photo driven portfolio site with an architectonic and intuitive navigation. //// Site portfolio de photographies doté d'un système de navigation architectonique et intuitif. //// **Eine von Fotografie bestimmte Portfolioseite mit architektonischer und intuitiver Navigation.**

Infos

DESIGN AND PROGRAMMING: Knowawall Design <www.knowawall.com>. /// **TOOLS:** Macromedia Flash, html. /// **COST:** 90 hours. /// **MAINTENANCE:** 5 hours per month.

HW PHOTOGRAPHY

JAPAN

www.hwphotography.com

2004

Concept

Simple for a novice, flexible for an expert. //// Simple pour un novice, souple pour un expert. //// Einfach verständlich für einen Anfänger, flexibel für einen Experten.

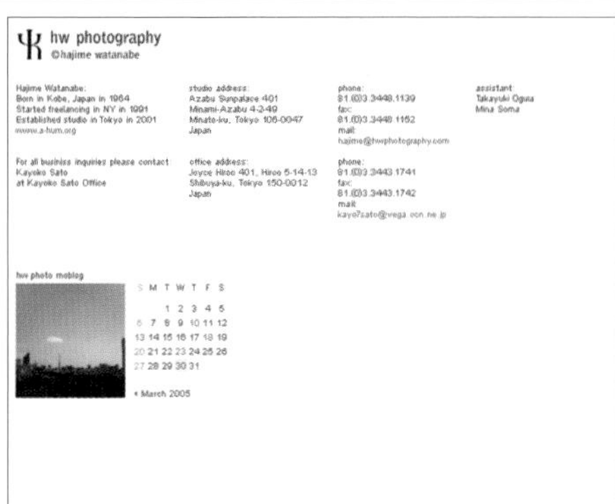

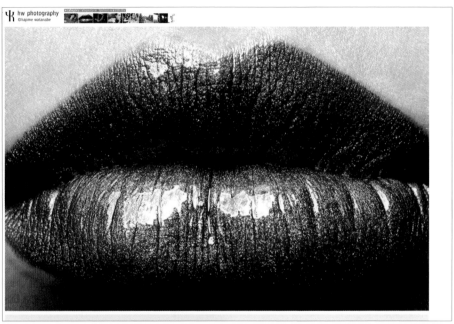

Infos

Design and Programming: Hitoshi Okazaki (FIRM NOT NAMED YET) <www.firmnotnamedyet.com>. /// **Awards:** I.D. Magazine Interactive Media Design Review (Honorable Mention). /// **Tools:** Macromedia Flash, Movable Type. /// **Cost:** 200 hours. /// **Maintenance:** 1 hour per month.

HYBRIDWORKS

JAPAN

www.hybridworks.jp

2003

Concept

Without any unified concept, this site contains graphics, illustrations, animations, etc. filled with humor. //// Dépourvu de tout concept global, ce site contient des graphismes, illustrations, animations, etc. remplis d'humour. //// Ohne unbedingt ein einheitliches Konzept aufzuweisen, beinhaltet diese Webseite Grafiken, Illustrationen, Animationen usw. und das nicht ganz ohne Humor.

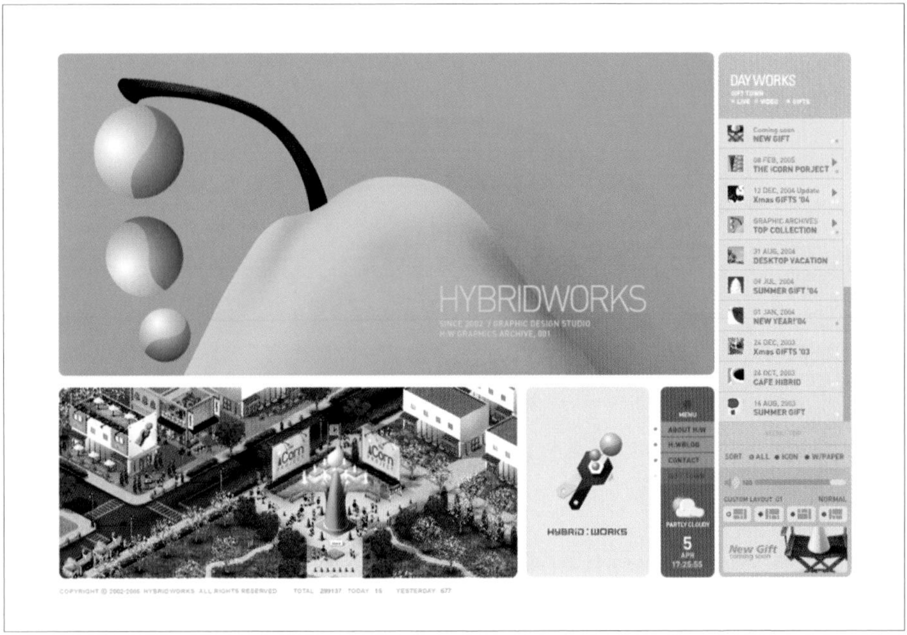

Infos

Design and Programming: Masaki Hoshino (HYBRIDWORKS). /// **Tools:** Adobe Photoshop, Adobe Illustrator, Macromedia Flash, xml. /// **Cost:** 2 years. /// **Maintenance:** 1-2 weeks per year.

IDIOM 3 MEDIA

USA

www.idiom3.com

2003

Concept

The concept behind was to create a pleasant atmosphere that displayed the work while also retaining full functionality and aesthetics. //// L'idée derrière ce site était de créer une atmosphère agréable dans laquelle présenter les travaux, tout en restant conservant une fonctionnalité totale et une esthétique. //// **Das Konzept dieser Seite bestand darin, eine angenehme Atmosphäre zu schaffen, die wiederum unsere Arbeiten wiederspiegelt, unter Beibehaltung voller Funktionalität und Ästhetik.**

Infos

DESIGN AND PROGRAMMING: John Cruz (Idiom 3 Media). /// **AWARDS:** Plasticpilots. /// **TOOLS:** Macromedia Flash, html. /// **COST:** 20 hours. /// **MAINTENANCE:** 5 hours per month.

ILLUSTRATOR.BE

BELGIUM

www.illustrator.be

2004

Concept

The site's metaphor is a 'physical light box' that illustrators used to sit and work on in the old days. //// La métaphore utilisée dans le site est une « table lumineuse physique », sur laquelle les illustrateurs d'autrefois s'asseyaient et travaillaient. //// **Die Metapher dieser Seite ist ein 'echter Leuchtkasten', den früher die Illustratoren zum Arbeiten benutzten.**

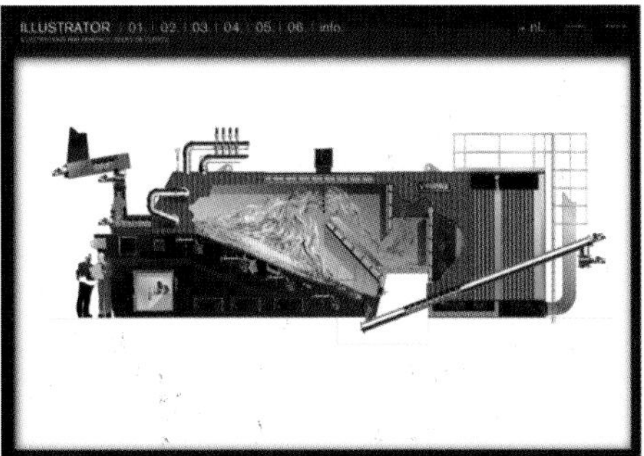

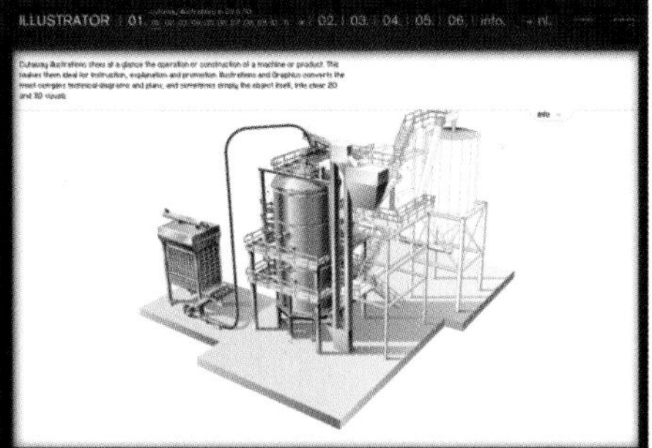

Infos

DESIGN AND PROGRAMMING: group94 <www.group94.com>. /// **TOOLS:** Macromedia Flash. /// **COST:** 3 weeks. /// **MAINTENANCE:** 1 day every 6 months.

INBREDBOY

CANADA

www.inbredboy.com

2003

Concept

A bug-eyed, deformed boy becomes lost in the swamp one day. He discovers a talent for art and makes a little portfolio for himself out of the odds and ends he finds laying around. //// Un garçon difforme aux yeux exorbités se perd dans un marais. Il se découvre un talent pour l'art et se constitue un petit portfolio à partir de tout ce qu'il trouve autour de lui. //// Ein froschäugiger, entstellter Junge verläuft sich eines Tages im Sumpf. Er entdeckt sein Talent für die Kunst und bastelt sein Portfolio aus allerlei Dingen, die er in seiner Umgebung findet, zusammen.

Infos

Design: Cameron Wilson (Inbredboy). /// **Programming:** Christian Ayotte. /// **Awards:** Digital Marketing Awards (Gold), Cannes Cyber Lion (Short List). /// **Tools:** html, Macromedia Flash, dhtml, xml. /// **Content:** music, film, etc. /// **Cost:** 300 hours.

J6 STUDIOS

USA

www.j6studios.com

2003

Concept

J6Studios.com was created to be a place where I can store and show my ideas and interests to the rest of the world. //// J6Studios a été créé comme un lieu où je peux conserver et montrer mes idées et centres d'intérêt au reste du monde. //// J6Studios.com ist ein Platz, an dem ich meine Ideen aufbewahren und sie ausserdem dem Rest der Welt zeigen kann.

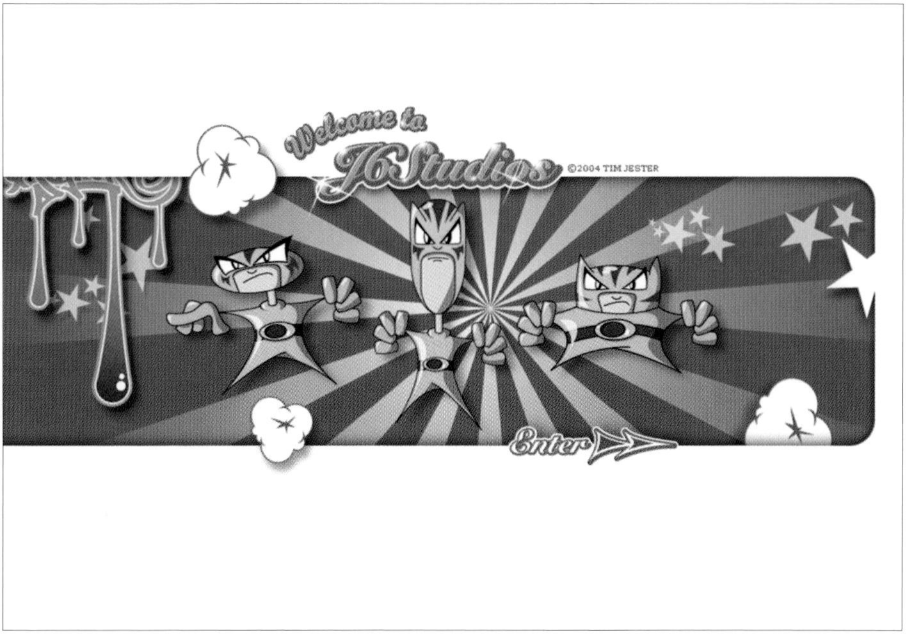

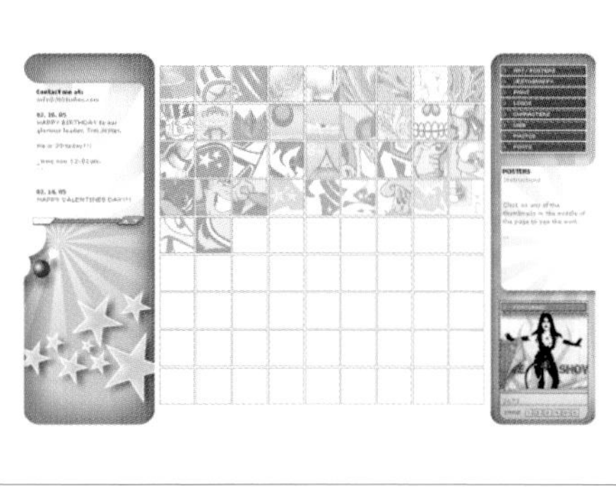

Infos

DESIGN: Tim Jester (J6Studios). /// **PROGRAMMING:** Tim Jester and Neal Desai. /// **TOOLS:** html, Macromedia Flash, music, xml. /// **COST:** the cost was zero. It was all done in my spare time. /// **MAINTENANCE:** it takes about 3 minutes for a new image, icon and text to be uploaded to the site.

JAN KNOFF PHOTOGRAPHY

GERMANY

www.janknoff.de

2004

Concept

The design doesn't intend to display the strength with complicated navigation. So the page is flash based in a way that the images are automatically updated. //// Le design ne vise pas à montrer la force à l'aide d'une navigation complexe. La page est donc au format Flash de façon à ce que les images soient automatiquement mises à jour. //// **Das Design beruht auf der Intention, die Wirkung der Fotos nicht durch eine umständliche Navigation zu beeinträchtigen. Darüber ist bei dieser Flash-Site gewährleistet, dass sich die Navigation bei einer Aktualisierung automatisch anpasst.**

Techno

Techno_06

Infos

DESIGN: Jan Knoff and Wolfgang Kohlert. /// PROGRAMMING: Wolfgang Kohlert <www.cybercartoon.de>. ///
TOOLS: html, Macromedia Flash. /// COST: 136 hours.

JASON SIU & CO

HONG KONG

www.jasonsiu.com

2002

Concept

Speak your mind. //// Exprimez-vous. //// Sag deine Meinung.

Infos

Design: DHKY <www.dhky.com> and Jason Siu. /// **Programming:** DHKY. /// **Awards:** FWA. /// **Tools:** Adobe Photoshop, Adobe Illustrator, Macromedia Flash. /// **Cost:** 2 months. /// **Maintenance:** 2-3 hours every 2 month.

JEEDOUBLEU DESIGN

CANADA

www.jeedub.com

2004

Concept

The concept for this site is to visualize the struggle that designers go through, trying to think "Outside The Box". //// Le concept de ce site consiste à visualiser la lutte à laquelle sont confrontés les designers en essayant de penser « hors de la boîte » (traduction d'une expression anglaise signifiant « de façon créative »). //// **Das Konzept dieser Seite visualisiert die Schwierigkeit der Designer, kein Schubladen-Denken (Outside The Box) zu entfalten.**

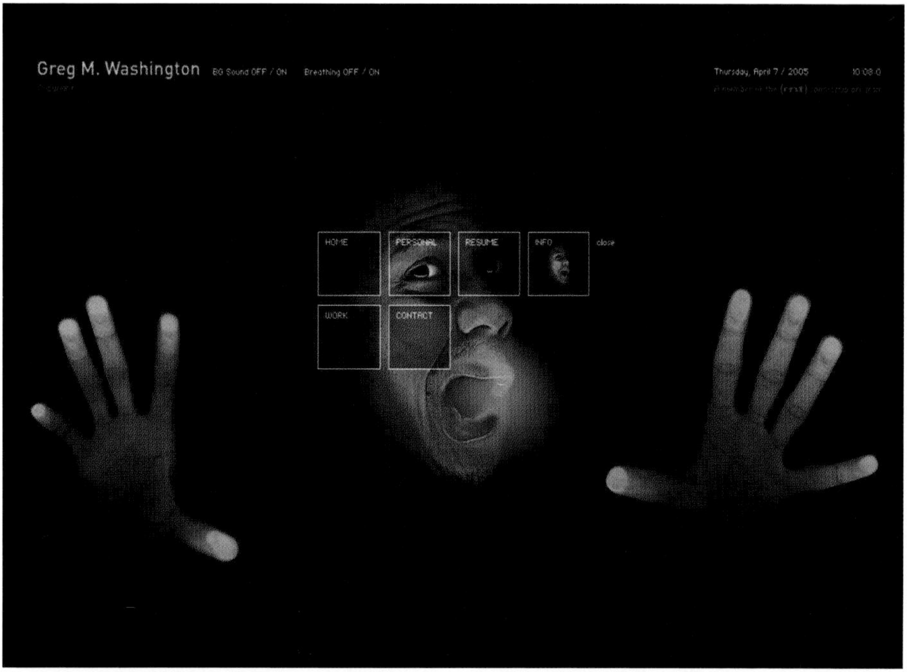

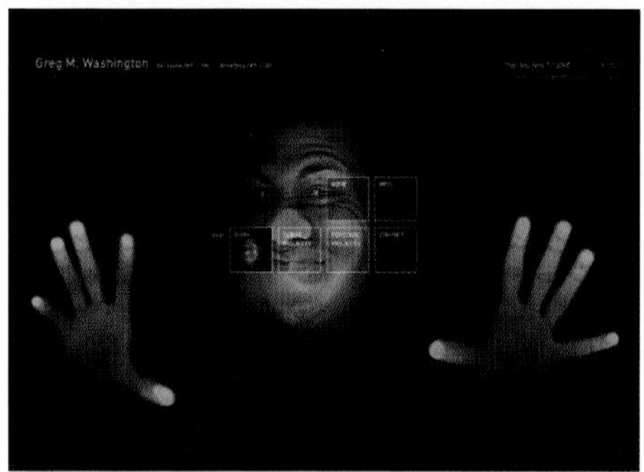

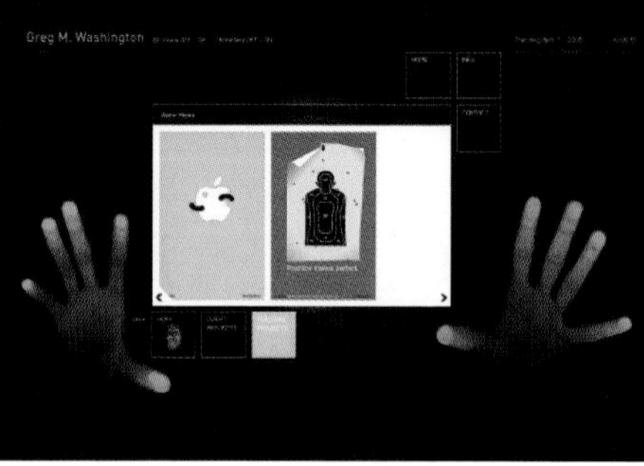

Infos

DESIGN AND PROGRAMMING: Greg M. Washington (JEEDUB). /// **AWARDS:** FWA, TINY, Flash Forward Festival. /// **TOOLS:** Adobe Illustrator, Adobe Photoshop, Adobe Premier, Macromedia Dreamweaver, Macromedia Flash, Actionscript, php, html, Javascript, music. /// **COST:** 20 hours. /// **MAINTENANCE:** 4 hours per month.

JENS GOERLICH PHOTO

GERMANY

www.jens-goerlich.de

2004

Concept

The reduction of navigation and info-elements should lead to a stronger focus on the main content of the site, the photography of Jens. ////
La navigation minimaliste et les info-éléments ont été pensés pour mettre en valeur le principal intérêt du site : les photographies de Jens. ////
Weniger Navigations- und Informationselemente ermöglichen, den Schwerpunkt auf den wesentlichen Inhalt der Seite zu lenken, nämlich die Fotografie von Jens.

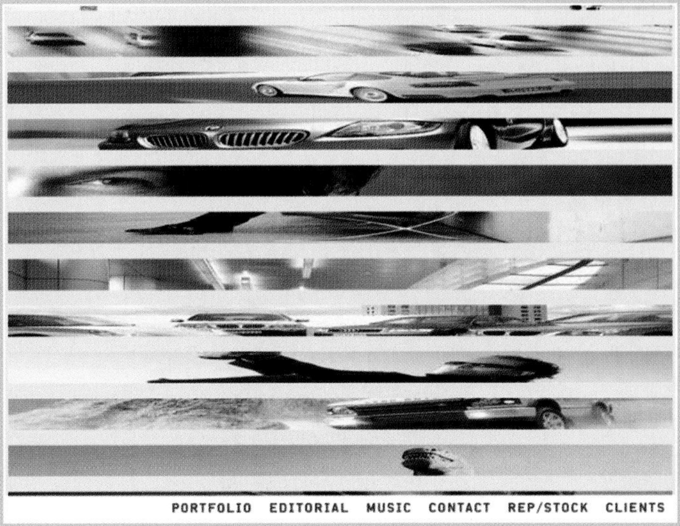

Infos

Design and Programming: Amin Weber <www.amination.net>. /// **Tools:** Macromedia Flash, html, scanned images of slide- and negative film. ///
Cost: 50 hours. /// **Maintenance:** 5 hours per month.

JIMMY MCGRATH PHOTO

USA

www.jimmymcgrathphoto.com

2003

Concept

By using the photos as inspiration for an illustration then presenting them as a single experience we achieved an experience that is very compelling and memorable. //// En utilisant les photos comme inspiration pour une illustration puis en présentant les photos et illustrations sous la forme d'une expérience unique, nous sommes parvenus à créer une expérience et mémorable. //// Indem wir die Fotos als Inspiration für Illustrationen verwenden und dann die Fotos und die Illustration als eine gemeinsame Erfahrung präsentieren, schaffen wir ein unwiderstehliches und nachhaltig Erlebnis.

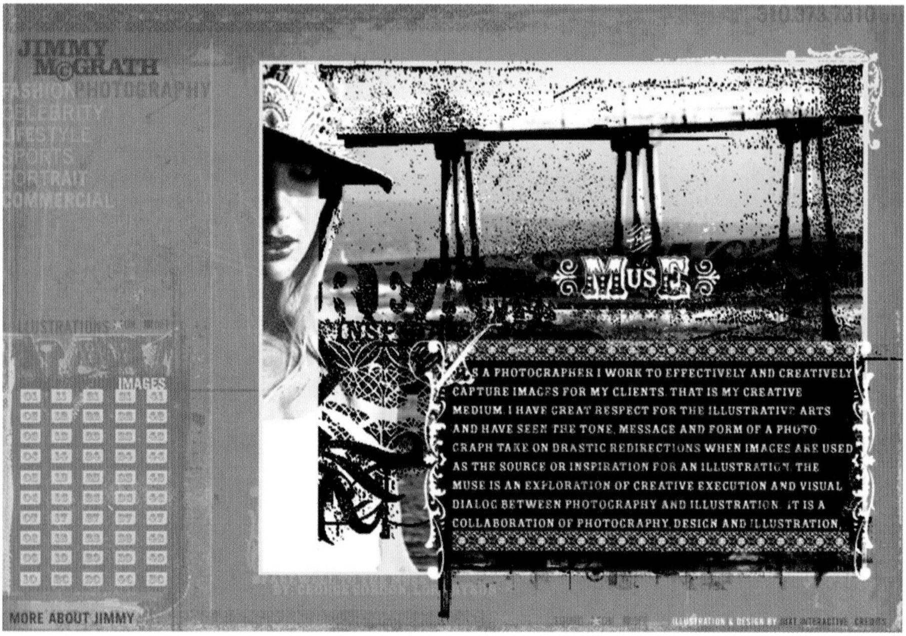

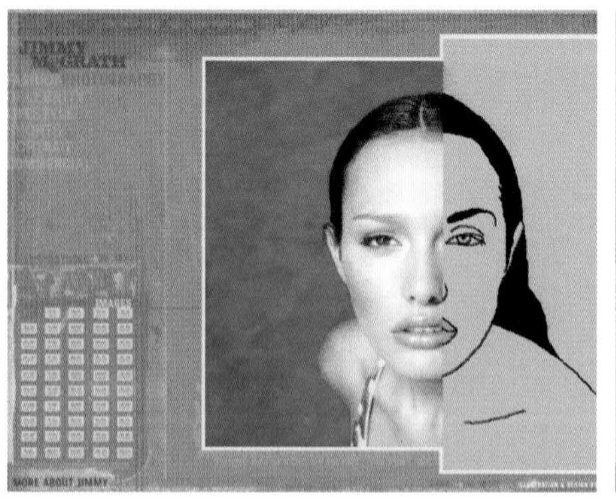

Infos

Design: Todd Purgason, Luis Escoril, Paul Drohan, Mike Hanson, Nate Smith and Shant Parseghian (Juxt Interactive) <www.juxtinteractive.com>. /// **Programming:** Todd Purgason. /// **Awards:** One show, Cannes Cyber Lion. /// **Tools:** Macromedia Flash. /// **Cost:** too many to count.

JOE VAUX, MY HAPPY PLACE

USA

www.joevaux.com

2003

Concept

I wanted it to have some of the qualities of my paintings as well as a life of its own. Sounds and animation strike a mood that I feel enhances the presentation of my work. //// Je voulais que mon site ait certaines des qualités de mes peintures mais aussi qu'il ait une vie propre. Les sons et l'animation créent une ambiance qui, je crois, met en valeur la présentation de mon travail. //// Die Seite sollte einerseits die Qualitäten wie die meiner Gemälde aufweisen, als auch als eigenes Project bestehen können. Sound und Animation spiegeln die Stimmung meiner Arbeiten wieder und bereichern deren Präsentation.

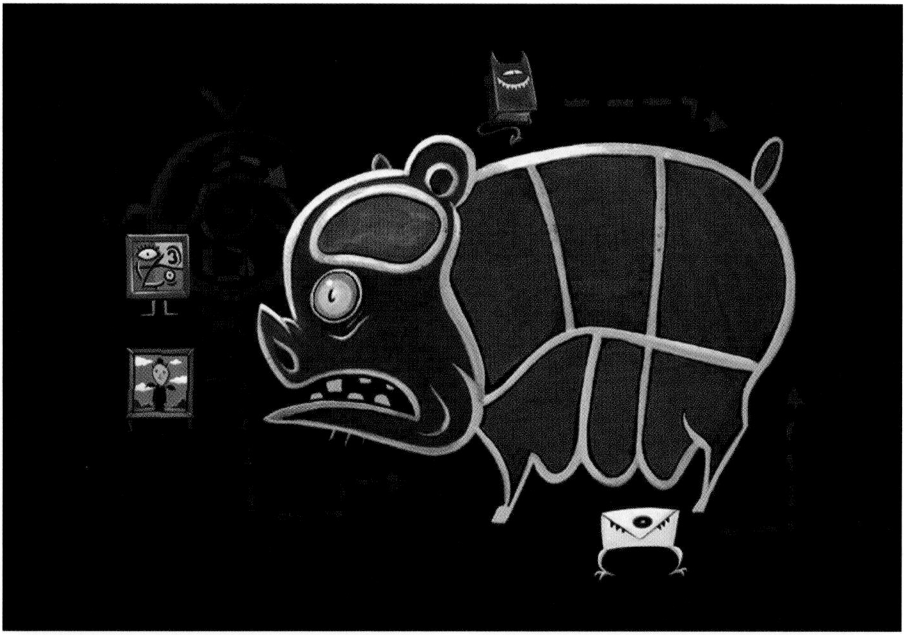

Infos

DESIGN: Squidhaven L.L.C. <www.squidhaven.com>. /// **PROGRAMMING:** Tom Martin. /// **TOOLS:** html, Macromedia Flash. /// **COST:** 100 hours. /// **MAINTENANCE:** $50 per month.

JOHN PARKER PHOTOGRAPHY UK

www.johnparker.biz 2004

Concept

Simple but effective navigation to showcase images. //// Une navigation simple mais efficace pour présenter les photos. //// Einfache, aber effektive Navigation zur Darstellung von Bildern.

Infos

DESIGN: Chris Christodoulou (Saddington & Baynes) <www.sb-showcase.com>. /// **PROGRAMMING:** Duncan Hart. /// **TOOLS:** html, Macromedia Flash.

JULIAN WATSON AGENCY UK

www.julianwatsonagency.com 2004

Concept

A fluid and calming environment to view artists work. //// Un environnement fluide et apaisant dans lequel découvrir les travaux d'artistes. //// Ein fliessendes und beruhigendes Ambiente für die Betrachtung künstlerischer Werke.

Infos

DESIGN: underwaterpistol <www.underwaterpistol.com>. /// **PROGRAMMING:** Gary Carruthers and Gary Belton. /// **TOOLS:** html, Macromedia Flash, php, MySQL. /// **COST:** 200 hours. /// **MAINTENANCE:** 4 hours per month.

JOHN ROSS PHOTOGRAPHY UK

www.johnross.co.uk 2004

Concept

The aim was to let the unobtrusive navigation remove all the clutter and let the photography do the talking. //// Le but était de laisser la discrète navigation ôter toute trace de désordre et de laisser la photographie faire la conversation. //// Das Ziel war es, durch eine einfache Navigation alles Hinderliche aus dem Weg zu räumen und die Fotografie für alles Weitere verantwortlich zu machen.

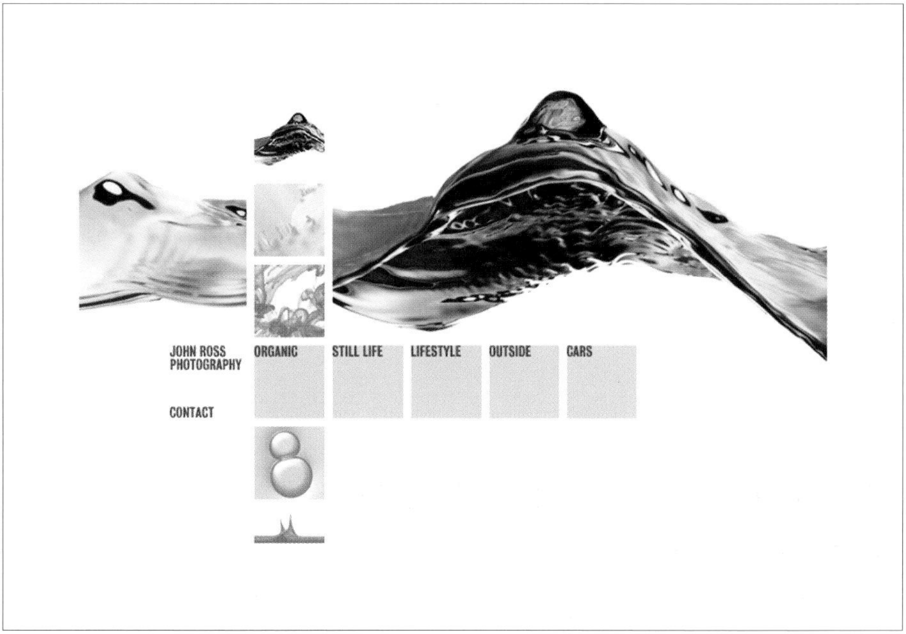

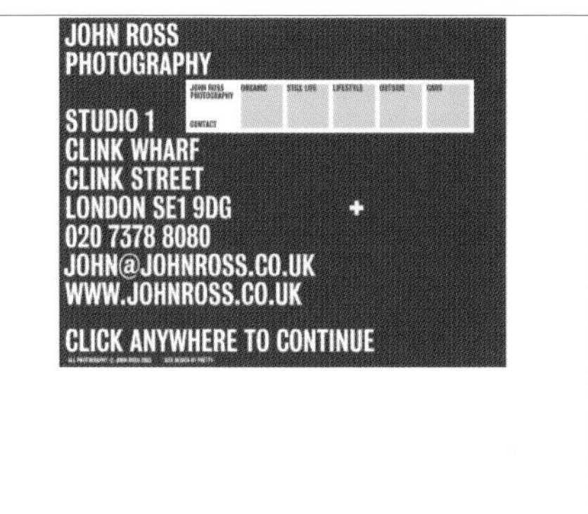

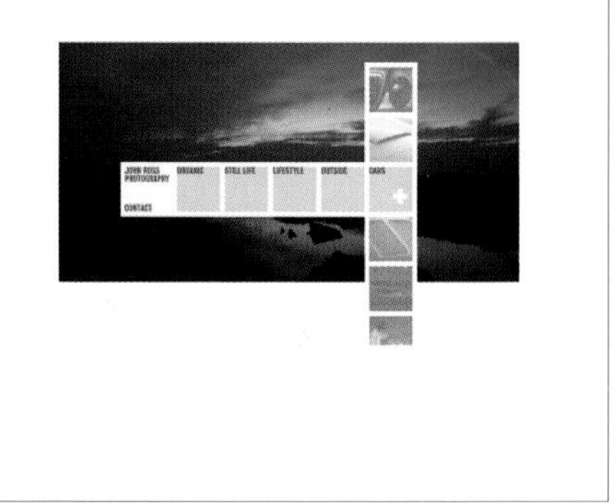

Infos

Design: Toby Stokes and Dominic McMahon (Pretty) <www.prettystudio.co.uk>. /// **Programming:** Simon Dixon. /// **Tools:** Macromedia Flash. /// **Cost:** 80 hours. /// **Maintenance:** 6 hours every 6 months

JULIE WEST ILLUSTRATION

USA

www.juliewest.com

2004

Concept

Created to be clean and simple, yet reflect the artist's illustration style throughout the site. //// Créé pour être clair et simple, ce site reflète toutefois de part en part le style de l'artiste. //// Trotz einfachem und klarem Design zeigt sich der Illustrationsstil des Künstlers auf der gesamten Webseite.

Infos

Design: Julie West. /// **Tools:** php, MySQL, html, CSS. /// **Cost:** 40 hours. /// **Maintenance:** 2 hours per week.

KARINA BEDNORZ PHOTO

GERMANY

www.karinabednorz.de

2004

Concept

A precise and clean shell that makes an easy overview of the portfolios presented. //// Un écrin précis et net qui donne un aperçu facile des portfolios présentés. //// Eine klare und präzise Struktur, die einen einfachen Überblick über die Portfolios verschafft.

Infos

Design and Programming: Rune Høgsberg <www.adoptdesign.com>. /// **Awards:** FWA, TAXI. /// **Tools:** Macromedia Flash. /// **Cost:** 2.200 € /// **Maintenance:** 1 hour per month.

KATY BARKER AGENCY

UK

www.katybarker.com

2004

Concept

Simple and elegant, ensuring the design did not intrude on the strength of the images. //// Simple et élégant, pour que le design ne nuisse pas à la force des images. //// **Einfach und elegant, und mit Sicherheit kein Einfluss des Designs auf die Dominanz der Fotografie.**

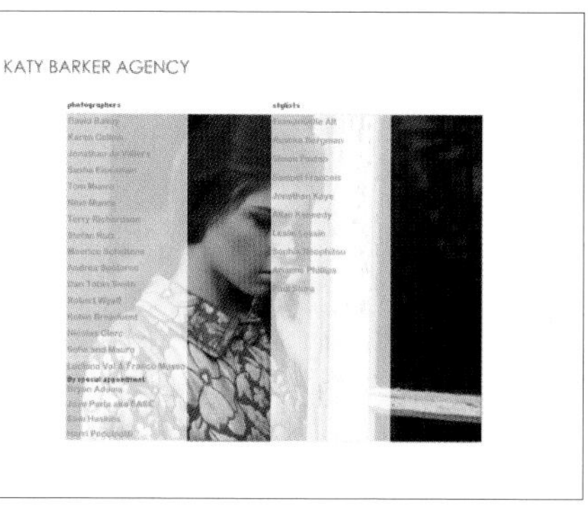

Infos

Design: underwaterpistol <www.underwaterpistol.com>. /// **Programming:** Gary Carruthers and Gary Belton. /// **Tools:** html, Macromedia Flash, php, MySQL. /// **Cost:** 240 hours. /// **Maintenance:** 6 hours per month.

KDLAB

USA

www.kdlab.net

2003

Concept

A framework defined by densities of transparency allowing for the viewing of content in a detailed arrangement, but one that does not distract from the content in focus. //// Un cadre défini par des densités de transparence permettant la consultation de contenus dans une disposition détaillée mais ne distrayant pas du contenu qu'elle sert. //// Eine Struktur, die sich durch die dichteren Stellen ihrer Transparenz definiert und somit ihren Inhalt in detaillierter Aufgliederung zur Schau stellt, ohne dabei vom Wesentlichen abzulenken.

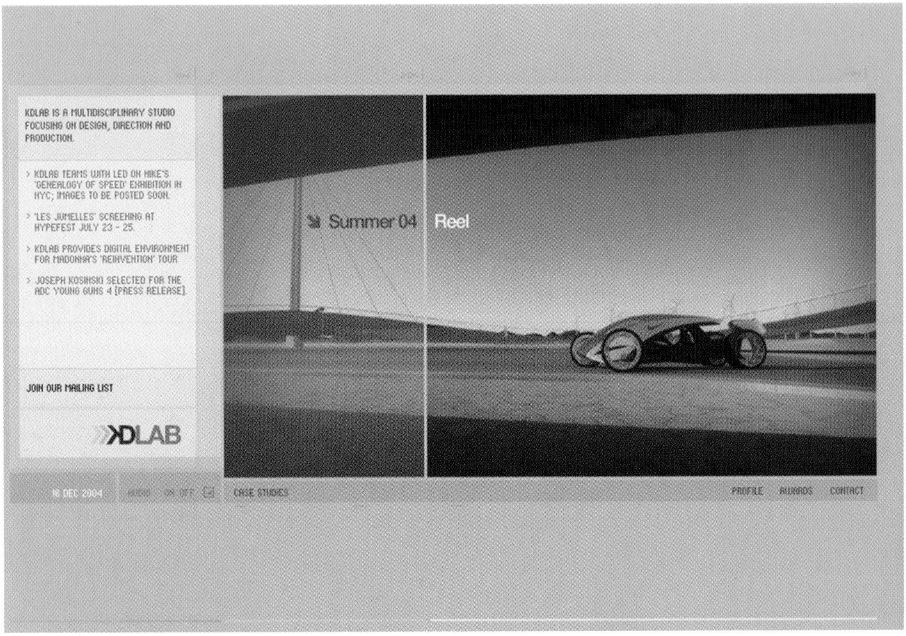

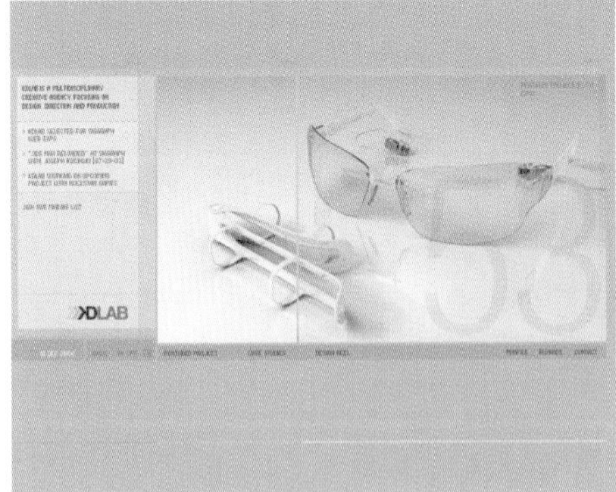

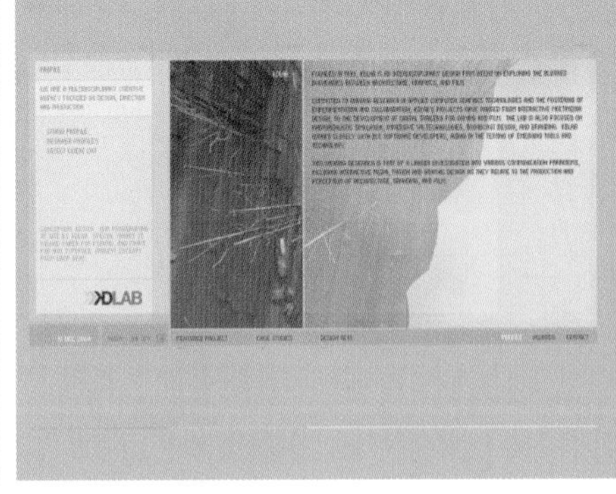

Infos

Design and Programming: Dean DiSimone (KDLAB). /// **Awards:** Web Expo Siggraph. /// **Tools:** html, Macromedia Flash, mp3, Quicktime.

KELAMALI

FRANCE

www.kelamali.com

2003

Concept

Conceived so as to immerge the user into the Manding kingdom by exciting his senses with interactive African music and images. //// Conçu pour immerger l'utilisateur dans le royaume mandingue en éveillant ses sens à l'aide de musique africaine et d'images interactives. //// Als ob der Nutzer in das Königreich Manding eintauchen und seine Sinne von interaktiver afrikanischer Musik und Bildern stimuliert würden.

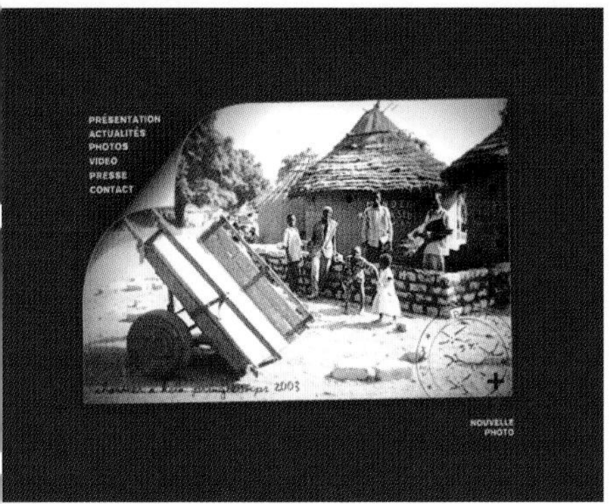

Infos

DESIGN: dunun <www.dunun.com>. /// **PROGRAMMING:** Micael Reynaud. /// **AWARDS:** fcukstar.com, TINY. /// **TOOLS:** Macromedia Flash, php, html. /// **CONTENT:** interactive music, photo, text, video. /// **COST:** 110 hours. /// **MAINTENANCE:** 5 hours per month.

KIRSTEN ULVE ILLUSTRATION USA

www.kirstenulve.com 2000

Concept

I wanted a 'Lite Brite' feel of saturated RGB color (my drawings) against pitch black in the portfolio sections. Plus there's entertaining animation and music! //// Je voulais qu'une touche « Lite Brite » de couleurs RVB (mes dessins) saturées contraste sur le noir d'encre des sections de portfolio. Je voulais aussi des animations et de la musique divertissantes ! //// Ich möchte ein 'leichtes, helles' Gefühl von saturierten RGB-Farben (die meiner Zeichnungen) vermitteln, die im Kontrast zum Tiefschwarz meines Portfolios stehen. Ausserdem gibt es unterhaltsame Animation und Musik.

Infos

DESIGN: Kirsten Ulve. /// PROGRAMMING: site and movement by Mike Faivre <www.sweatboxdesign.com>. Sound by Chad Pearson. /// TOOLS: Adobe Photoshop, Adobe Illustrator, Macromedia Dreamweaver, Macromedia Flash, Quicktime, xhtml, CSS, Pro Tools, Reason, Garage Band. /// COST: 50-60 hours. /// MAINTENANCE: 1-2 hours per month.

NORBERT KNIAT PHOTO

AUSTRIA

www.kniat.de

2004

concept

To create a website that is fast, beautiful and easy to use and works without a "techy" interface... //// Pour créer un site Web, rapide, beau, facile à utiliser et fonctionnant sans interface technique... ////Eine Webseite kreieren, die schnell, wunderschön und einfach anzuwenden ist und ohne ein "techy" Interface arbeitet.

infos

DESIGN: Matthias Netzberger (Lessrain) <www.lessrain.com>. /// **PROGRAMMING:** Matthias Netzberger (Frontend) & Peter Pokorny (Backend). /// **TOOLS:** Adobe Photoshop, Macromedia Flash, Macromedia Dreamweaver, xml. /// **CONTENT:** music, photos. /// **COST:** 50 hours. /// **MAINTENANCE:** 10 hours per month.

KOLLEKTIEF INTERIOR

BELGIUM

www.kollektief.be

2003

concept

The portfolio is presented on a system of floating panes. The navigation system consists of exactly 1 button, that contains all functionality. //// Le portfolio est présenté à l'aide d'un système de fenêtres flottantes. Le système de navigation consiste en un unique bouton, qui contient toutes les fonctionnalités. //// Das Portfolio wird auf einem System schwebender Scheiben präsentiert. Das Navigationssystem besteht aus nur einem Knopf, der alle Funktionen ausführt.

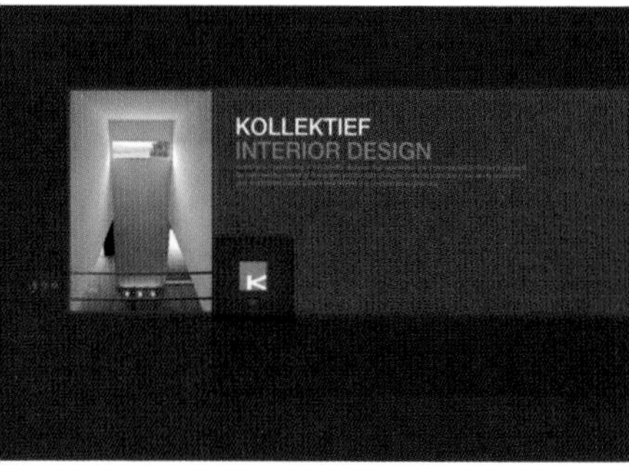

infos

DESIGN AND PROGRAMMING: group94 <wwwgroup94.com>. /// **AWARDS:** FWA (Site of the Day), TAXI (Site of the Day), Visueller Orgasmus (Top20 Sites). /// **TOOLS:** Macromedia Flash, php. /// **COST:** 3 weeks. /// **MAINTENANCE:** 1 day every year.

KREATIVKOLLEKTIV

GERMANY

www.kreativkollektiv.de

2003

Concept

The main concept is to have dynamic and modular construction in order to allow ner contents and designs to be inserted anytime. //// L'idée principale repose sur une construction modulaire et dynamique permettant d'insérer à tout moment de nouveaux contenus et design. //// Das Grundkonzept besteht im modularen und dynamischen Aufbau der es ermöglicht inhaltlich und gestalterisch jederzeit neue Ideen einfließen zu lassen.

Infos

DESIGN: Stefan Richter and André Grünhoff (Kreativkollektiv). /// **PROGRAMMING:** Karsten Koch (Kreativkollektiv). /// **TOOLS:** Macromedia Flash. /// **CONTENT:** audio, video, text. /// **COST:** 200 hours. /// **MAINTENANCE:** 10 hours per month.

LA FILLE D'O

BELGIUM

www.lafilledo.com

2004

Concept

It's just sexy. Hot. A little bit bad. Don't be afraid to use your mouse and **click**! //// C'est sexy, chaud, un rien osé. N'ayez pas peur de **cliquer** avec votre souris ! //// Es ist einfach sexy. Heiss. Ein klein bischen verdorben. Habe keine Angst, die Maus in die Hand zu nehmen und einfach **anzuklicken**.

Infos

DESIGN: Stijn Pauwels (Milkandcookies) <www.milkandcookies.be>. /// **PROGRAMMING:** Milkandcookies. /// **TOOLS:** Macromedia Flash, Adobe Photoshop, and dirty pictures! /// **COST:** 2 weeks. /// **MAINTENANCE:** a lot!

LANA LANDIS

USA

www.lanalandis.com

2003

Concept

I was listening to old scratched Marilyn Monroe tunes and was thinking about the feeling of how it used to be to drive in an Pink Chevy down the highway. //// J'écoutais des vieilles chansons de Marilyn Monroe en me demandant ce que ça devait faire autrefois de conduire une Chevrolet rose sur l'autoroute. //// Ich hörte mir alte Marilyn-Monroe-Lieder an und dachte darüber nach, wie es damals war, in einem rosafarbenen Chevy den Highway entlangzufahren.

Credits

Design and Programming: 247 Media Studios <www.24-7media.de>. /// **Awards:** Flash Film Festival San Francisco. /// **Tools:** Macromedia Flash. /// **Cost:** 40 hours. /// **Maintenance:** none.

LENNY

www.lenny.com.br

BRAZIL
2003

Concept

A main website with an additional hotsite for every new season of the brazilian fashion calendar. //// Un site Web principal qui complète un site branché à chaque saison de la mode brésilienne. //// Eine Webseite mit zusätzlichem Link zum brasilianischen Modekalender, der zu jeder Saison neu erscheint.

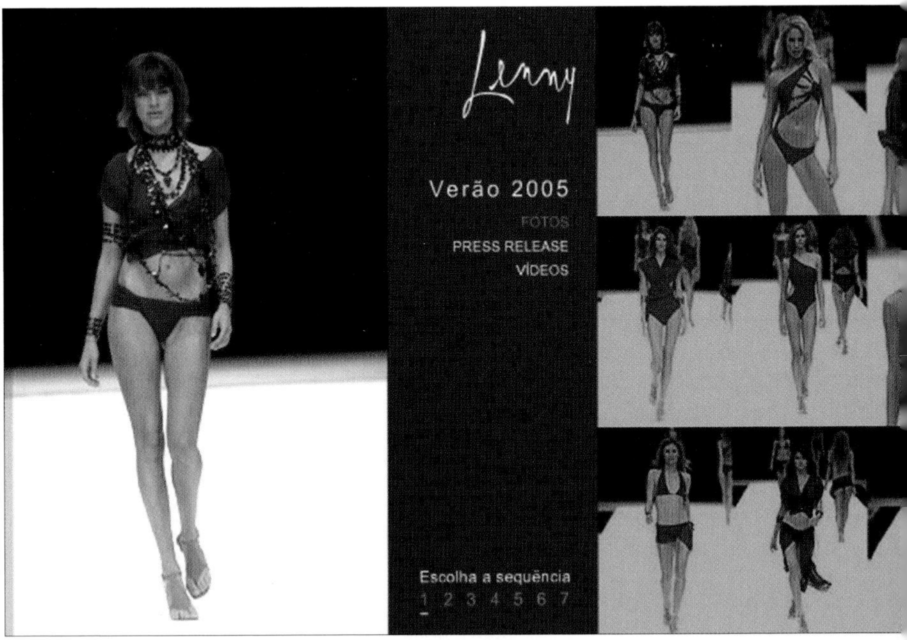

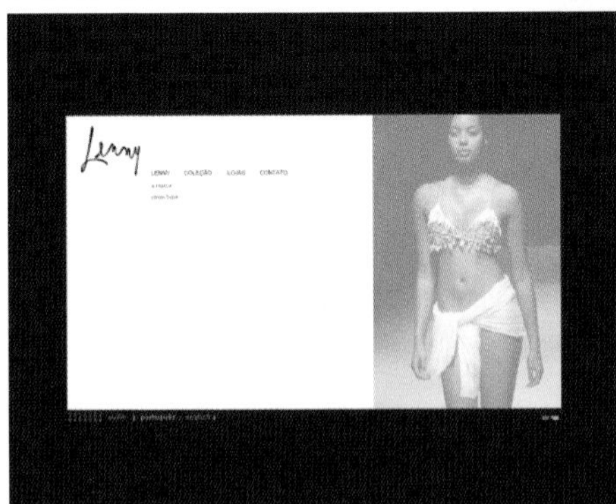

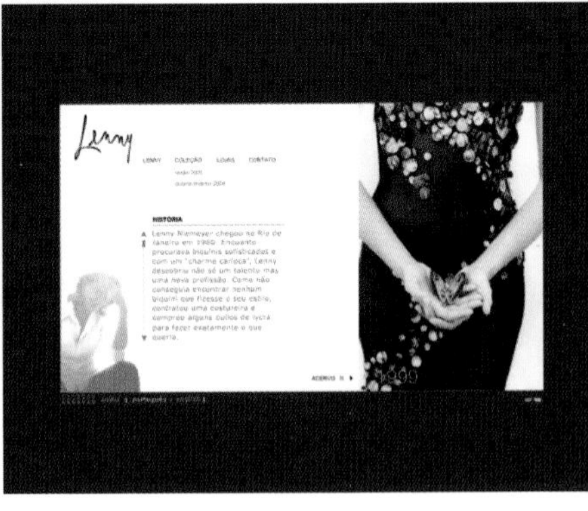

Infos

Design: 6D estúdio <www.6destudio.com.br>. /// **Programming:** Gabriel Marques (6D estúdio). /// **Tools:** Macromedia Flash. /// **Content:** films (fashion shows edited by 6D estúdio), music (ocean sounds edited by 6D estúdio). /// **Cost:** 240 hours. /// **Maintenance:** 48 hours every 6 months.

LIFE BEACH

ESTONIA

www.lifebeach.ee

2004

Impressive site to remember. Unique navigation. //// Un site impressionnant à ne pas manquer. Une navigation vraiment originale. ////
Eine beeindruckende Seite, die Ihnen in Erinnerung bleibt. Einzigartige Navigation.

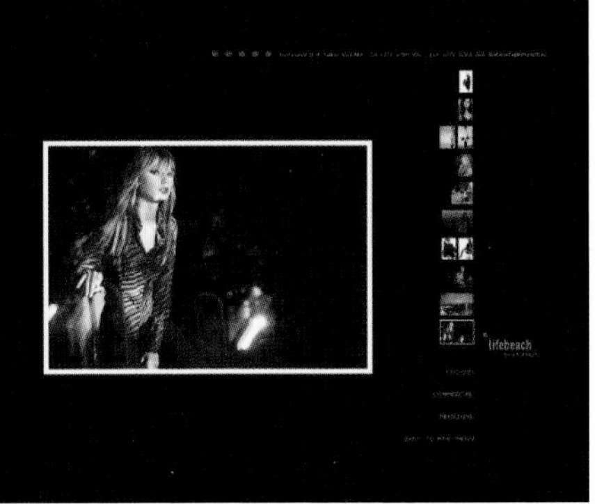

DESIGN: Sander Sellin (Lime Creative) <www.lime.ee>. /// **PROGRAMMING:** Sander Sellin and Vladimir Morozov /// **AWARDS:** styleboost.com. ///
TOOLS: Macromedia Flash, html. /// **COST:** 100 hours. /// **MAINTENANCE:** 5-15 hours per month.

LIME CREATIVE

ESTONIA

www.lime.ee

2004

Concept

Clean and simple magazine layout. To archive the right order of photo illustrations the magazine idea was used for navigation. //// Une mise en page nette et simple s'inspirant des pages d'un magazine. Pour parvenir au classement correct des illustrations photographiques, l'idée du magazine a été utilisée pour la navigation. //// Klares und einfaches Layout einer Zeitschrift. Um eine optimale Archivierung der Fotoillustrationen vornehmen zu können, wurde die Idee der Zeitschrift auch für die Navigation genutzt.

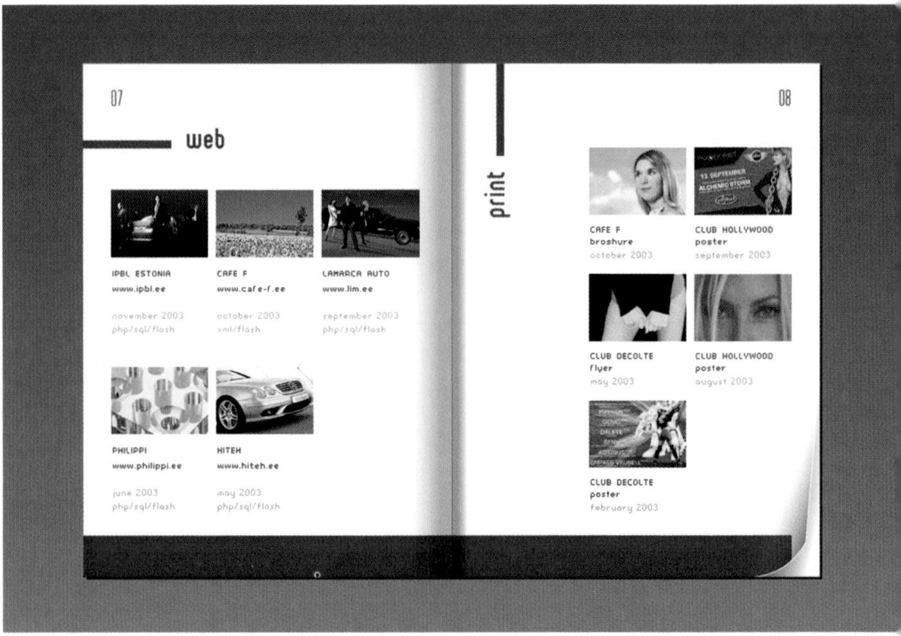

07
web
IPBL ESTONIA
www.ipbl.ee
november 2003
php/sql/flash
CAFE F
www.cafe-f.ee
october 2003
xml/flash
LAMARCA AUTO
www.lim.ee
september 2003
php/sql/flash
PHILIPPI
www.philippi.ee
june 2003
php/sql/flash
HITEH
www.hiteh.ee
may 2003
php/sql/flash
print
08
CAFE F
broshure
october 2003
CLUB HOLLYWOOD
poster
september 2003
CLUB DECOLTE
flyer
may 2003
CLUB HOLLYWOOD
poster
august 2003
CLUB DECOLTE
poster
february 2003

01
02
lime creative
online portfolio
winter/spring
2004

05
showcase
06
selected works

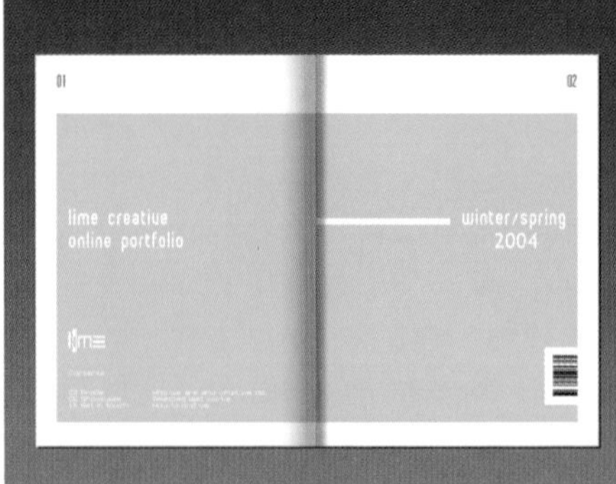

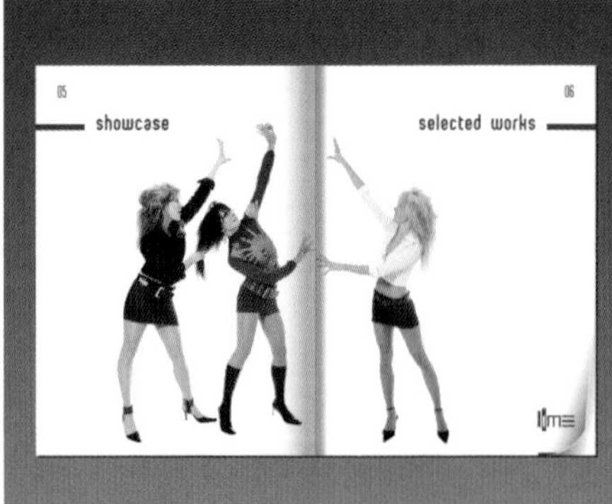

Infos

DESIGN: Vladimir Morozov, Sander Sellin (Lime Creative). /// **PROGRAMMING:** Sander Sellin. /// **AWARDS:** FWA (Site of the Day), fcukstars.com. /// **TOOLS:** Macromedia Flash, html. /// **CONTENT:** photos. /// **COST:** 70 hours. /// **MAINTENANCE:** 5-10 hours per month.

LITTLELOUD

UK

www.littleloud.com

2002

concept

We wanted something based on an environment and to show some of our cinematic influences. //// Nous voulions quelque chose de basé sur un environnement et montrer certaines de nos influences cinématographiques. //// Wir wollten sowohl unsere Ambitionen zum Film als auch den Bezug zur Umwelt miteinfliessen lassen.

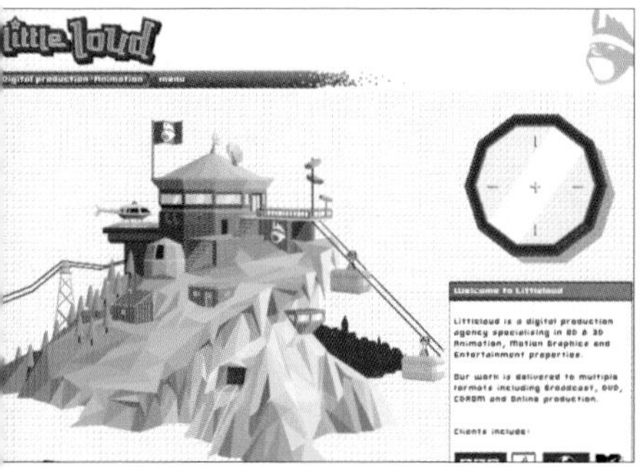

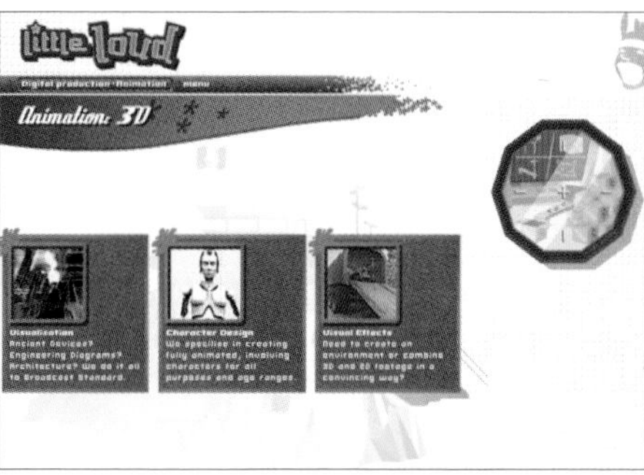

infos

Design: David Jacklin, Darren Garrett, Iestyn Lloyd And Paul Simpson (LITTLELOUD). /// **Programming:** Iestyn Lloyd. /// **Awards:** Best Creative Agency, Sussex Business Awards, Future Uk Internet Awards. /// **Tools:** Macromedia Flash, html, Quicktime, Adobe Photoshop, Adobe Illustrator, pens, pencils, and paper. /// **Cost:** many hours and still working on it. /// **Maintenance:** roughly 1 day or 2 each month.

MAGNET STUDIO

UK

www.magnetstudio.com

1996

concept

The site was designed to be as simple as possible, with the idea of showing off the work rather than the site itself. //// Le site a été créé avec l'idée d'être aussi simple que possible et de donner la part belle au travail plutôt qu'au site lui-même. //// Das Design dieser Seite wurde so einfach wie möglich gehalten, um die Arbeiten und nicht die Webseite zur Geltung kommen zu lassen.

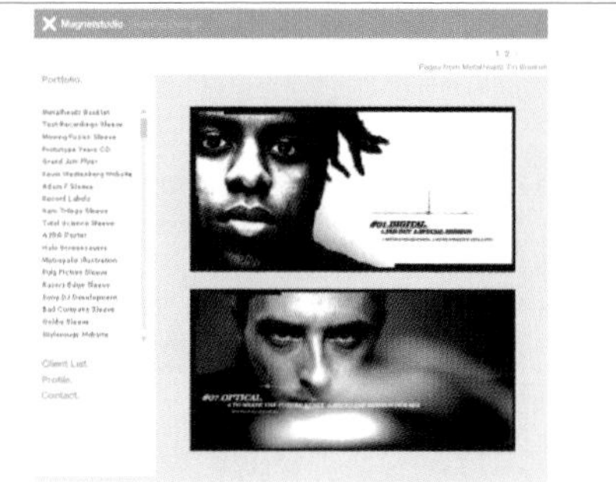

infos

Design and Programming: Jon Black (Magnetstudio). /// **Tools:** Macromedia Flash. /// **Cost:** 2 days. /// **Maintenance:** 3 hours per month.

LOCOGRAFIX

THE NETHERLANDS

www.locografix.com

2002

Concept

The concept and navigation is derived from the name Locografix. (LOCO)grafix stands for 'Living Online Coorperation'. //// Le concept et le système de navigation de ce site sont inspirés du nom Locografix. (LOCO)grafix est un condensé de « Living Online Cooperation ». //// Konzept sowie Navigation basieren auf dem Namen Locografix. (LOCO)grafix steht für 'Living Online Cooperation'.

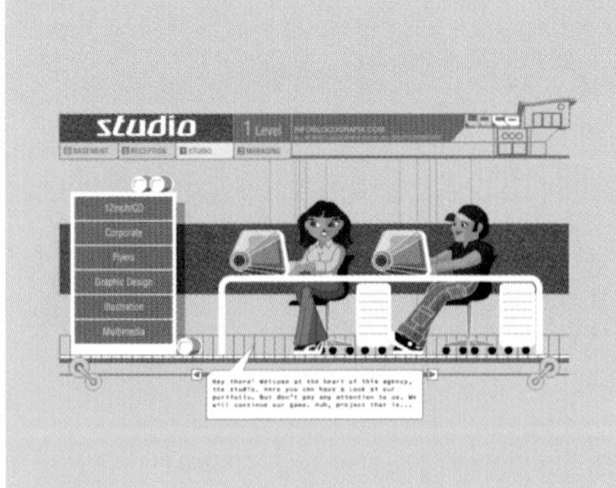

Infos

Design: Locografix. /// **Programming:** Jurgen van Zachten. /// **Awards:** Best Webpick Award, Daags (Site of the Month). /// **Tools:** html, Macromedia Flash, Adobe Illustrator. /// **Cost:** 3 months. /// **Maintenance:** 1 hour per month.

LOMP

www.lomp.de

GERMANY

2003

concept

Work in progress. //// Un travail en constante évolution. //// **Wir arbeiten dran.**

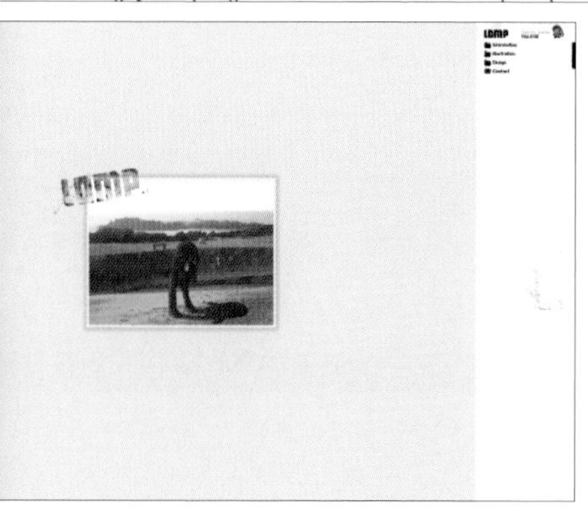

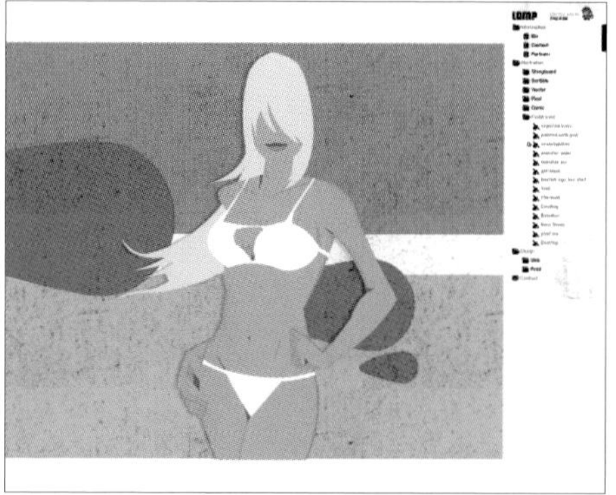

credits

DESIGN AND PROGRAMMING: Stephan Lomp. /// **AWARDS:** FWA. /// **TOOLS:** Macromedia Flash, html. /// **COST:** I'm still working on it. /// **MAINTENANCE:** 5–10 hours per month.

LOW PROFILE

CANADA

www.lowprofile.ca

2001

Concept

To allow easy access to the work and information, to present it in a simple and elegant way and most importantly, to offer a experience that would enhance artists' work. //// Assurer un accès aisé aux travaux et aux informations, présenter les photos de manière simple et élégante et, surtout, offrir une expérience qui mettrait en valeur la beauté du travail des artistes. //// Problemloser Zugang zu Arbeiten und Information, Fotografie auf einfache und elegante Art und Weise, und diese präsentiert mit besonderem Schwerpunkt auf dem Erfahrungswert, der die Schönheit eines Kunstwerkes hervorhebt.

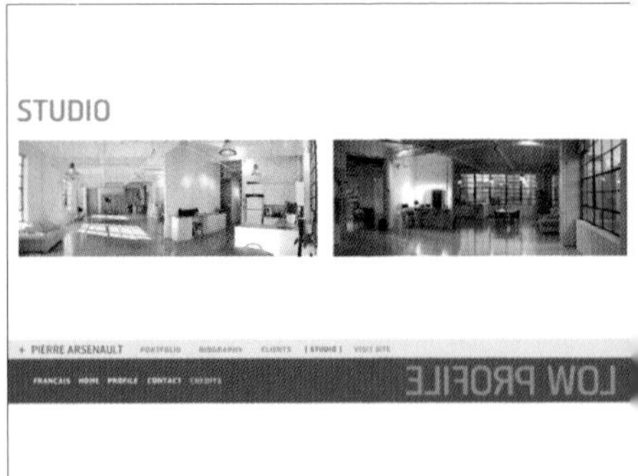

Infos

DESIGN: Plank <www.plankdesign.com>. /// **PROGRAMMING:** Geoffrey Weeks. /// **TOOLS:** Macromedia Flash, Adobe Photoshop. /// **COST:** 100 hours. /// **MAINTENANCE:** average of 10 hours quarterly.

MAAG PICTURES

DENMARK

www.maagpictures.com

2004

Concept

A fun loving look into the illustration of Luke Magee. //// Une incursion amusante dans les illustrations de Luke Magee. //// Ein lustiger, liebevoller Blick auf die Illustration von Luke Magee.

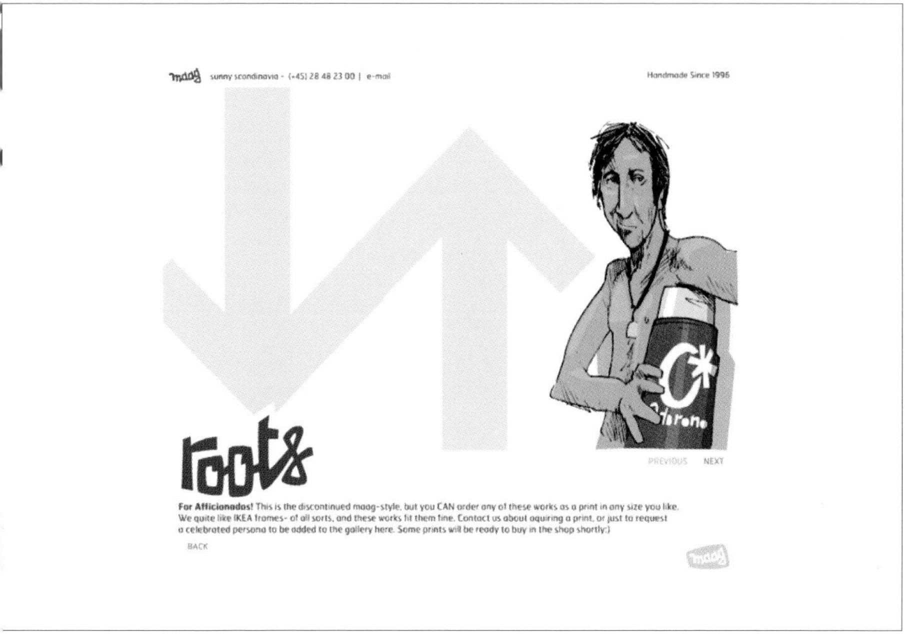

maag sunny scandinavia - (+45) 28 48 23 00 | e-mail
Handmade Since 1996
roots
PREVIOUS
NEXT
For Afficionados! This is the discontinued maag-style, but you CAN order any of these works as a print in any size you like. We quite like IKEA frames- of all sorts, and these works fit them fine. Contact us about aquiring a print, or just to request a celebrated persona to be added to the gallery here. Some prints will be ready to buy in the shop shortly:)
BACK

maag
When you've gotta have it.

Choose a style gallery:
krispy
roots

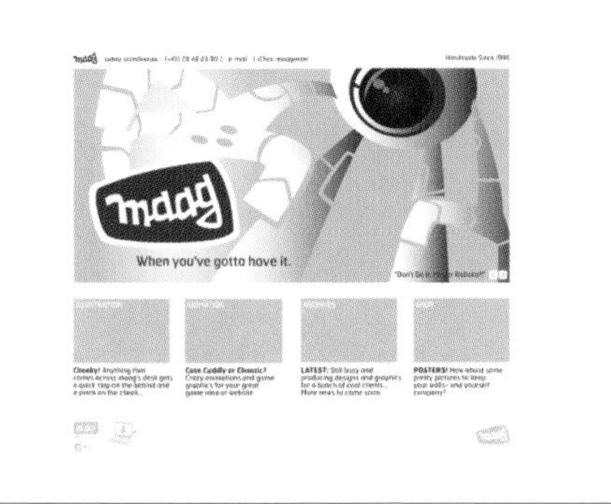

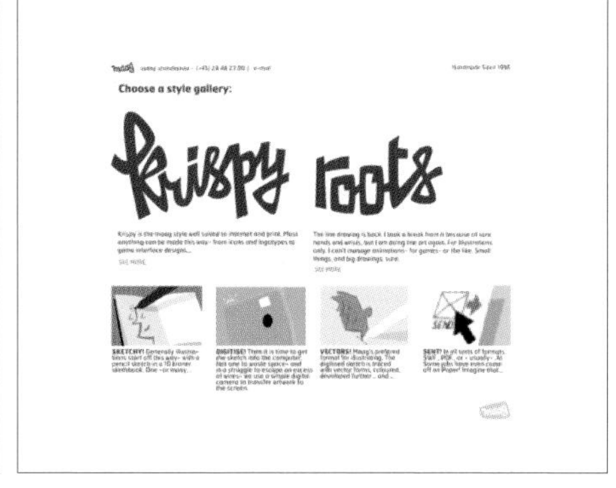

Infos

DESIGN AND PROGRAMMING: Luke Magee (Maag Pictures). /// AWARDS: Linkdup. /// TOOLS: Macromedia Flash, html. /// COST: 16 hours. /// MAINTENANCE: 2-3 hours per month.

MARTIN HOLTKAMP PHOTO

UK

www.ma-ho.com

2001

Concept

An interactive light box, and an elastic interface, which works by means of dynamic sliders. User can dynamically and quite precisely slide images onto the light box. //// Une table lumineuse interactive et une interface élastique qui fonctionne à l'aide de diapos dynamiques. L'utilisateur peut faire glisser dynamiquement et assez précisément les diapos sur la table lumineuse. //// Eine interaktive Leuchtplatte und ein elastisches Interface, das mit dynamischen Schiebern funktioniert. Der Benutzer kann dynamisch und ziemlich genau die Bilder auf die Leuchtplatte ziehen.

Infos

Design: Artificial Environments <www.ae-pro.com>. /// **Programming:** Tom Elsner, Hilla Neske. /// **Awards:** we were given some awards, but I haven't kept records about it. /// **Tools:** html, Macromedia Flash.

MAX LAUTENSCHLÄGER

GERMANY

www.maxlautenschlaeger.de

2004

Concept

A simple yet elegant layout displays the variety of works, all through an interface that can be easily maintaind and updated by the artist. //// Une mise en page simple mais élégante présente la variété des travaux, via une interface qui peut facilement être mise à jour par l'artiste. //// Ein einfaches und doch elegantes Layout, das eine Vielzahl von Arbeiten auf einem leicht instandzuhaltenden Interface präsentiert. Vom Künstler selbst können problemlos Aktualisierungen vorgenommen werden.

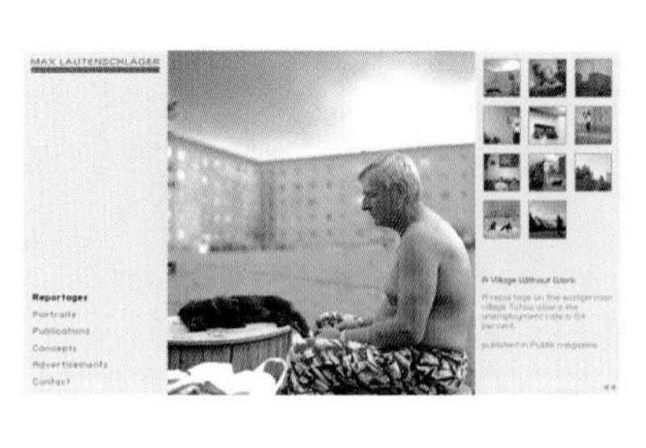

Infos

Design and Programming: Jan Illmann <www.jan-illmann.de>. /// **Tools:** Macromedia Flash, php, MySQL. /// **Cost:** 35 hours.

MALCOLM TARLOFSKY

USA

www.malcolmtarlofsky.com

2001

Concept

The dynamic main navigation was designed to be "out of the box." Getting away from standard left, top, and lower navigation is a constant design challenge. //// Dynamique, la navigation principale a été conçue pour sortir du lot. Se départir des systèmes de navigation typiques constitue un défi constant en matière de design. //// Das Design dieser Seite sowie seine dynamische Navigation sollte "ausserhalb der Schachtel" angeordnet werden. Sich aus dem typischen Schema der Navigation zu lösen, bedeutet eine ständige Herausforderung bei der Gestaltung.

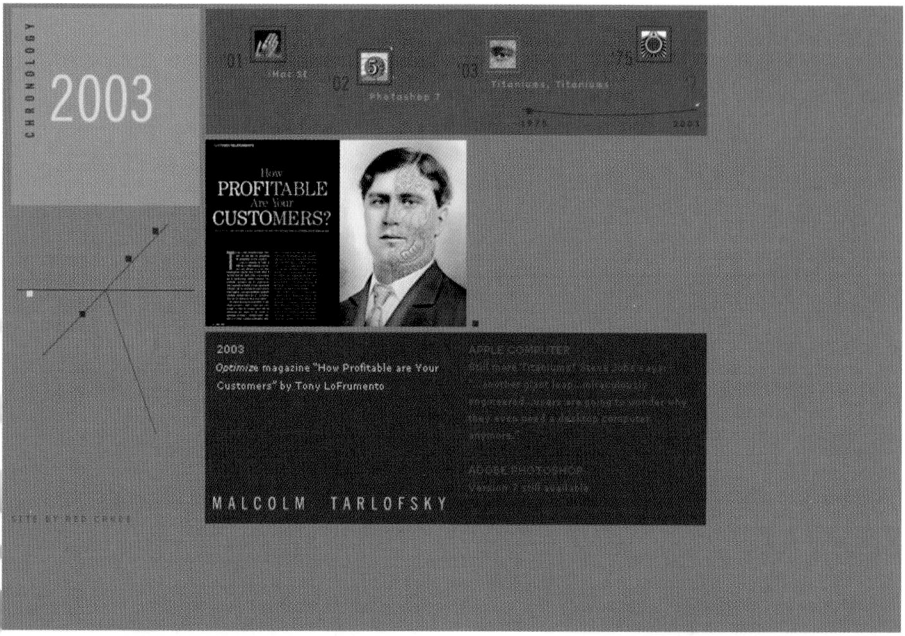

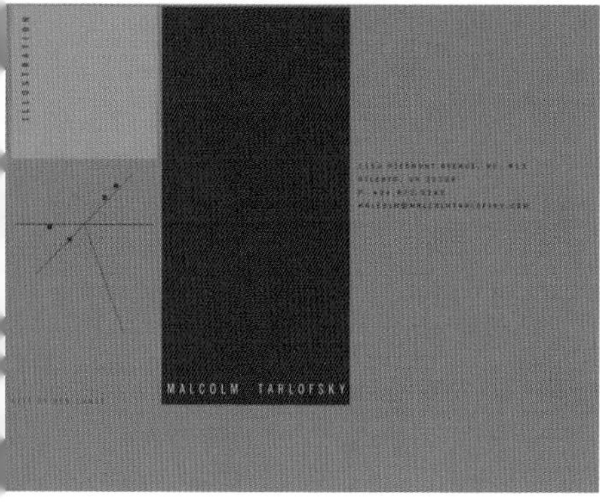

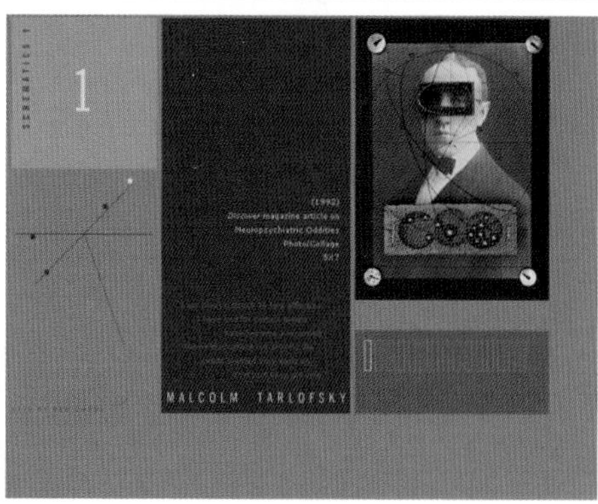

Infos

Design: Deb Koch and Caroline Kavanagh (Red Canoe) <www.redcanoe.com>. /// **Programming:** Deb Koch, Benjamin Kaubisch /// **Awards:** HOW Interactive, Graphis Design Annual. /// **Tools:** Macromedia Flash, html, javascript.

MANIPULATOR STUDIOS

USA

www.manipulator.com

2004

Concept

The photographic style required fluid transitions on menu page and image pages and between pages, which was a challenge, given the large image sizes. //// Le style photographique a exigé des transitions fluides sur la page de menu, les pages d'images et entre les pages : un véritable défi compte tenu de la taille des images. //// **Der fotografische Stil fordert fliessende Übergänge sowohl bei Menü- und Bildseiten als auch bei Zwischenseiten – aufgrund der Bildgrössen eine echte Herausforderung.**

manipulator

jill greenberg studio

PORTFOLIO
NAMES
BIO & PRESS
NEWS
CONTACT
CLIENT ZONE

ENTERTAINMENT

MUSIC

Infos

DESIGN AND PROGRAMMING: group94 <www.group94.com> /// **AWARDS:** FWA (Site of the Day), Wow-factor.com (Site of the Week). /// **TOOLS:** Macromedia Flash, php. /// **COST:** 5 weeks.

MARCO GROB PHOTO

SWITZERLAND

www.marcogrob.com

2004

Concept

Reduced design to leave enough space to leave the pictures to speak for themselves. Each strip is telling it's own story. //// Un design réduit pour donner suffisamment d'espace aux images de sorte qu'elles puissent s'exprimer. Chaque bande raconte sa propre histoire. //// Minimales Design, bei denen die Bilder für sich selbst sprechen. Jede Reihe hat ihre eigene Geschichte.

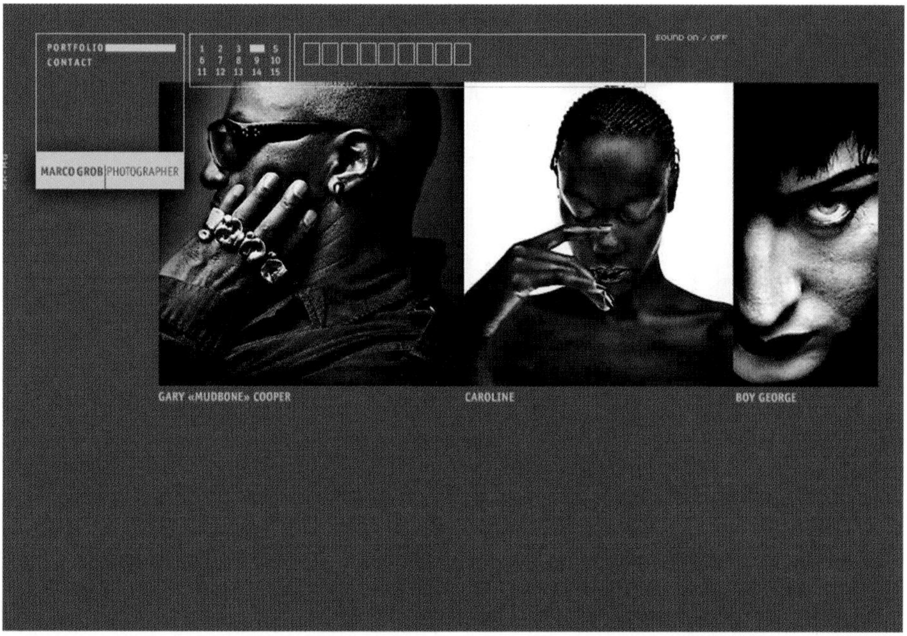

PORTFOLIO
CONTACT
1 2 3 5
6 7 8 9 10
11 12 13 14 15
SOUND ON / OFF
MARCO GROB PHOTOGRAPHER
GARY «MUDBONE» COOPER
CAROLINE
BOY GEORGE

MARCO GROB PHOTOGRAPHER
NEWS
PORTFOLIO No. 13
T3K
PORTFOLIO No. 12
MARKHAM
PORTFOLIO No. 11
ALBUM COVER / BOOKLET «SEVEN»
PORTFOLIO No. 5
NEW STORY «SUNNINGDALE»
PORTFOLIO No. 7
GQ STORIES
PORTFOLIO No. 3
FASHION

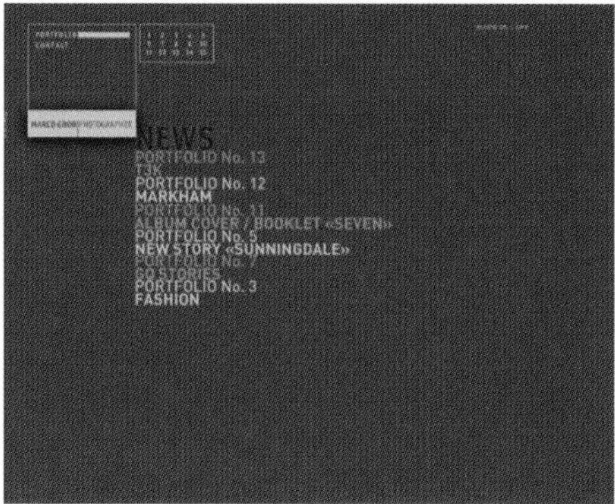

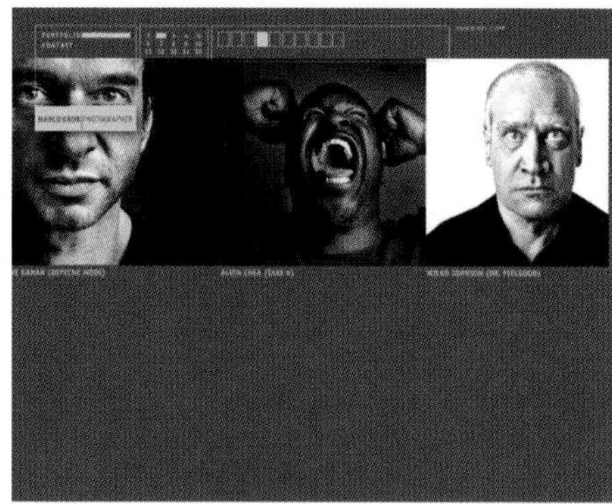

Infos

DESIGN: KK,MG Advertising Agency <www.kk-mg.com>. /// **PROGRAMMING:** Patrick Schnyder. /// **AWARDS:** Moluv's Picks, k10k.net, etc. /// **TOOLS:** html, Macromedia Flash, music, php. /// **COST:** 80 hours. /// **MAINTENANCE:** 2 hours per month.

MARGE CASEY & ASSOCIATES USA

www.margecasey.com 2004

Concept

Besides fast loading images, the main concern here was how to present a complex system in such a way that it would be most intuitive at use. //// Hormis un chargement rapide des images, la préoccupation majeure ici a été de présenter un système complexe de façon à ce qu'il soit des plus intuitifs. //// Schnell zu ladende Bilder sowie die Präsentation eines komplexen Systems, das rein intuitiv benutzt werden kann, waren das Hauptanliegen bei der Erstellung dieser Seite.

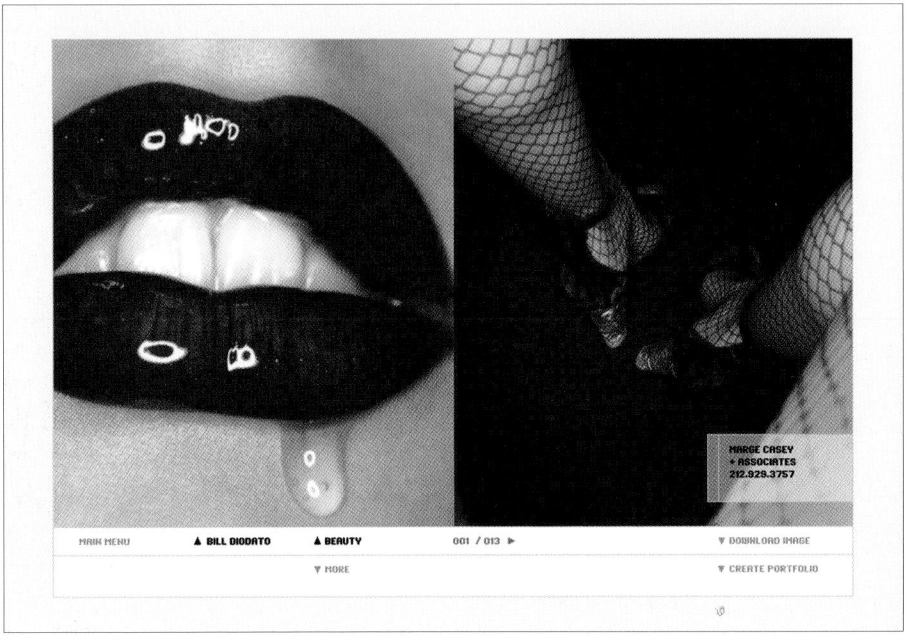

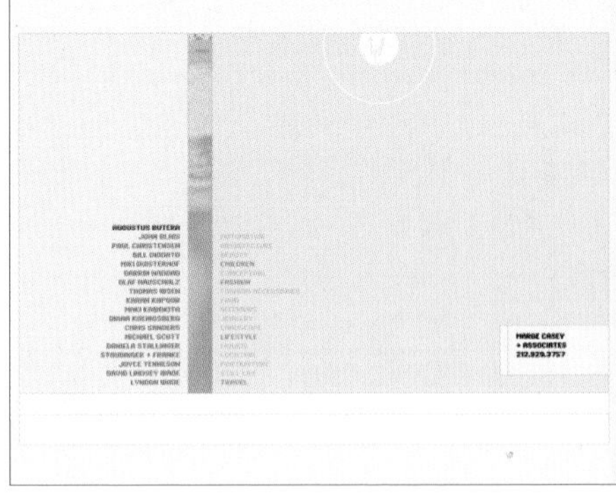

Infos

DESIGN: group94 (in collaboration with Liska NY) <www.group94.com>. /// **PROGRAMMING:** group94. /// **AWARDS:** FWA (Site of the Day), QBN (Certified on Newstoday), TAXI (Site of the Day), Wow-factor.com (Site of the Week). /// **TOOLS:** Macromedia Flash, php, MySQL. /// **COST:** 8 weeks.

MARIO LALICH PHOTOGRAPHY

USA

www.mariolalich.com

2003

Concept

Mario Lalich's site is an authentic interpretation of his aesthetics. The simple navigation effortlessly leads user to his unique photographs, framed in bold colors. //// Le site de Mario Lalich est une interprétation authentique de son esthétique. Simple, la navigation conduit sans effort l'utilisateur vers ses photographies uniques, encadrées de couleurs vives. //// Mario Lalichs Seite ist eine authentische Interpretation seiner Ästhetik. Die einfache Navigation führt den Besucher ohne Umstand zu seinen einzigartigen Fotografien, von kräftigen Farben umrahmt.

PORTFOLIOS

ONE

1 of 20

T

SS

site by HUGE

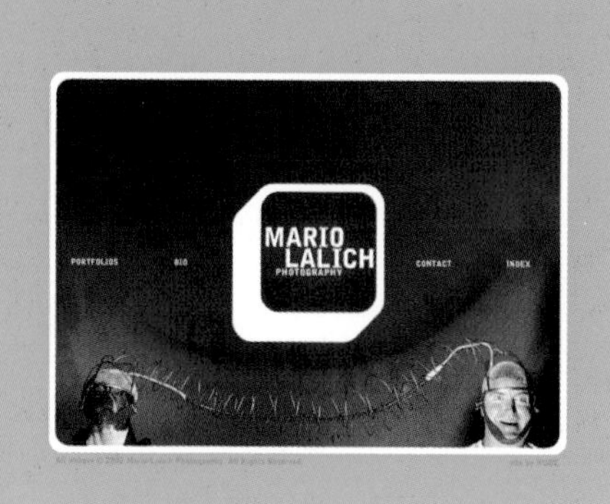

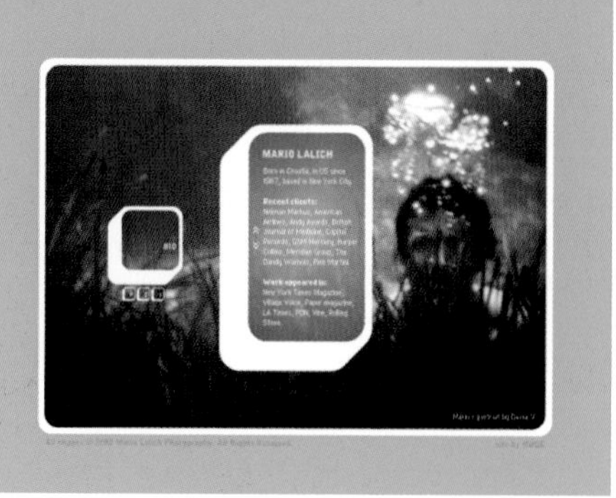

Infos

Design and Programming: HUGE <www.hugeinc.com>. /// **Tools:** Macromedia Flash. /// **Cost:** 2 months. /// **Maintenance:** 5 hours every 2 months.

MARKESE PHOTOGRAPHY

USA

www.markesephotography.com

2004

Concept

Distinguishing design with an easy to comprehend navigation system supported by a layout that has amazing longevity. //// Un design résolument différent assorti d'un système de navigation facile à comprendre et s'appuyant sur une mise en page d'une longévité incroyable. //// **Andersartiges Design mit einem leicht verständlichen Navigationssystem sowie ein Layout mit beeindruckender Langlebigkeit.**

Infos

DESIGN: Branislav S. Cirkovic (Revolution Interactive) <www.revolutioninteractive.com>. /// **PROGRAMMING:** Scott Ysebert. /// **AWARDS:** FWA, TINY (Site of the Week), DOPE, Visueller Orgasmus (Site of the Week). /// **TOOLS:** Macromedia Flash, html, php, xml, MySQL, MP3 (with original music by Rich Markese), Discreet 3D Studio Max, Adobe Photoshop, Adobe AfterEffects. /// **COST:** 350 hours. /// **MAINTENANCE:** all work is handled through an admin panel. The database is so easy to use that its under a minute to get a new photo in.

MARK HOLTHUSEN PHOTOGRAPHY USA

www.markholthusen.com 2004

Concept

Minimalist, the site expands and contrasts to showcase each image according to its unique construction. The images are presented as they if they were going to print. //// Minimaliste, le site s'agrandit et offre des contrastes différents au gré des images, afin de s'adapter à la structure de chacune d'entre elles. Les images sont présentées comme si elles étaient sur le point d'être imprimées. //// Minimalistisch: Die Seite entfaltet sich und untersucht jedes Foto entsprechend seiner Besonderheiten. Die Fotos werden druckreif präsentiert.

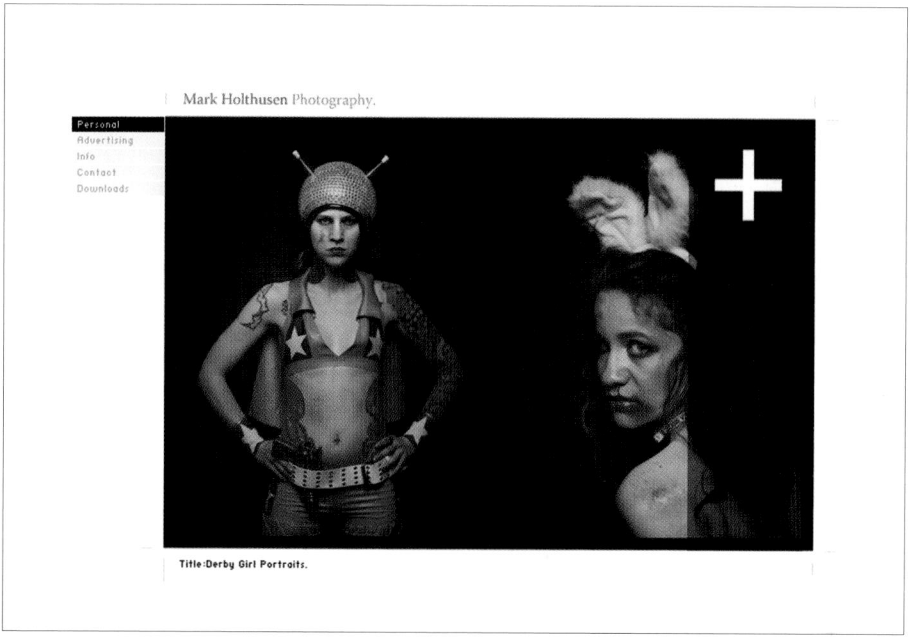

Mark Holthusen Photography.
Personal
Advertising
Info
Contact
Downloads
Title:Derby Girl Portraits.

Mark Holthusen Photography.
Title: Nokia.

Mark Holthusen Photography.

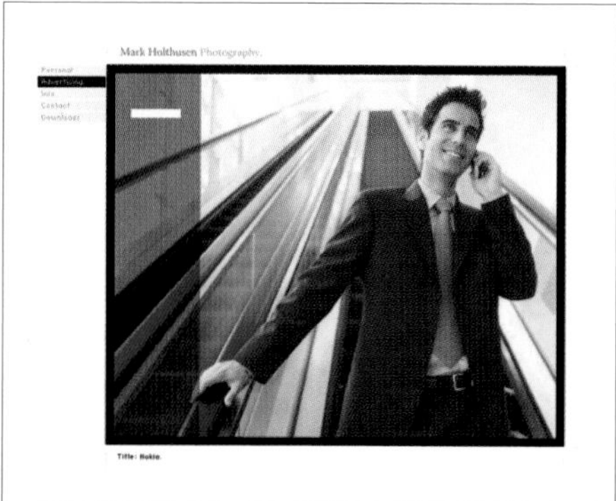

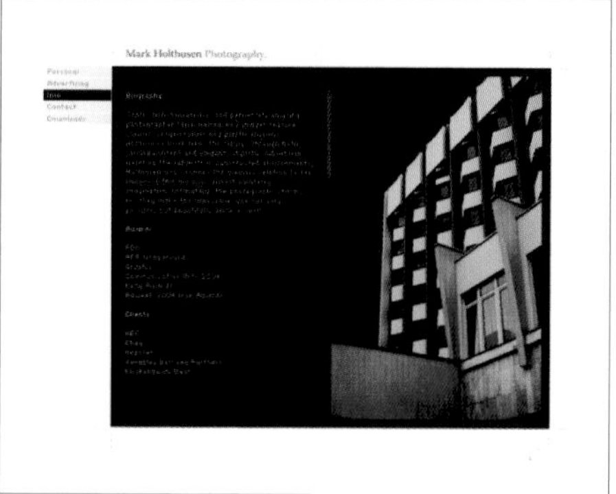

Infos

DESIGN: Ever Growing Studio <www.evergrowing.net>. /// **PROGRAMMING:** Arron Bleasdale. /// **TOOLS:** Adobe Photoshop, Macromedia Flash, html, xml. /// **COST:** 80-100 hours.

MATTISIMO

USA

www.mattisimo.com

2004

Concept A simple, easy-to-navigate display of the work that is also a functional piece of design. //// Une vitrine simple et facile à naviguer d'un travail qui constitue aussi un design fonctionnel. //// Ein einfaches, leicht zu navigierendes Display unserer Arbeiten, das gleichzeitig einen Teil des funktionellen Designs darstellt.

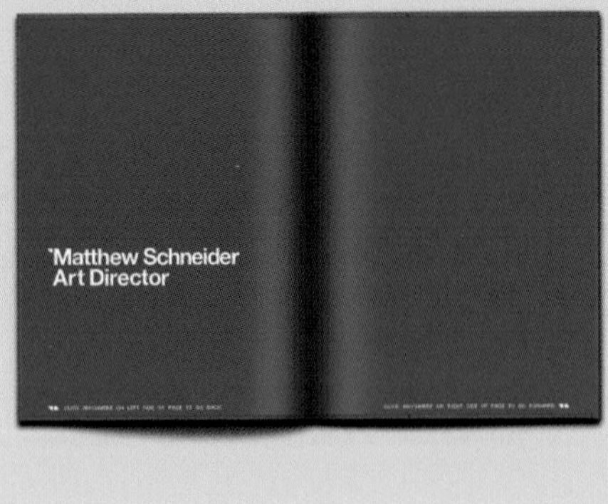

Infos **DESIGN:** Matthew Schneider (Mattisimo). /// **TOOLS:** Adobe Photoshop, Macromedia Flash. /// **COST:** Many, many weekends and evenings. /// **MAINTENANCE:** many a night and weekend preparing files, cleaning up work and building. Truly a labor of love.

MICHEL HENAU

BELGIUM

www.michelhenau.com

2004

Concept

The concept was to present MH's collection in a clean & simple way the minimalistic setup and look&feel of the site draws full attention to the collection. //// L'idée était de présenter la collection de Michel Henau de façon claire et simple. Le style et la configuration minimaliste du site attirent toute l'attention sur la collection. //// Das Konzept bestand darin, die Kollektion MH's auf eine klare und einfache Art und Weise darzustellen. Dank der minimalistischen Aufmachung sowie dem look & feel dieser Seite steht die Kollektion im Mittelpunkt.

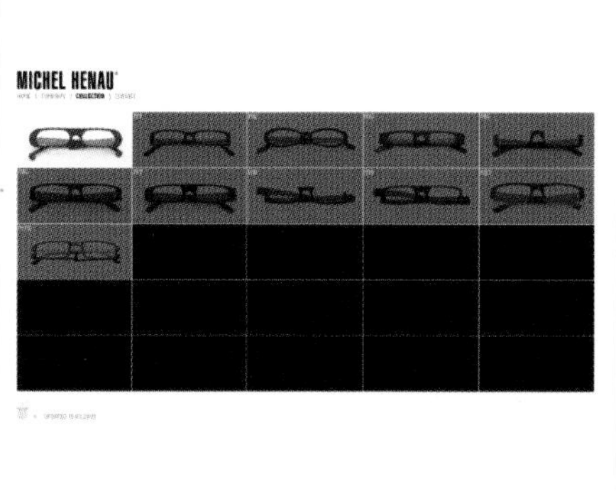

Infos

DESIGN: Deluxe Graphique <www.deluxe.be>. /// PROGRAMMING: Thomas Baert. /// AWARDS: TINY, Plasticpilots. /// TOOLS: Macromedia Flash, xml. /// COST: 120 hours. /// MAINTENANCE: that will depend on the growth of the collection the site is xml driven so it goes quite fast to update.

MIKE T ARTWORKS

USA

www.miketartworks.com

2002

Concept

Hip Hop Norman Rockwell. //// Hip Hop Norman Rockwell. //// **Hip Hop Norman Rockwell.**

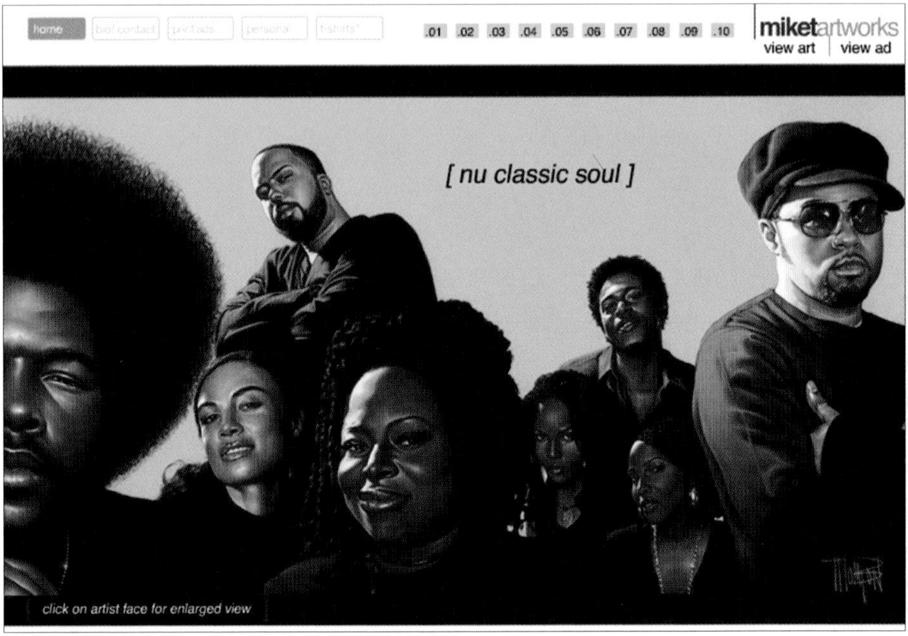

Infos

DESIGN AND PROGRAMMING: Mike Thompson. /// **TOOLS:** Macromedia Flash. /// **COST:** too many.

MILES ALDRIDGE

UK

www.milesaldridge.com

2003

Concept

Less is more was the main concept. We wanted to present Miles' images completely untouched, in all their RGB glory. //// Jouer la carte de l'économie a été l'idée principale ici. Nous voulions présenter les photos de Miles sans retouche aucune, dans toute leur gloire RVB. //// "Weniger ist mehr" lautet das Konzept. Miles Bilder sollten ganz ohne Bearbeitung und in ihrem vollen RGB-Glanz präsentiert werden.

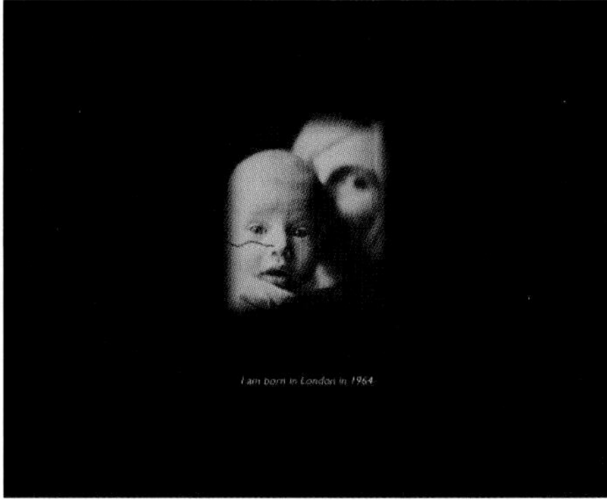

Infos

DESIGN AND PROGRAMMING: Hi-Res! <www.hi-res.net>. /// TOOLS: Macromedia Flash, Logic Pro, php, images, sound. /// COST: spread over almost 2 years, it's one of the longest running projects we have had so it's impossible to trace back how much time we spent.

MORTEN LAURSEN

UK

www.mortenlaursen.com

2005

Concept

Replicates the feel of flicking through Morten Laursens fantastic leather portfolios that are sent to. //// Donne la sensation de feuilleter l'un des fantastiques portfolios de cuir de Morten Laursens. //// **Gibt das Gefühl, durch Morten Laursens fantastische, in Leder gebundene Porfolios zu blättern.**

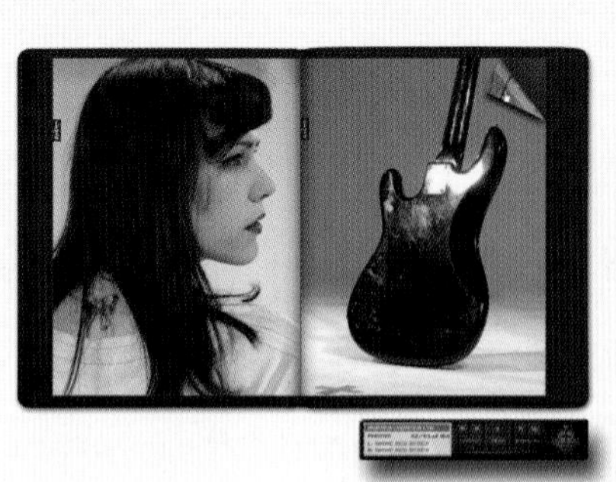

Infos

DESIGN AND PROGRAMMING: Weidemann Ltd. <www.weidemann.com >. /// **TOOLS:** Macromedia Flash, html, xml, CMS. /// **CONTENT:** sound, music, video. /// **MAINTENANCE:** maintained for free by owner using CMS.

NERO GIARDINI

ITALY

www.nerogiardini.it

2004

Concept

The photographic pictures are playing an important role in the construction of this website and they unify the web content with the advertising campaign for the press. //// Les photos jouent un rôle important dans la construction de ce site. Elles sont le pendant de la campagne publicitaire conçue pour la presse. //// **Die fotografischen Bilder spielen eine wichtige Rolle bei der Konstruktion dieser Webseite und sie verbinden ihren Inhalt mit der Werbekampagne für die Presse.**

Infos

Design: Roberto Crippa <www.blover.com>. /// **Programming:** Dario Tubaldo. /// **Tools:** html, Macromedia Flash, Adobe Photoshop. ///
Cost: 150 hours. /// **Maintenance:** 10 hours per month.

NEUMEISTER + PARTNER

GERMANY

www.neumeister-partner.de

2003

Concept

The elegant and clear structured website is transmitting N+P's design philosophy: Intelligent, creative and durable solutions for high-technology and high-quality projects. //// Ce site Web élégant et clairement structuré transmet parfaitement la philosophie du design de N+P : Des solutions intelligentes, créatives et durables pour des projets de haute technologie et de haute qualité. //// Die elegant und klar strukturierte Webseite vermittelt die Design-Philosophie von N+P: Intelligente, kreative und dauerhafte Lösungen für hochtechnische und hochqualifizierte Projekte.

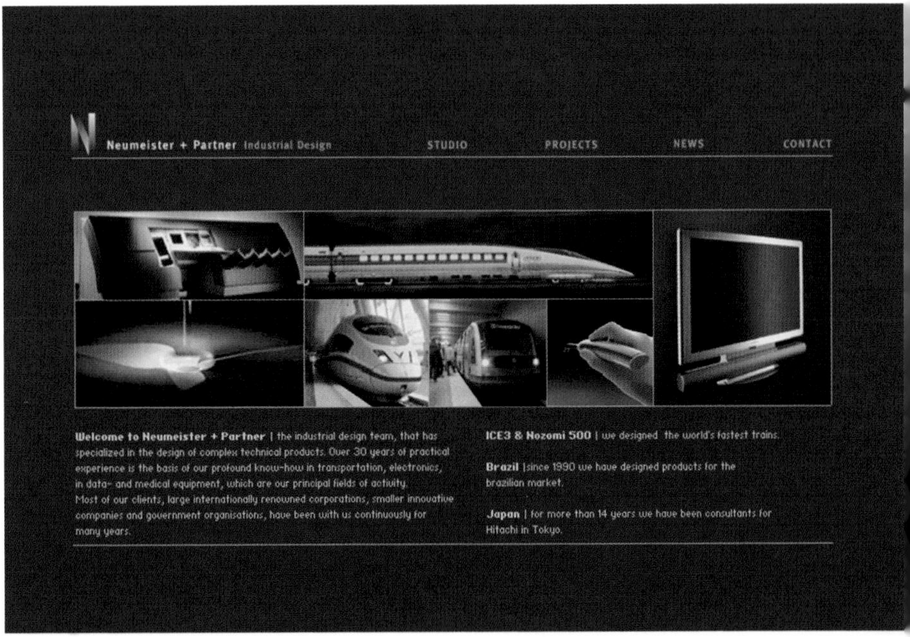

Neumeister + Partner Industrial Design STUDIO PROJECTS NEWS CONTACT

Welcome to Neumeister + Partner | the industrial design team, that has specialized in the design of complex technical products. Over 30 years of practical experience is the basis of our profound know-how in transportation, electronics, in data- and medical equipment, which are our principal fields of activity.
Most of our clients, large internationally renowned corporations, smaller innovative companies and government organisations, have been with us continuously for many years.

ICE3 & Nozomi 500 | we designed the world's fastest trains.

Brazil | since 1990 we have designed products for the brazilian market.

Japan | for more than 14 years we have been consultants for Hitachi in Tokyo.

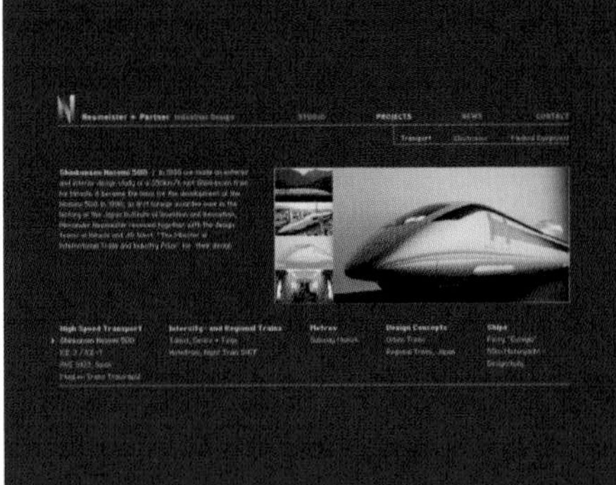

Infos

DESIGN: Joana Leal (Neumeister + Partner Industrial Design). /// **PROGRAMMING:** Christopher N. Friedmann (DESIGN : INSTINKT). /// **AWARDS:** Golden Web Award. /// **TOOLS:** Macromedia Flash, Adobe Photoshop, Allaire Homesite, Adobe Acrobat, html, JavaScript, VBS, Action Script. /// **COST:** 180 hours. /// **MAINTENANCE:** 30 hours every year.

NEW EZRA

USA

www.newezra.com

2004

Concept

Explores both interactive Flash and, providing a standards compliant, usability focused xhtml version as well. //// Explore les possibilités interactives de Flash ainsi que celles, centrées sur la convivialité, du format xhtml. //// Behandelt interaktiven Flash als auch die Zulieferung von Standardanwendungen, ausserdem Nutzbarkeit von xhtml-Version.

Infos

Design and Programming: Jonathan Moore (New Ezra). /// **Awards:** Web Standards Award, Kirupa (Site of the Week), TINY /// **Tools:** xhtml, CSS, W3C Standards Compliance, php, Macromedia Flash, xml. /// **Cost:** 60 hours. /// **Maintenance:** 5 hours per month.

NINJACRUISE

USA

www.ninjacruise.com

2006

Concept

NinjaCruise is an ever evolving space online. The navigation is a reflection of the visual style of each update. //// NinjaCruise est un espace en ligne en constante évolution. La navigation reflète le style visuel de chaque mise à jour. //// NinjaCruise ist ein sich ständig weiterentwickelnder Platz online. Die Navigation reflektiert den visuellen Stil eines jeden Updates.

The Drama Presents: A to Z
@ New Image on 1005 N Fairfax
This is a one-night only event,
lasting from 7pm - 10pm on April 6, 2005

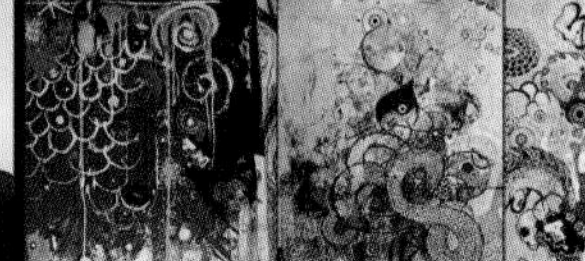

Infos

DESIGN AND PROGRAMMING: Matthew Curry (NinjaCruise). /// AWARDS: Coolstop.com, American Design Awards (Gold). /// TOOLS: Macromedia Flash, html. /// COST: thousands! /// MAINTENANCE: 5-30 hours a week.

NOTBENT

NORWAY

www.notbent.com

2002

Concept

Photography showcase with navigation fun. //// Une vitrine de photographies avec une navigation amusante. //// **Fotografisches Showcase mit einer Navigation, die einfach Spass macht.**

Infos

DESIGN AND PROGRAMMING: Are Bu Vindenes <www.arervindenes.com>. /// **TOOLS:** Macromedia Flash, html. /// **COST:** 40 hours. /// **MAINTENANCE:** 1 hour per month.

OLAF VELTMAN PHOTO THE NETHERLANDS

www.olaf-veltman.com 2003

Concept

Clear, simple, clean web portfolio that feels like a printed one. //// Un portfolio Web clair et simple qui a tout d'un portfolio imprimé. //// **Klares, einfach und sauberes Portfolio, das den Eindruck eines gedruckten Portfolios hinterlässt.**

Infos

Design: Chris Christodoulou (Saddington & Baynes) <www.sb-showcase.com>. /// **Programming:** Duncan Hart. /// **Tools:** html, Macromedia Flash.

ONCE BLIND PHOTOGRAPHY

USA

www.onceblindphotography.com

2004

Concept

Everything was pared down to the essentials; elements like the subtle grey palette, silky animation, and unobtrusive, intuitive navigation keep visitors solely focused on his photos. //// Tout a été réduit à l'essentiel : des éléments tels que la subtile palette de gris, les animations fluides et la navigation discrète et intuitive concentrent l'attention des visiteurs sur les photos. //// **Alles Unwichtige wurde entfernt; Elemente, wie die Palette der Grautöne, seidenweiche Animation, sowie angenehme und intuitive Navigation lassen den Besucher einzig und allein den Fotografien ihre Aufmerksamkeit schenken.**

Infos

DESIGN AND PROGRAMMING: Lawrence Aaron Buchanan <www.lab-media.com>. /// **AWARDS:** Linkdup, TINY, Plasticpilots [Two Star], fcukstar.com, Ades Design, Strange Fruits, American Design Award, Net Inspiration, Best Flash Designs, e-Creative, Cool Home Pages, Design Firms, GOUW, DOPE, DesignLinks.org. /// **TOOLS:** Macromedia Flash, html. /// **COST:** 60 hours. /// **MAINTENANCE:** 1 hour per month.

SAMO VIDIC PHOTOGRAPHY

SLOVENIA

www.onlysamo.com

2004

Concept

The site focuses on Samo Vidic's excellent photography, emphasizing its clarity and conciseness through the use of minimalist design patterns. //// Le site se concentre sur l'excellente photographie de Samo Vidic, mettant en valeur sa précision et sa concision grâce à l'usage de motifs minimalistes //// Der Schwerpunkt dieser Seite liegt auf Samo Vidics genialer Fotografie, seiner Klarheit und Prägnanz durch Anwendung von minimalistischen Designmustern.

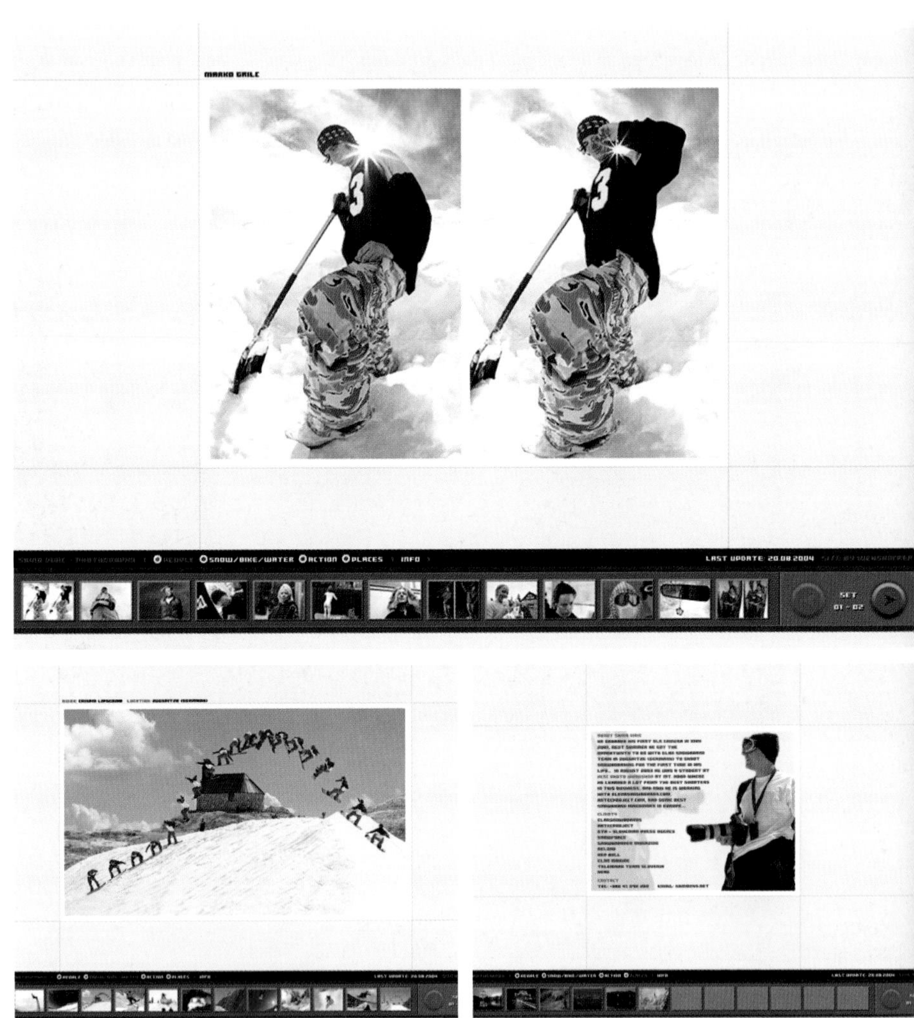

Infos

DESIGN: Webshocker <www.webshocker.net>. /// **PROGRAMMING:** Matjaz Valentar /// **AWARDS:** FWA, ITA, fcukstar.com, DOPE, King For a Week, and more. /// **TOOLS:** Macromedia Flash, Adobe Photoshop. /// **COST:** 60 hours.

PABLO MARQUES

BRAZIL

www.pablomarques.com

2004

Concept

An environment that represents the way I see the world that surrounds me and how it influences my work. //// Un environnement qui représente la façon dont je vois le monde qui m'entoure et son influence sur mon travail. //// Ein Umgebung, die die Welt aus meinem Blickpunkt wiederspiegelt und zeigt, wie dies meine Arbeit beeinflusst.

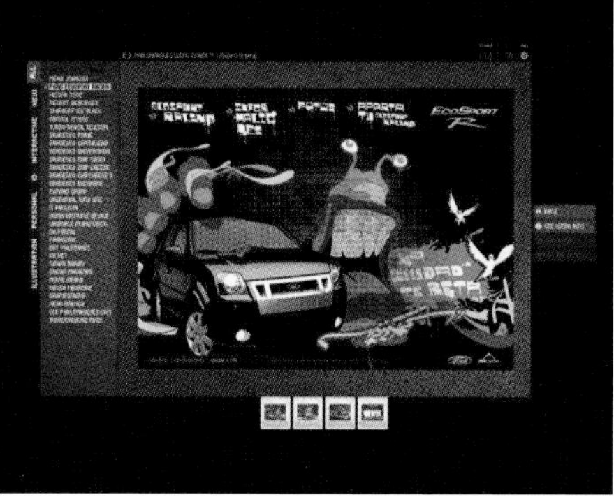

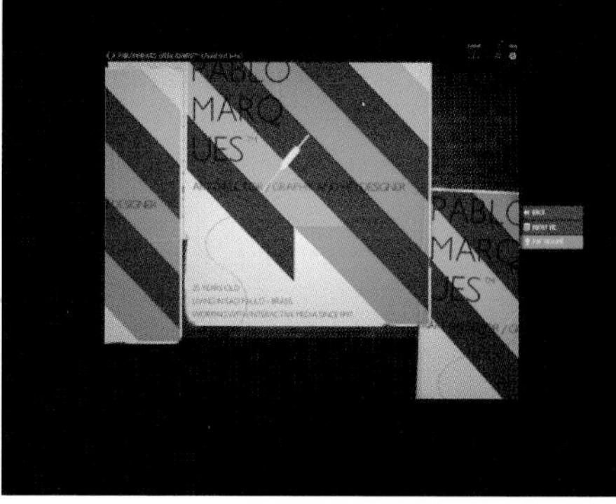

Infos

Design: Pablo Marques. /// **Programming:** Pablo Marques, Zé Rorshack and Flávio Ensiki. /// **Awards:** FWA, Bombshock, TINY. /// **Tools:** Adobe Photoshop, html, Macromedia Flash, xml, Sound Edition in Peak LE. /// **Cost:** 200 hours. /// **Maintenance:** 5-10 hours per month.

PETER FUNCH PHOTOGRAPHY

USA

www.peterfunch.com

2003

Concept

Portfolio for a photographer in a tight and need design which projects photographs powerfull. //// Portfolio d'un photographe dans un cadre sec et net qui projète les photos de manière puissante. //// Das Portfolio eines Fotografen mit unabdingbarem, eng geschnürtem Design, welches die Fotografie kraftvoll zur Geltung kommen lässt.

Infos

DESIGN: Adoptdesign <www.apoptdesign.com>. /// **AWARDS:** Masterclass Student. /// **TOOLS:** Adobe Photoshop, html, Macromedia Flash. /// **COST:** 3 weeks. /// **MAINTENANCE:** zero till next update.

INGO PETERS PHOTOGRAPHY GERMANY

www.peters-photography.de 2004

Concept

Less is more. //// Le minimalisme comme mot d'ordre. //// Weniger ist mehr.

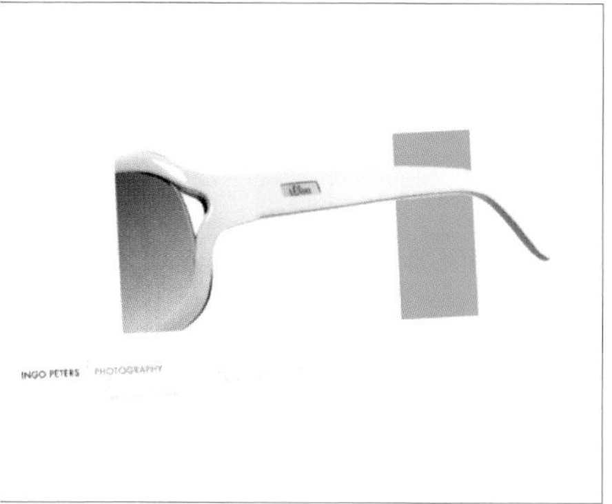

Design: ZUM KUCKUCK <www.zumkuckuck.com>. /// **Programming:** Werner Goldbach, Steven Schmidt and Daniel Rothaug. /// **Awards:** fcukstar.com, mypixeloryours.com, puraraza.net. /// **Tools:** Macromedia Flash, JavaScript, html. /// **Cost:** 102 hours. /// **Maintenance:** 3h every 3 months.

PHOTOPIX PHOTOGRAPHY

USA

www.photopix.net

2004

Concept

This site is part of a double photographers portfolio website. Both sites have a fully updateable portfolio, based on the same site engine and with similar functionality. //// Ce site fait partie d'un double site de portfolio de photographes. Les deux sites comportent un portfolio qui peut être entièrement mis à jour et partagent le même moteur et les mêmes fonctionnalités ou presque. //// Diese Seite ist Teil einer doppelten Portfolio-Webseite eines Fotografen. Beide Seiten weisen ein komplett aktualisierbares Portfolio auf, mit der gleichen Suchmaschine und vergleichbarer Funktionalität.

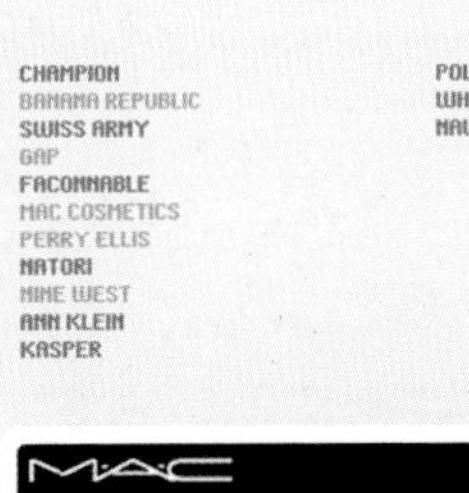

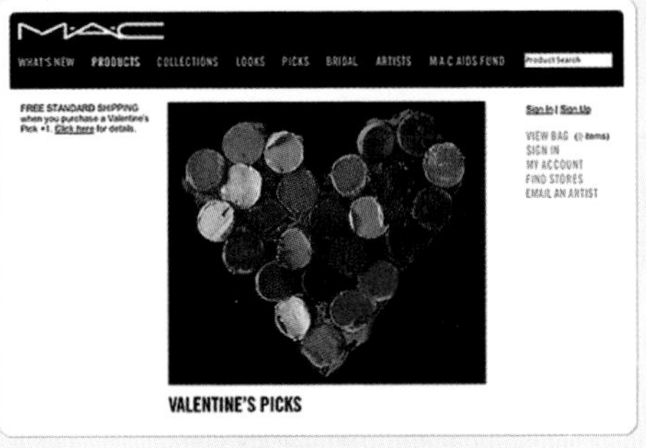

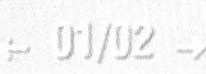

PHOTOPIX CLIENTS CONTACT · PORTFOLIO

Infos

DESIGN AND PROGRAMMING: group94 <www.group94.com>. /// TOOLS: Macromedia Flash, php. /// COST: 5 weeks.

PIXELRANGER

USA

www.pixelranger.com

2002

I created an experience based upon sounds and image manipulation that anyone could experience as if they were actually there. //// J'ai créé une expérience basée sur des sons et des manipulations d'image que tout le monde peut vivre « en live ». //// Soundeffekte und Bildmanipulation werden zu einem Erlebnis für den Besucher, die ihm den Eindruck vermitteln, direkt bei dem Geschehen dabei zu sein.

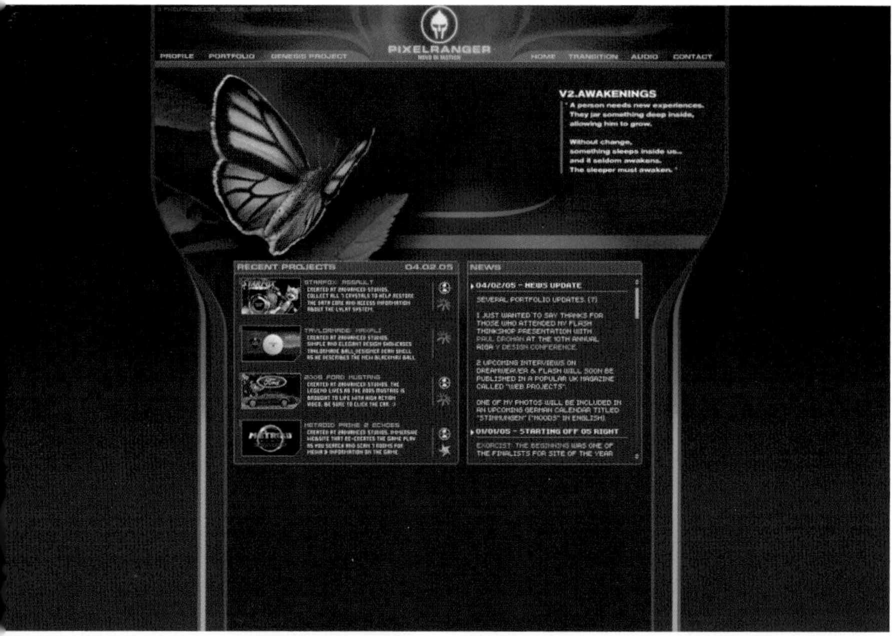

Design and Programming: Shane Seminole Mielke <www.pixelranger.com>. /// **Awards:** FWA (Site of the Day). /// **Tools:** html, Macromedia Flash, xml, audio, photography. /// **Cost:** 40 hours to design and create the core site. /// **Maintenance:** 1 hour per month to update the portfolio.

MAREK WEIHBERG PHOTO

POLAND

www.pixelriot.pl/mwp

200

Concept The site was designed to be very “minimal”. I thought that it is not about using loads of “extras” but about having interesting ideas, which can b expressed in a simple form. //// Le site a été conçu dans un esprit très « minimal ». L'important n'est pas d'utiliser beaucoup d' « extras » mais d'avoir des idées intéressantes, qui peuvent être exprimées de façon simple. //// Das Design dieser Seite ist minimalistisch. Anstatt eine Menge “Extras” zu präsentieren, geht es mir vielmehr darum, interessante Ideen aufweisen zu können, die sich durch einfache Art ausdrücken lassen.

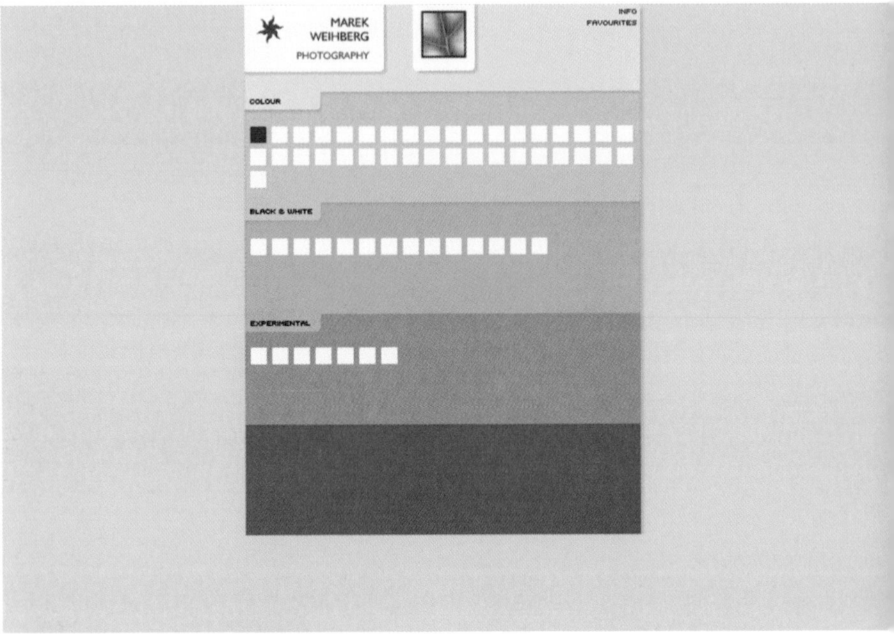

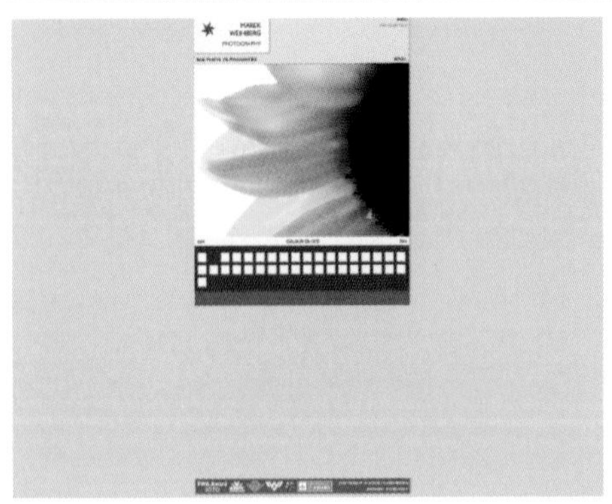

Infos **Design and Programming:** Marek Weihberg (Pixel Riot) <www.pixelriot.pl>. /// **Awards:** FWA (Site Of The Day), DOPE, e-Creative (Site Of The Day), NewWebPick, American Design Award. /// **Tools:** Macromedia Flash, xml. /// **Cost:** 60 hours. /// **Maintenance:** thanks to the use of xml keeping my site updated takes a little time. I only have to add a proper lines to the xml file and the site is automatically updated.

ww.planetb.hr

CROATIA

2004

The concept was user experience of imaginative planet "planetB", on which they can explore services of production house specialized in commercials. //// L'idée du site Web était que les utilisateurs découvrent une planète imaginaire « planetB » sur laquelle ils pourraient explorer les services d'une maison de production spécialisée dans des publicités télévisées. //// Grundlage dieser Webseite sind die Erfahrungswerte der Nutzer des imaginären Planeten "planetB", eine Produktionsfirma, die spezialisiert in Fernsehreklame.

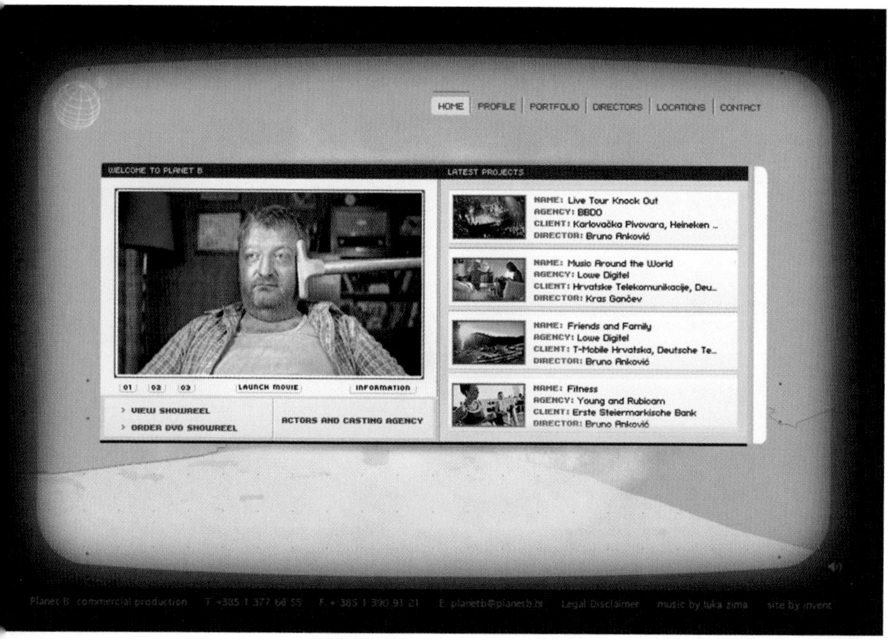

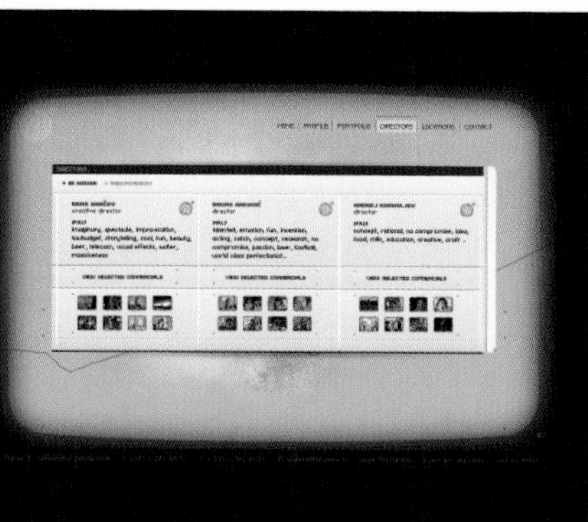

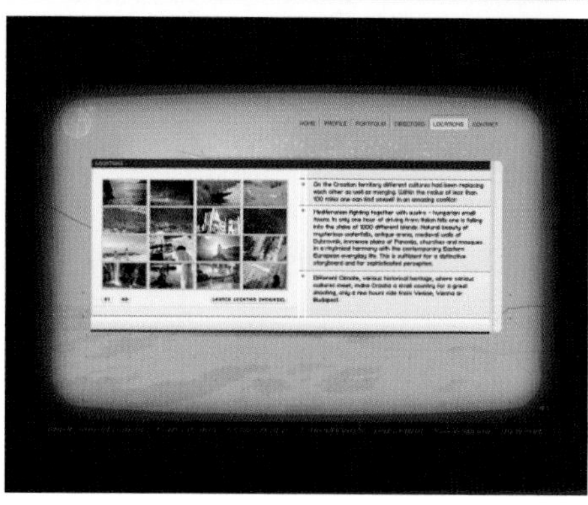

DESIGN: Igor Skunca (invent : multimedia studio) <www.invent.hr>. /// **PROGRAMMING:** invent : multimedia studio. /// **AWARDS:** Croatian Advertising Festival. /// **TOOLS:** Macromedia Flash, Macromedia Dreamweaver, Adobe Photoshop. /// **CONTENT:** music by Luka Zima; films by blanetB. /// **COST:** 350 hours. /// **MAINTENANCE:** 25 hours per month.

PORTE-VOIX.COM

FRANCE

www.porte-voix.com

199

Concept

A very clear and simple design to don't kill the work inside. //// Un design très clair et simple, afin de ne pas porter préjudice aux travaux présentés. /
Ein sehr klares und einfaches Design, um die eigentliche Arbeit damit nicht zu überlagern.

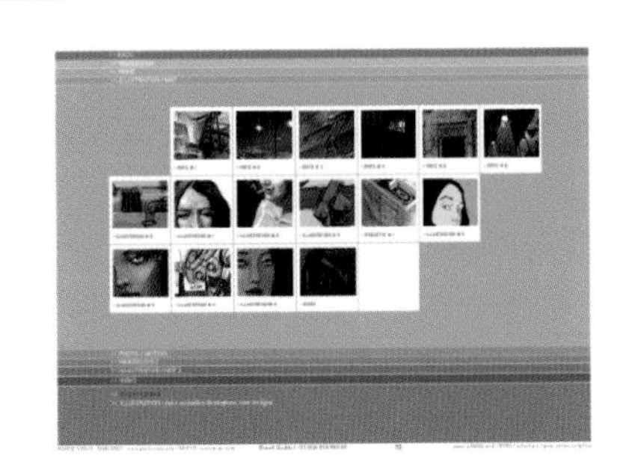

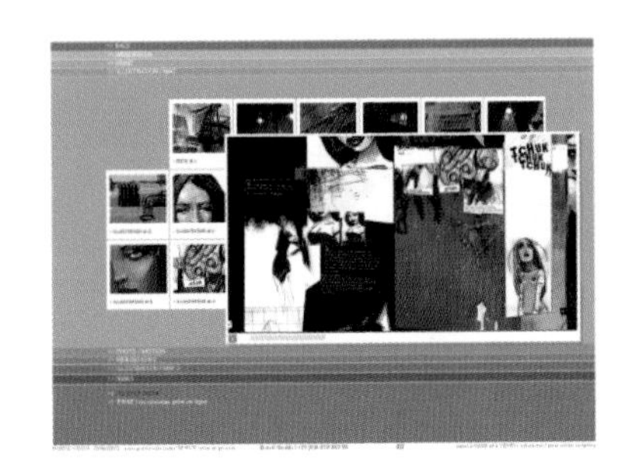

Infos

DESIGN AND PROGRAMMING: Benoit Godde <www.porte-voix.com>. /// **TOOLS:** Macromedia Flash, html, dhtml, xml. /// **COST:** to much. ///
MAINTENANCE: to much again—I love Sophie, my girlfriend.

PRECURSOR

U

www.precursorstudio.com

200

Concept

The site was designed to be very easy to use, and to give utmost importance to the work contained within it, the site is not over designed or in y face, it is the work and nothing more. //// Le site a été conçu pour être facile d'utilisation et donne l'importance la plus extrême au travail qu'il présente Il n'est pas « surdesigné » ou agressif, c'est une vitrine de mon travail un point c'est tout. //// Die Seite wurde zur einfachen Anwendung bestimmt, mit besonderem Schwerpunkt auf dessen Inhalt, sie ist weder überdesigned noch aufdringlich, die Konzentration liegt allein auf den Arbeiten.

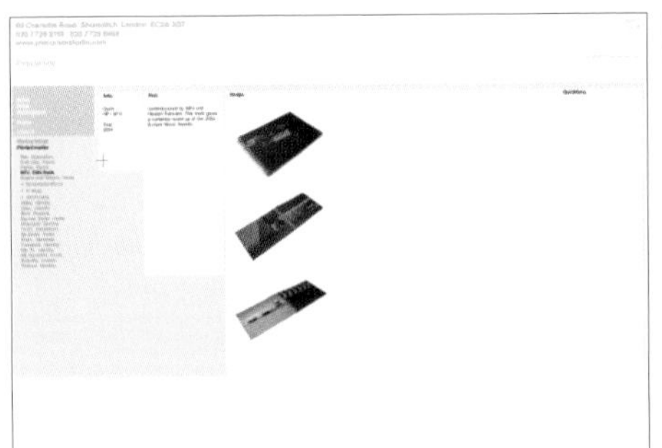

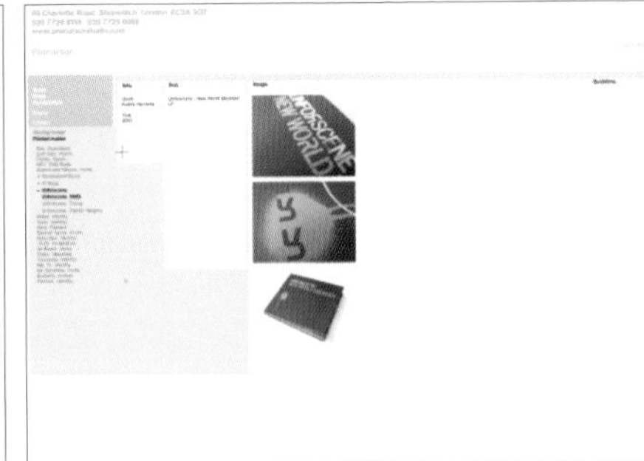

Infos

DESIGN: Precursor. /// **PROGRAMMING:** Chris Bond and Jon Spain. /// **TOOLS:** Adobe Photoshop, Macromedia Fireworks, Macromedia Dreamweaver, dhtml, x asp. Content is an asp/xml based management system /// **COST:** 35 hours. /// **MAINTENANCE:** all updating is done in house and it varies from month to mo

QUIDANTE

BELGIUM

www.quidante.com

2004

Her angel's face as the great eye of heaven shined bright, and made a sunshine in the shady place. //// Tel l'œil splendide du paradis, son visage d'ange était illuminé et éclaira l'ombre. //// Ihr Engelsgesicht erstrahlte wie das grosse Auge des Himmels, und erfüllte den schattigen Ort mit Sonnenschein.

Design: Valentijn Destoop (Quidante). /// **Programming:** Front-end: Thomas Spiessens; Back-end: Stefan Colins and Vic Rau. /// **Awards:** TAXI (Site of the Day), MultiMediaMadness (Best Web Application), Golden Website (Best Flash Designs), NewWebPick (Superpick of the World), DOPE, BD4D, fcukstar.com, LinkDup, De Lijst, Moluv's Picks. /// **Tools:** Macromedia Flash, xml, html. /// **Cost:** 1 month. /// **Maintenance:** 10 hours per month.

RAFAEL GARCIA STUDIOS

BRAZIL

www.rafaelgarcia.com.br

200

Concept

The site was born when I did my first graphic drawing, it's a 13 years compilation of my graphic work. //// Ce site est né en même temps que mon premier dessin graphique. C'est une compilation vieille de 13 ans de mon travail de graphiste. //// Diese Seite wurde mit meiner ersten graphischen Zeichnung ins Leben gerufen, eine Zusammenstellung aus 13 Jahren Arbeit im graphischen Bereich.

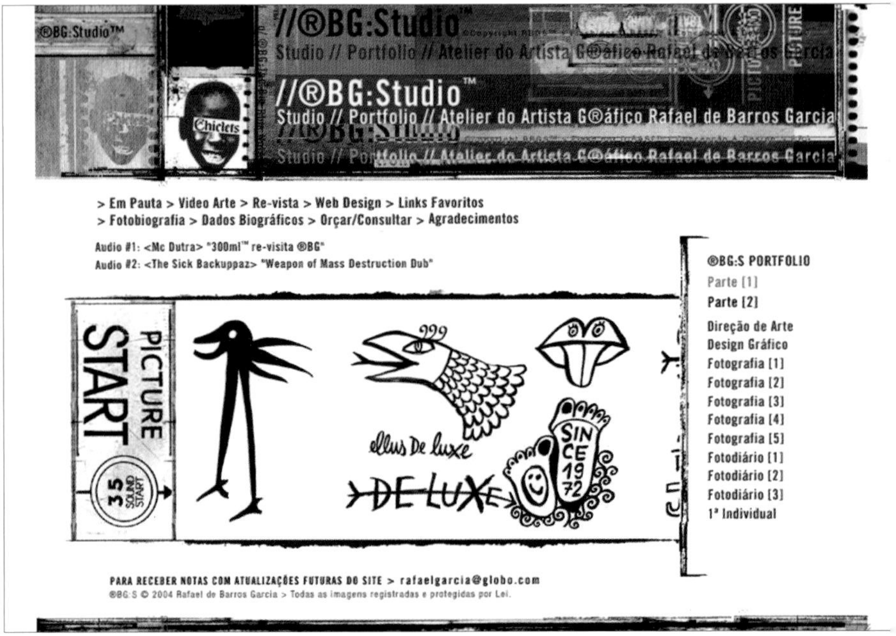

®BG:Studio™
//®BG:Studio™
Studio // Portfolio // Atelier do Artista G®áfico Rafael de Barros Garcia
> Em Pauta > Video Arte > Re-vista > Web Design > Links Favoritos
> Fotobiografia > Dados Biográficos > Orçar/Consultar > Agradecimentos
Audio #1: <Mc Dutra> "300ml™" re-visita ®BG"
Audio #2: <The Sick Backuppaz> "Weapon of Mass Destruction Dub"
PICTURE START
35 SOUND START
ellus De luxe
DE LUXE
SIN CE 19 72
®BG:S PORTFOLIO
Parte [1]
Parte [2]
Direção de Arte
Design Gráfico
Fotografia [1]
Fotografia [2]
Fotografia [3]
Fotografia [4]
Fotografia [5]
Fotodiário [1]
Fotodiário [2]
Fotodiário [3]
1ª Individual
PARA RECEBER NOTAS COM ATUALIZAÇÕES FUTURAS DO SITE > rafaelgarcia@globo.com
®BG:S © 2004 Rafael de Barros Garcia > Todas as imagens registradas e protegidas por Lei.

//®BG:Studio™
> Em Pauta > Video Arte > Re-vista > Web Design > Links Favoritos
> Fotobiografia > Dados Biográficos > Orçar/Consultar > Agradecimentos
®BG:S™ Video Arte
01: "Volume MAX"
02: "The President does not"
03: "Bush Speech"
04: "Innocent Target War"
05: "Driving Miss Bush"
06: "Com Vovó Dirce"
07: "Com PEQ"
08: "Com Tio M&M"
09: "Com Cronai"
10: "Com Zequinha"
11: "Com Jú Bukowitz"
12: "With Bruce Brown"
®BG:S PORTFOLIO

//®BG:Studio™
> Em Pauta > Video Arte > Re-vista > Web Design > Links Favoritos
> Fotobiografia > Dados Biográficos > Orçar/Consultar > Agradecimentos
®BGSTUDIO > RAFAEL DE BARROS GARCIA STUDIO

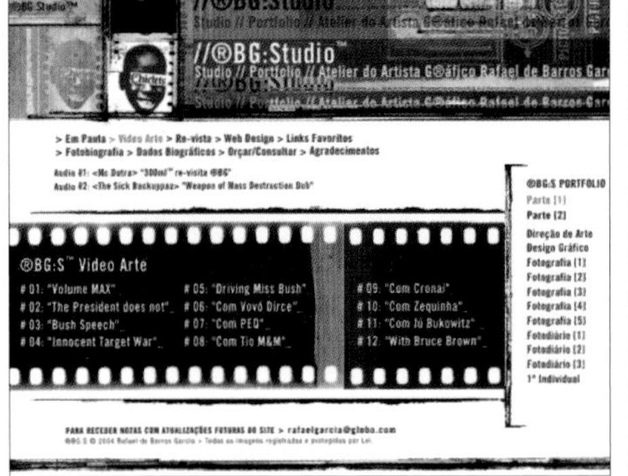

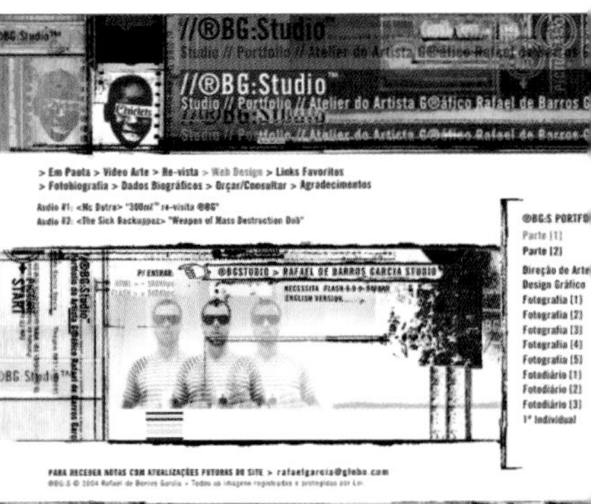

Infos

DESIGN: Rafael de Barros Garcia. /// PROGRAMMING: Daniel Maia and Marcelo de Paula. /// TOOLS: html, Macromedia Flash. /// CONTENT: music, film. /// COST: over 1.000 hours. /// MAINTENANCE: 6 hours per month.

R BEHRENS PHOTOGRAPHY USA

behrens.com 2004

ouble photographers portfolio website. Both sites have a fully updateable portfolio, based on the same site engine and with '/// Ce site fait partie d'un double site de portfolio de photographes. Les deux sites comportent un portfolio qui peut être entièrement le même moteur et les mêmes fonctionnalités ou presque. //// Diese Seite ist Teil einer doppelten Portfolio-Webseite eines en weisen ein komplett aktualisierbares Portfolio auf, mit der gleichen Suchmaschine und vergleichbarer Funktionalität.

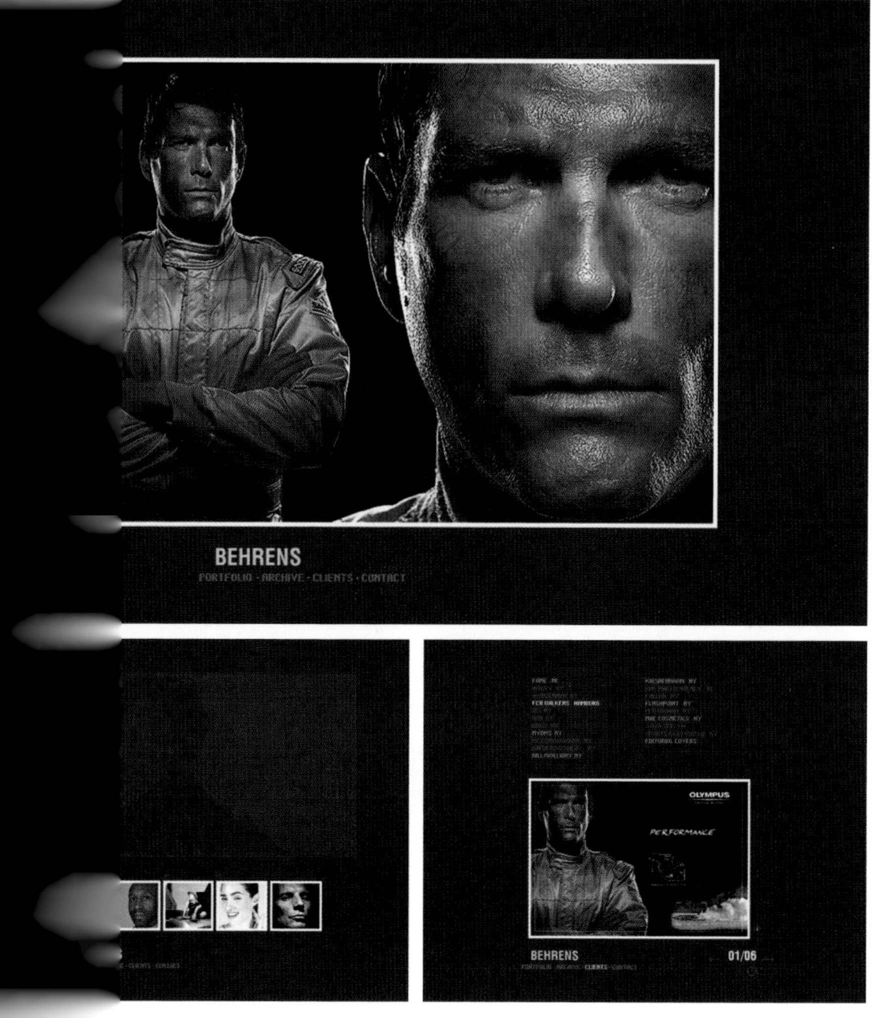

NG: group94 <www.group94.com>. /// **AWARDS:** axesart.com (Site of the day), wow-factor.com (Site of the week), e-Creative
OLS: Macromedia Flash, php. /// **COST:** 5 weeks.

RALF WENGENMAYR

GERMANY

www.ralfwengenmayr.com

2001

Concept

The target was to present Ralf Wengenmayr's broad composer abilities and the projects he has realized so far. //// L'objectif était de présenter l'étendue des qualités de compositeur de Ralf Wengenmayr et les projets qu'il a réalisés jusqu'ici. //// Ziel war es, sowohl Ralf Wengenmayrs breitgefächerte Fähigkeiten als Komponist zu präsentieren sowie auch seine bisherigen Projekte.

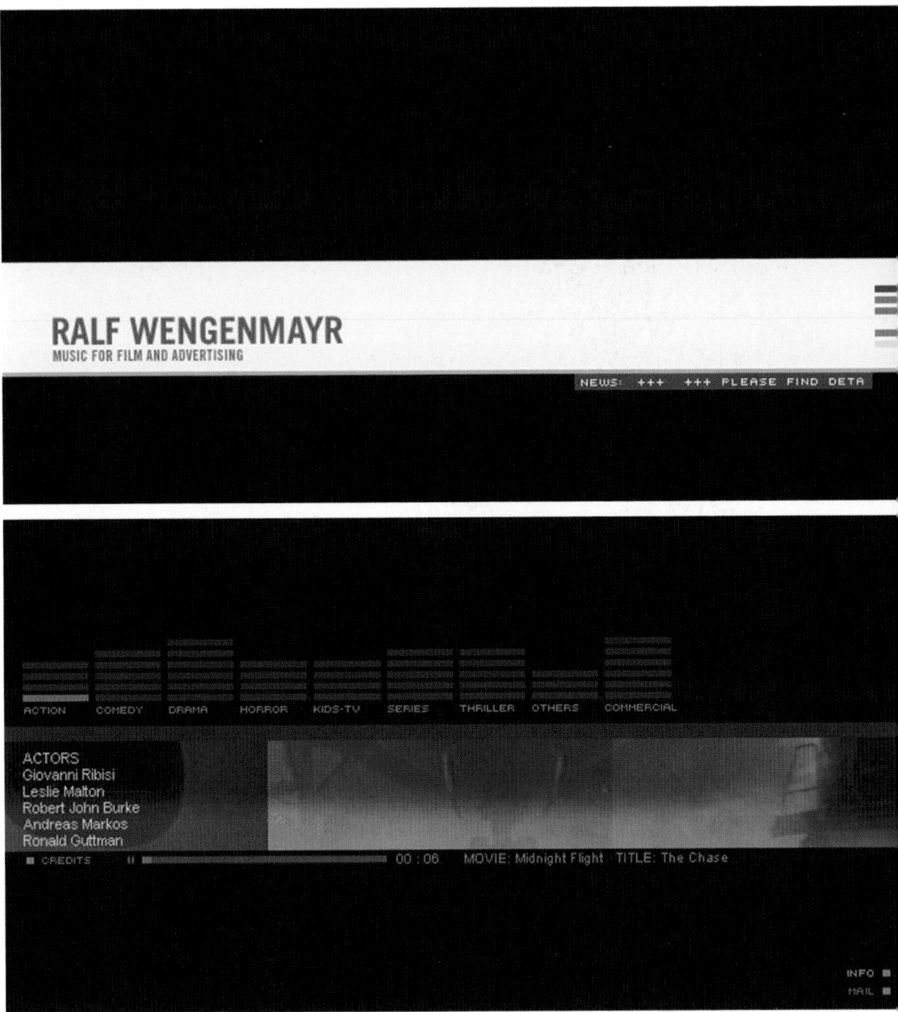

Infos

Design and Programming: SCHOLZ & VOLKMER <www.s-v.de>. /// **Awards:** Cannes Cyber Lion, Best of Business-to-Business, Red Dot Communication Design, EPICA, iF Interaction Design, HOW Interactive Design, Art Directors Club New York, International Web Page, One Show Interactive, ANDY, Clio, Design and Art Annual, London International Advertising Award. /// **Tools:** html, Macromedia Flash, xml. /// **Content:** music, film.

RAPHAEL JUST PHOTO

AUSTRIA

www.raphaeljust.com

2002

Concept

The website looks & feels very much like a photographer's portfolio. To keep the experience authentic, the navigation reveals itself when the user is interacting with the site. //// L'interface à l'image d'un cahier en cuir contribue à ce que le site Web ait tout du portfolio de photographe. Pour que l'expérience reste aussi authentique que possible, la navigation ne se dévoile que lorsque l'utilisateur interagit avec le site. //// Das Interface ist wie ein Buch aufgebaut, was der Seite den Eindruck eines Portfolios eines Fotografen verleiht. Um diesen Eindruck zu halten, ist die Navigation nur bei Aktivierung der Seite ersichtlich.

Infos

Design and Programming: Matthias Netzberger (Lessrain) <www.lessrain.com>. /// **Awards:** Reboot, Golden Web, Platinum. /// **Tools:** Adobe Photoshop, Macromedia Flash, Macromedia Dreamweaver, xml, music, photos. /// **Cost:** 100 hours. /// **Maintenance:** 10 hours per month.

RED SQUARE PHOTOGRAPHY

USA

www.redsquarephoto.com

2002

Concept

The 3 level deep, database-driven navigation is a system of 'morphing' red squares. //// La navigation repose sur une base de données et est profonde de 3 niveaux, il s'agit d'un système de carrés rouges soumis aux lois du morphing. //// Das auf 3 Ebenen aufgebaute, database- gesteuerte Navigateionssystem basiert auf "morphinroten" Vierecken.

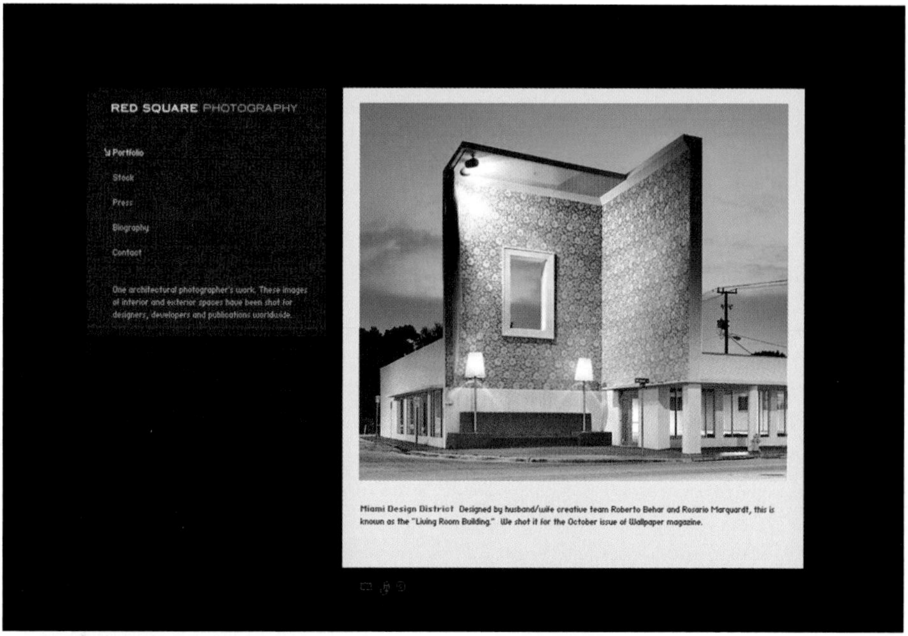

RED SQUARE PHOTOGRAPHY
Portfolio
Stock
Press
Biography
Contact
One architectural photographer's work. These images of interior and exterior spaces have been shot for designers, developers and publications worldwide.
Miami Design District Designed by husband/wife creative team Roberto Behar and Rosario Marquardt, this is known as the "Living Room Building." We shot it for the October issue of Wallpaper magazine.

RED SQUARE PHOTOGRAPHY

RED SQUARE PHOTOGRAPHY
ART FOR BUSINESS' SAKE.
Small Business

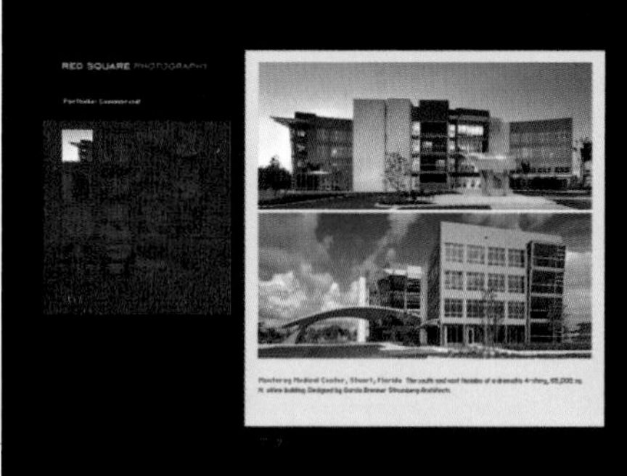

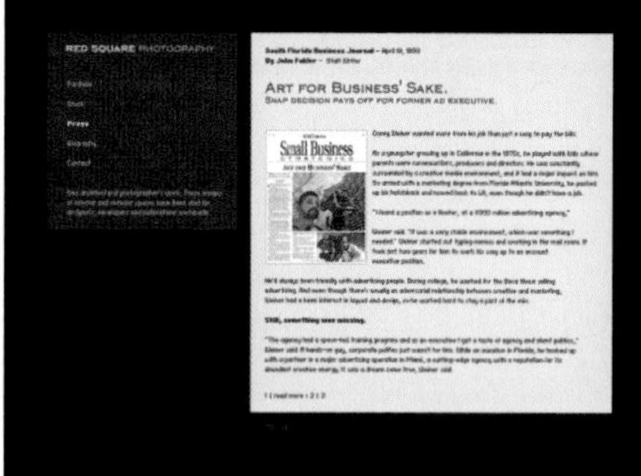

Infos

DESIGN AND PROGRAMMING: group94 <www.group94.com>. /// TOOLS: Macromedia Flash, php, MySQL. /// COST: 5 weeks.

RICE 5 WORKSHOP

HONG KONG

www.rice5.com

2003

Concept

A grass-root scene of Hong Kong. //// Une scène populaire de Hong Kong. //// Aus der Grassroot-Szene Hong Kongs.

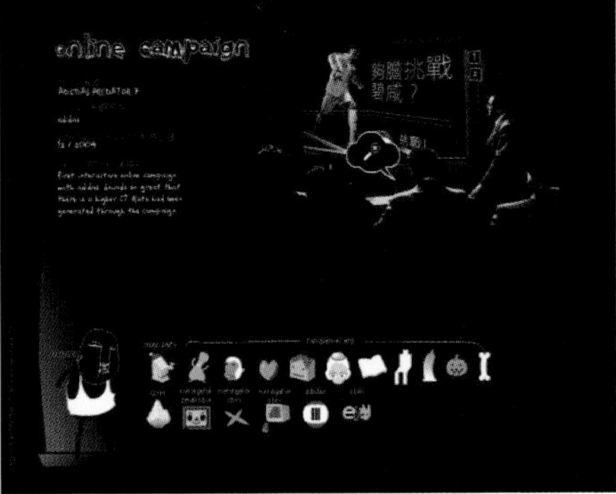

Infos

Design: Tom Shum, Kevin Tsang, Andrew Lee <www.rice5.com>. /// **Programming:** Daniel Yuen. /// **Awards:** HK 4As Interactive Awards - Best Use of Interactive Single (Silver), Bombshock, FWA (Site of the Day), American Design Award (Site of the Month) /// **Tools:** html, Macromedia Flash, xml. /// **Cost:** 1 month. /// **Maintenance:** 2-3 hours per month.

RON BERG PHOTOGRAPHY

USA

www.ronbergphoto.com

2004

Concept

The copy was meant to give the audience an alternate version of the bio, establishing a tone of sarcasm and humor, each a component of Ron's personality. //// Le texte situé sous les chiffres est destiné à donner au public une version alternative de la bio, établissant un ton de sarcasme et d'humour, deux aspects de la personnalité de Ron. //// **Die persönliche Information dient dem Besucher als Alternative zum Original, begleitet von Sarkasmus und Humor, beides Komponenten in Rons Persönlichkeit.**

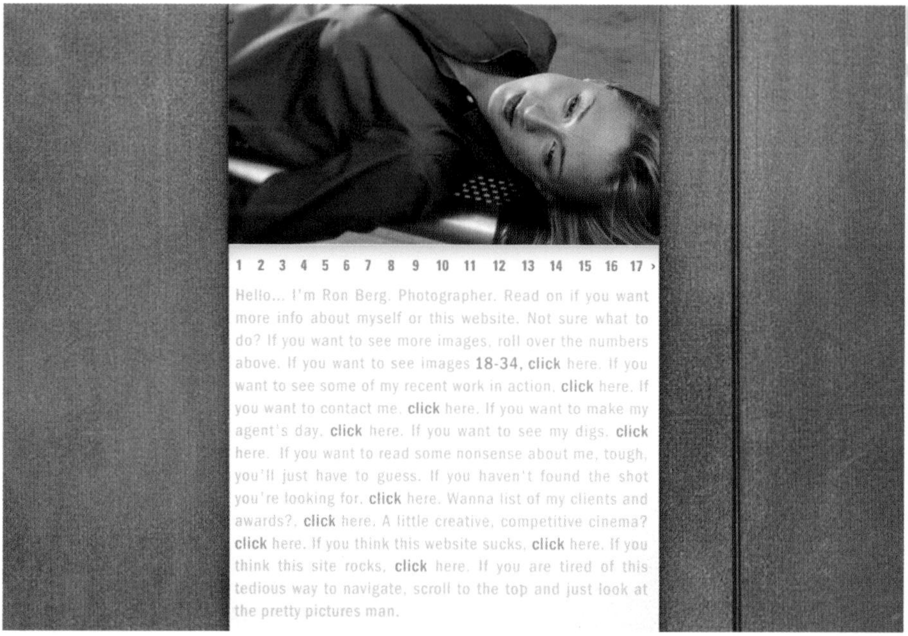

1 2 3 4 5 6 7 8 9 10 11 12 13 14 15 16 17 ›

Hello... I'm Ron Berg. Photographer. Read on if you want more info about myself or this website. Not sure what to do? If you want to see more images, roll over the numbers above. If you want to see images **18-34, click** here. If you want to see some of my recent work in action, **click** here. If you want to contact me, **click** here. If you want to make my agent's day, **click** here. If you want to see my digs, **click** here. If you want to read some nonsense about me, tough, you'll just have to guess. If you haven't found the shot you're looking for, **click** here. Wanna list of my clients and awards?, **click** here. A little creative, competitive cinema? **click** here. If you think this website sucks, **click** here. If you think this site rocks, **click** here. If you are tired of this tedious way to navigate, scroll to the top and just look at the pretty pictures man.

Infos

DESIGN: Todd Eaton (Mojo Studios) <www.mojostudios.com>; and Karen Knecht (KonnectDesign) <www.konnectdesign.com>. /// **PROGRAMMING:** Todd Eaton. /// **AWARDS:** FWA, fcukstar.com, DOPE, NewWebPick, TINY. /// **TOOLS:** Macromedia Flash, Macromedia Dreamweaver, Sorenson Squeeze, Adobe Premier, Adobe Audition, html, mp3, FLV. /// **COST:** 200 hours. /// **MAINTENANCE:** only minimal updating of images and videos.

ROYAL BOTANIA

BELGIUM

www.royalbotania.com

2003

Concept

A visual click-through system allows the visitor to switch easily and efficiently from atmosphere imagery to technical product sheets and back. //// Un système visuel basé sur les clics permet au visiteur de passer facilement et efficacement d'images d'ambiance à des fiches techniques et inversement. //// Ein visuelles 'click-through'-System zur einfachen und effizienten Sichtung von atmosphärischem Bildmaterial bis hin zu technischer Produktinformation.

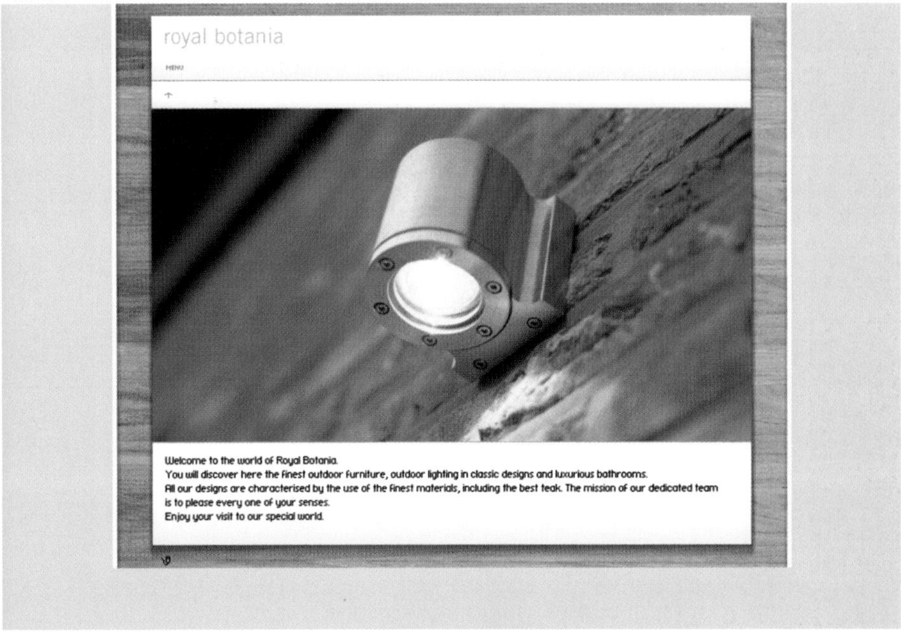

royal botania
MENU
Welcome to the world of Royal Botania.
You will discover here the finest outdoor furniture, outdoor lighting in classic designs and luxurious bathrooms.
All our designs are characterised by the use of the finest materials, including the best teak. The mission of our dedicated team is to please every one of your senses.
Enjoy your visit to our special world.

products
new products
next
E-Z

events & exhibitions
11-15.02.05
AMBIENTE
09-13.02.05
SWEDEN FURNITURE FAIR
13-18.04.05
Frankfurt
STOCKHOLM
MILANO

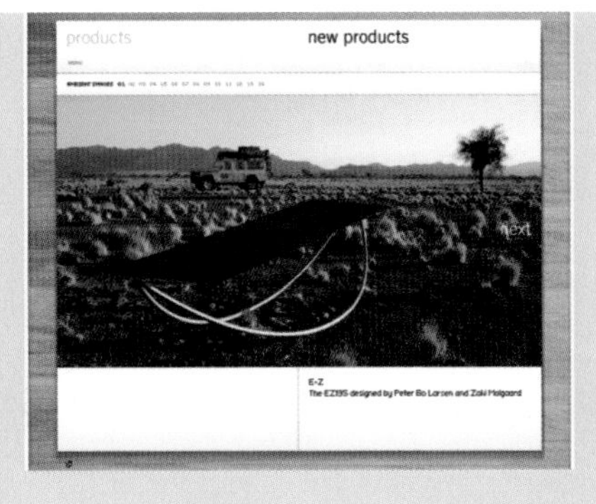

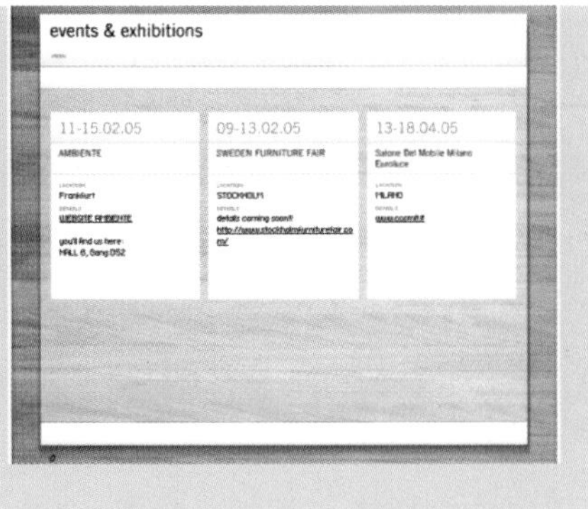

Infos

DESIGN AND PROGRAMMING: group94 <www.group94.com>. /// **AWARDS:** FWA (Site of the Day). /// **TOOLS:** Macromedia Flash, php, MySQL. /// **COST:** 7 weeks.

S2PHOTO

CZECH REPUBLIC

www.s2photo.cz

2004

Concept

Maximum space for the presented photographers versus bold, colorful and playful typography. //// Un espace maximum pour les photographes présentés avec une typographie ludique aux couleurs vives. //// Maximaler Raum für die vorgestellten Fotografen im Kontrast zu fettgedruckter, farbenfroher, verspielter Typografie.

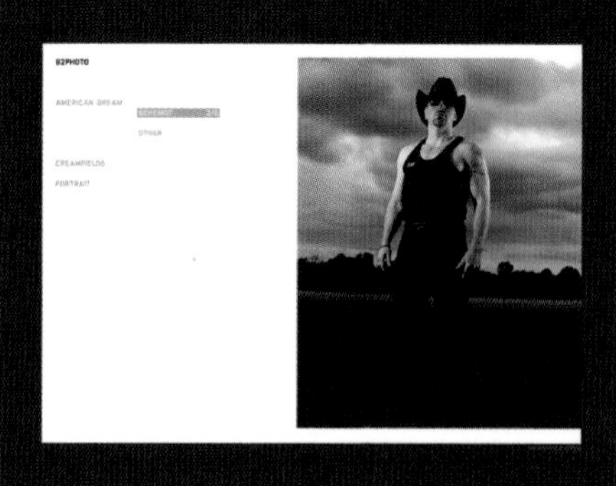

Infos

Design and Programming: Tomas Celizna (dgu) www.dgu.cz. /// **Tools:** Macromedia Flash, amfphp, php, MySQL, html. /// **Cost:** 90 hours. /// **Maintenance:** 250 hours per month.

SAGMEISTER

USA

www.sagmeister.com

2003

Concept

Presents the work of Sagmeister Inc. in a clear and easily accessible way. //// Présente le travail de Sagmeister Inc. De façon claire, simple et accessible. //// Präsentiert die Arbeit von Sagmeister Inc. in einer klaren und leicht zugänglichen Art und Weise.

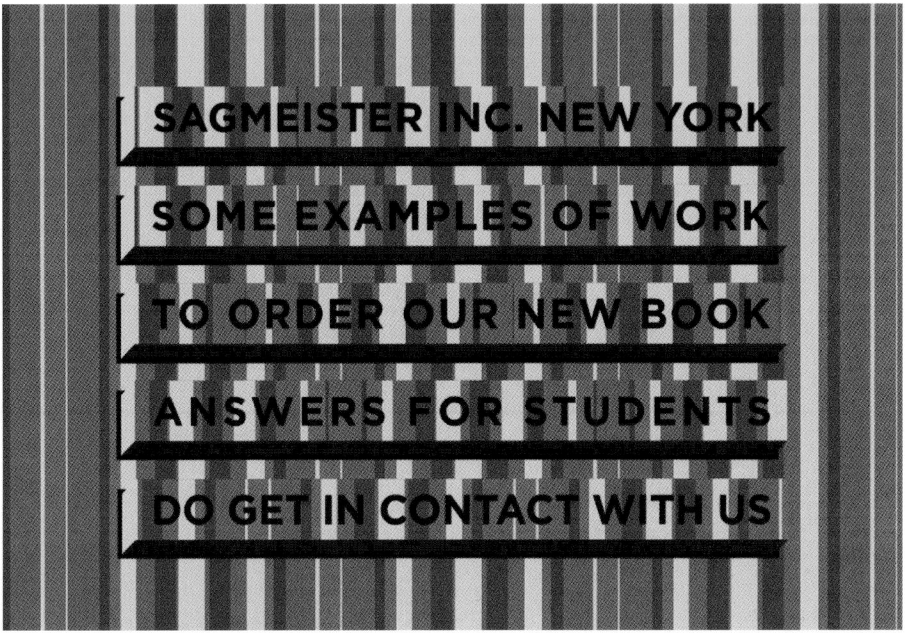

SAGMEISTER INC. NEW YORK
SOME EXAMPLES OF WORK
TO ORDER OUR NEW BOOK
ANSWERS FOR STUDENTS
DO GET IN CONTACT WITH US

LOU REED
BACK

SKELETON KEY
BACK

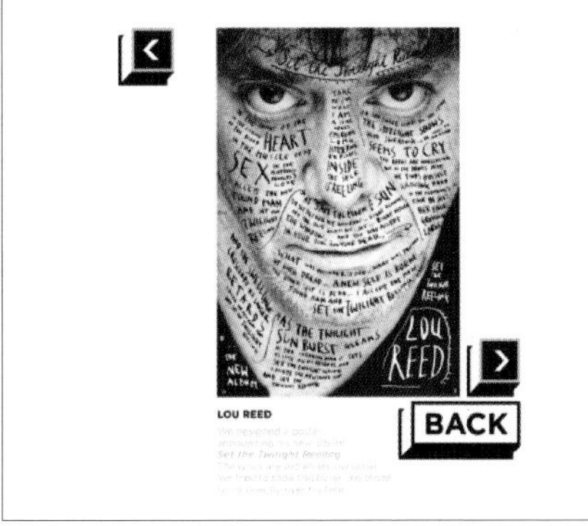

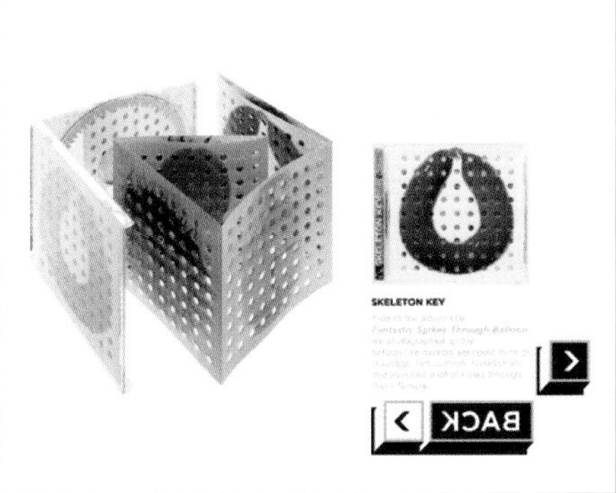

Infos

DESIGN: Sagmeister Inc. /// **PROGRAMMING:** Francisco J. Castro Lopez. /// **TOOLS:** Macromedia Flash. /// **COST:** 80 hours. /// **MAINTENANCE:** 1 hour per month.

SALVA CAMPILLO

SPAIN

www.salvacampillo.com

2003

Concept

The idea was to be very clear and give as more prominence as possible to the pictures with an easy and intuitive navigation system. //// L'idée était d'être clair et de donner autant d'importance que possible aux images, avec une navigation simple et intuitive. //// Die Idee lag darin, klar und präzise zu sein und die Bilder für sich sprechen zu lassen, basierend auf einem intuitiv und leicht anwendbaren Navigationssystem.

Infos

Design and Programming: Diego Laredo de Mendoza <www.lary.it>. /// **Awards:** TINY, Plasticpilots (3 Stars), fcukstar.com, American Design Awards. /// **Tools:** Macromedia Flash, Macromedia Dreamweaver. /// **Cost:** 100 hours. /// **Maintenance:** 1-2 hours per month.

SADDINGTON & BAYNES

UK

www.sb-showcase.com

2003

Concept

Comprehensive site to showcase creative retouching. //// Un site complet faisant office de vitrine pour le retouching créatif. //// **Eine gut verständliche Webseite zur Präsentation von kreativem Retouching.**

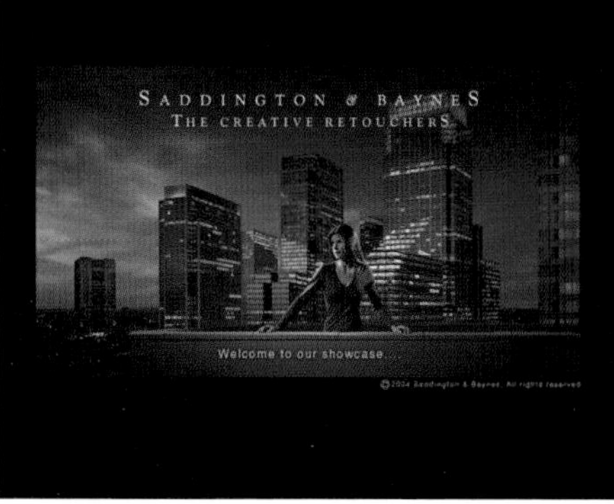

Infos

DESIGN AND PROGRAMMING: James Digby-Jones (Saddington & Baynes). /// **AWARDS:** IDEA Digital Imaging Interactive. /// **TOOLS:** html. /// **MAINTENANCE:** updated whenever new images are needed.

SCARYGIRL

AUSTRALIA

www.scarygirl.com

2003

Concept

A fast, fun site to showcase the Scarygirl toys and related projects. //// Un site rapide et amusant qui sert de vitrine aux jouets Scarygirl et aux projets qui y sont associés. //// Eine schnelle, unterhaltsame Seite, eine Demonstration der Spielsachen von Scarygirl sowie der damit zusammenhängenden Projekte.

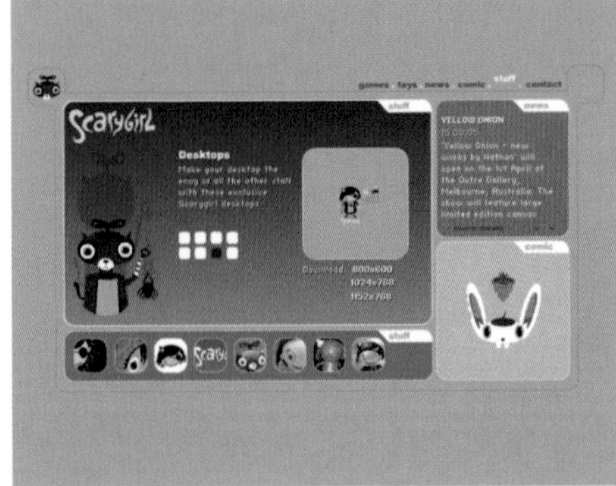

Infos

DESIGN: Nathan J (Soap Creative) <www.nathanj.com.au>; <www.soap.com.au>. /// **PROGRAMMING:** Ashley Ringrose. /// **TOOLS:** html, Macromedia Flash. /// **COST:** 40 hours. /// **MAINTENANCE:** 5 hours per month.

SCOT LAUGHTON

CANADA

www.scotlaughton.com

2003

Concept

We wanted a clean and simple design which put focus on the work, yet made the user's experience unique and playful. //// Nous avons voulu un design simple et clair mettant en avant nos travaux tout en assurant que la visite de l'utilisateur soit unique et ludique. //// Wir haben uns für ein klares und einfaches Design entschieden, mit Schwerpunkt auf unserer Arbeit. Für den Benutzer eine Erfahrung auf ganz besondere und gleichzeitig spielerische Art und Weise.

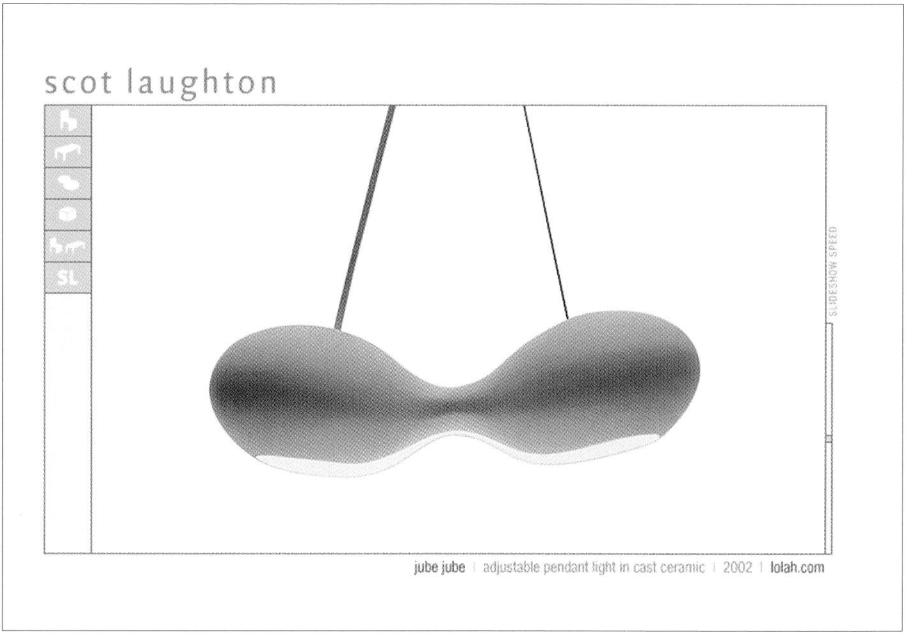

scot laughton
SL
SLIDESHOW SPEED
jube jube | adjustable pendant light in cast ceramic | 2002 | lolah.com

scot laughton
SL

scot laughton
SL
biography
bio

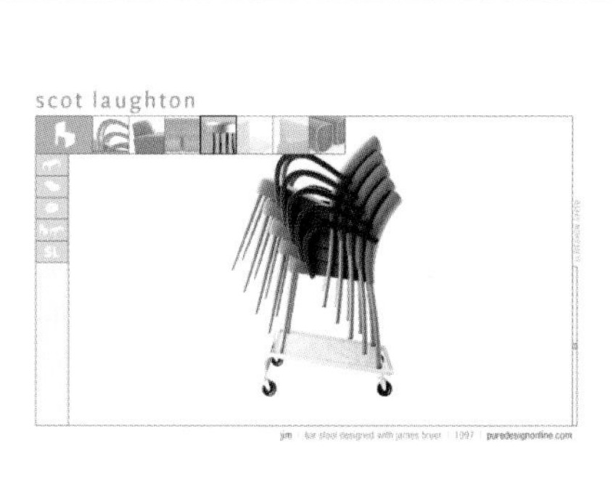

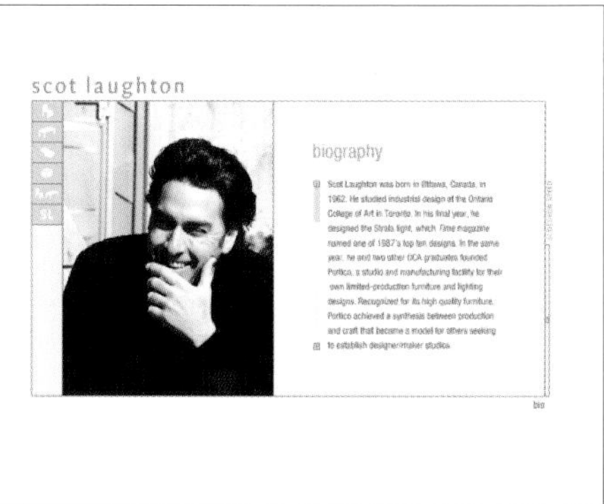

Infos

Design and Programming: Thomas Klepl (Pivot Design) <www.pivotdesign.ca>. /// **Tools:** Macromedia Flash. /// **Cost:** 120 hours. /// **Maintenance:** 2 hours per month.

THE ART OF SHAWN BARBER

USA

www.sdbarber.com

2002

Concept

Graphic simplicity; letting the work speak for itself. //// Une simplicité graphique, les mots parlent d'eux-mêmes. //// Graphische Klarheit; die Arbeit spricht für sich selbst.

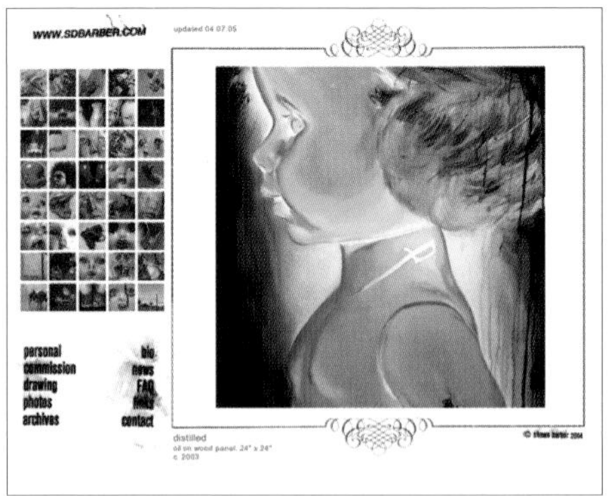

Infos

DESIGN AND PROGRAMMING: Shawn Barber. /// TOOLS: html, Adobe Golive.

SERGIO ROSSI

ITALY

www.sergiorossi.com

2001

Concept

The concept was jump-started by Sergio Rossi's ad campaign featuring models reflected in mirrors. The navigation here is minimal, elegantly complementing the design aesthetic of Sergio Rossi. //// L'idée est issue de la campagne publicitaire Sergio Rossi dans laquelle les modèles étaient reflétés dans des miroirs. La navigation est ici minimale, c'est un complément élégant de l'esthétique du style Sergio Rossi. //// Das Konzept hatte seine Durchbruch mit Sergio Rossis Werbekampagne: Models, die sich in Spiegeln reflektieren. Die Navigation hierbei ist minimal, eine elegante Ergänzung zu Sergio Rossis ästhetischem Design.

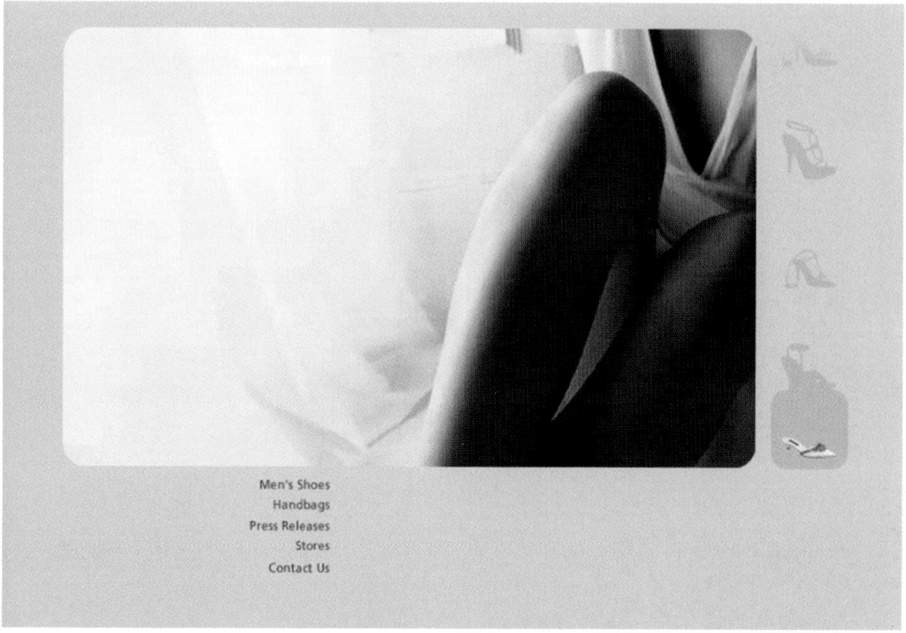

Men's Shoes
Handbags
Press Releases
Stores
Contact Us

Men's Shoes
Handbags
Press Releases
Stores
Contact Us
Register
sergio rossi

Women's Shoes
Men's Shoes
Handbags
Press Releases
Stores
SERGIO ROSSI'S NEW GLOBAL STORE CONCEPT
Contact Us
Register
sergio rossi

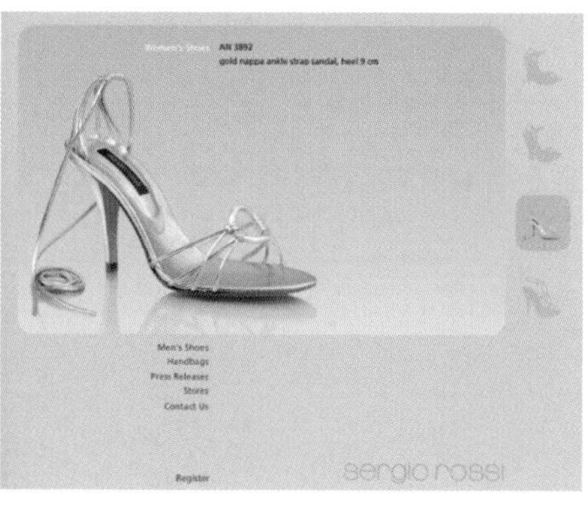

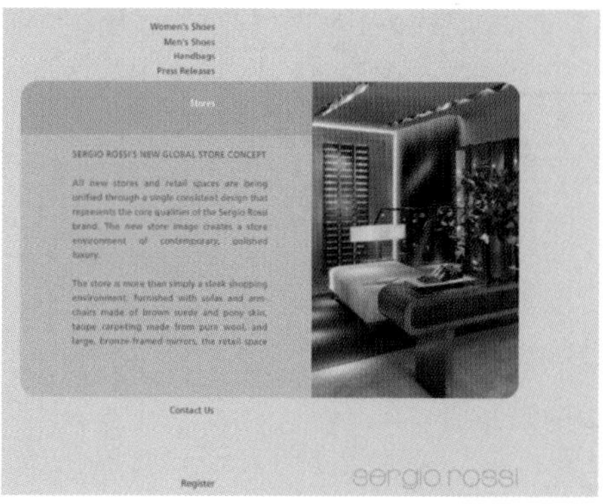

Infos

Design: Vas Sloutchevsky (Firstborn) <www.firstbornmultimedia.com>. /// **Programming:** Shea Gonyo and Josh Ott /// **Tools:** Macromedia Flash.

SHADOW AND LIGHT

USA

www.shadowandlight.net

2004

Concept

Interactive black and white photography exhibit containing a collection of 90 photographs taken during three months of travel and architectural study throughout Europe and Scandinavia. //// Une exposition interactive de photographies en noir et blanc composée de 90 images prises au cours de trois mois de voyage et d'étude architecturale en Europe et en Scandinavie. //// **Interaktive Ausstellung von Schwarz-Weissfotografie, eine Sammlung von 90 Fotografien, die eine dreimonatige Reise durch Europa und Skandinavien sowie diverse Architekturstudien reflektiert.**

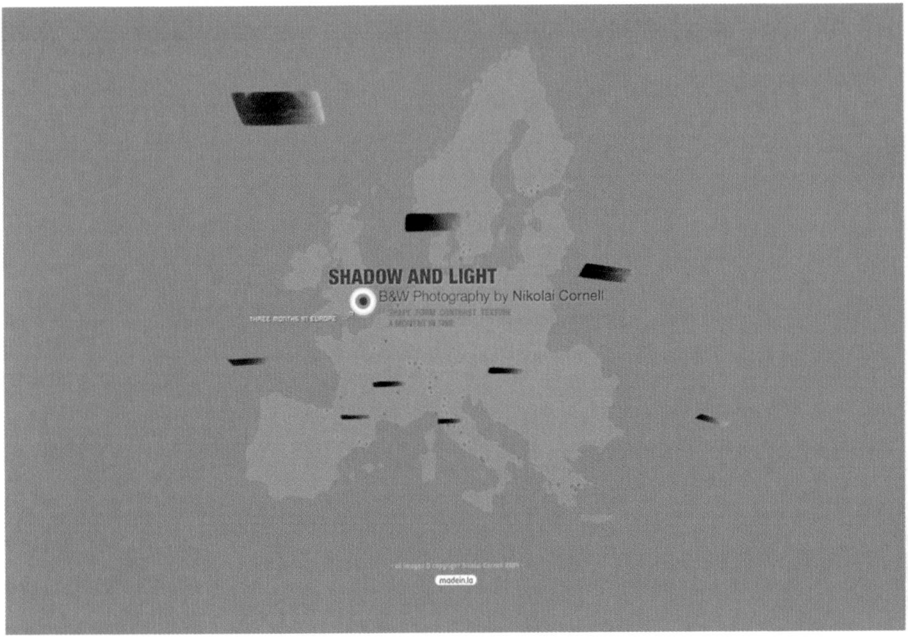

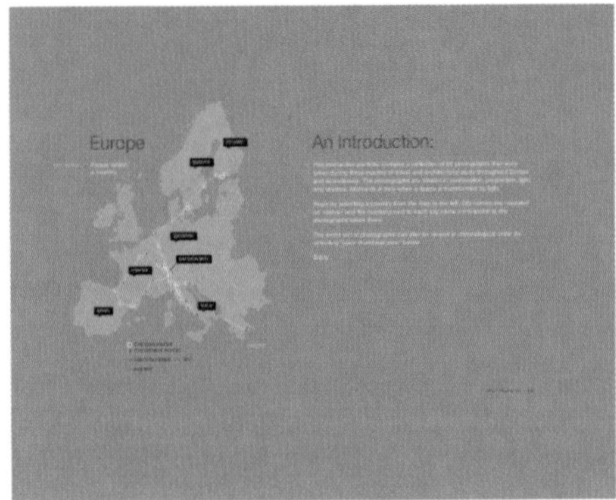

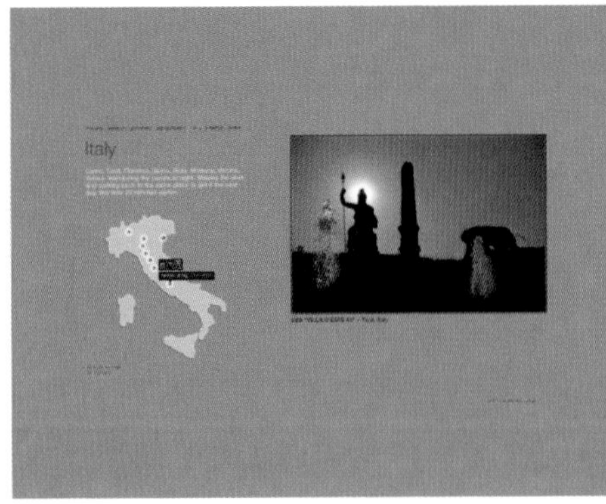

Infos

Design and Programming: Nikolai Cornell (madeinLA) <www.madein.la>. /// **Awards:** I.D. Interactive Media Design Review (Bronze), STEP design 100, Flash in the Can Design and Technology Festival, Thailand New Media Art Festival, Yahoo Picks (Site of the Day), Flashkit. /// **Tools:** 35mm "analog" camera, Macromedia Flash, Adobe Photoshop, Adobe ImageReady. /// **Cost:** I worked on the website on and off for 2 years. Really about 2 months of solid work. /// **Maintenance:** maybe 1 hour a month answering emails.

SHAMROCK

THE NETHERLANDS

www.shamrocking.com

2000

Concept

I see this site as my personal playground, and I hope visitors will feel my enthusiasm. //// Je conçois ce site comme mon terrain de jeu personnel et j'espère que les visiteurs éprouveront mon enthousiasme. //// Ich betrachte diese Seite als meinen ganz persönlichen Spielplatz, mit der Hoffnung, die Besucher können darin meinen Enthusiasmus wiedererkennen.

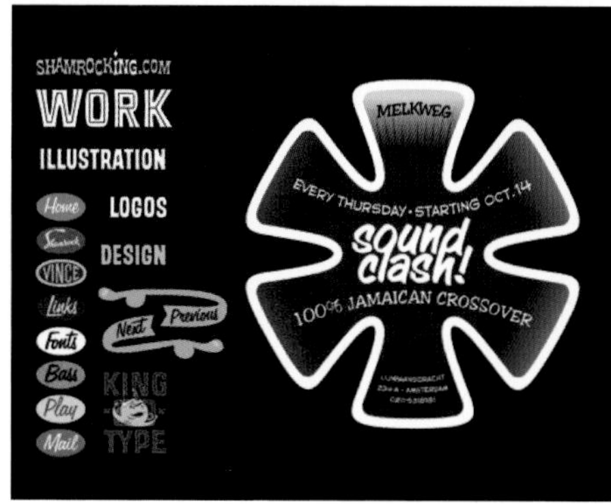

Infos

DESIGN: Jeroen Klaver (Shamrock Int.). /// **TOOLS:** Macromedia Flash. /// **COST:** 1 week. /// **MAINTENANCE:** That reminds me... should update again!

SHERRI O'CONNOR PHOTO

USA
2004

www.sherriphoto.com

Concept

By creating an intuitive navigation and by using Flash, we tried to make it an experience, immersing the user in the photography. //// En créant une navigation intuitive et en ayant recours à Flash, nous avons tenté de faire de la visite de ce site une expérience, en immergeant l'utilisateur dans la photographie plutôt que de faire du site un simple site Web de référence. //// **Durch die Kreation intuitiver Navigation sowie der Anwendung von Flash sollte dies zu einer Erfahrung werden, die den Besucher in die Welt der Fotografie eintauchen lässt.**

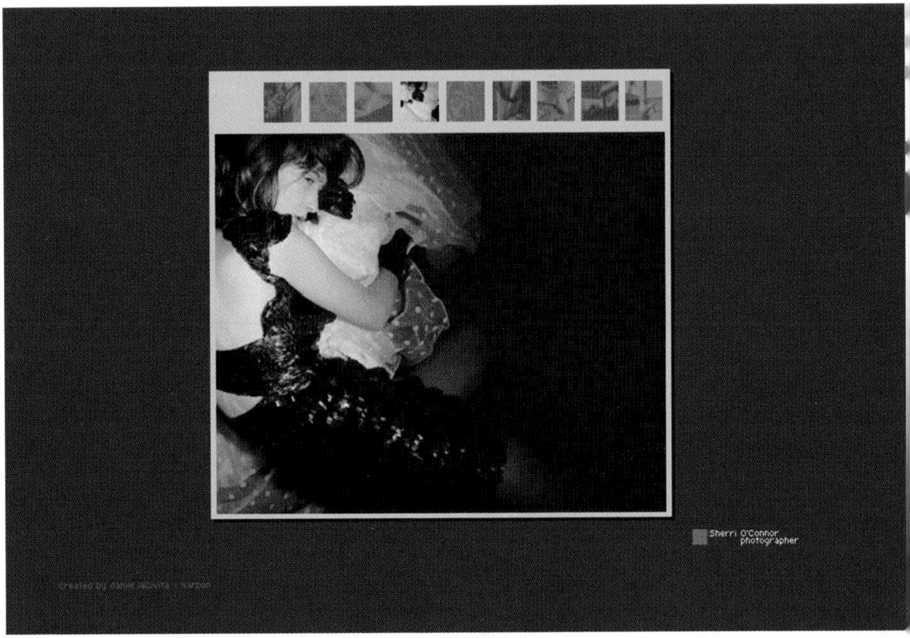

Infos

Design and Programming: Daniel LaCivita (Karbon Studios) <www.karbonstudios.com>. /// **Awards:** FWA. /// **Tools:** Macromedia Flash. /// **Cost:** 1 week. /// **Maintenance:** 2 hours per month.

SHOONYA DESIGN

INDIA

www.shoonyadesign.net

2003

Concept

The site Shoonya design is a design portfolio site. The prime objective of the site is to showcase my strength as creative professional in the interaction/graphic design domain. //// Le site Shoonya design est un site portfolio de design. L'objectif principal de ce site est de présenter mes compétences en tant que professionnel dans le domaine du design d'interaction et graphique. //// Shoonya Design ist ein Portfolio sowie eine Designerseite. Der Schwerpunkt liegt darin, meine professionelle Kreativität in der Welt des Designs, der Interaktivität und der Grafik zu behaupten.

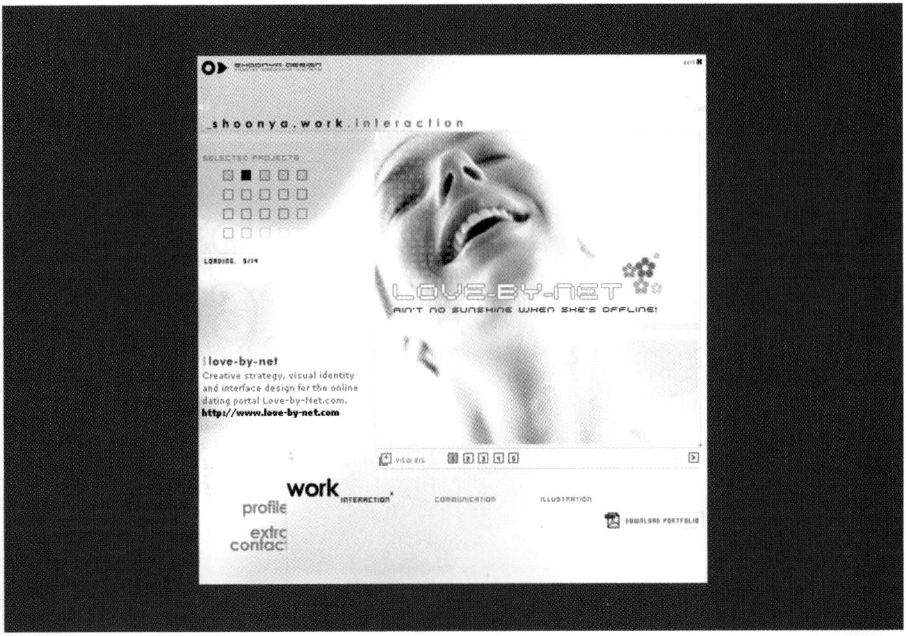

Infos

Design and Programming: Shoonya Design. /// **Awards:** TAXI (Site of the Week), Americal Design Award, Plasticpilots, DOPE, Golden Web (Site of the Month), Style Boost, NewWebPick (Superpick of the World), Flash Vista, Spoono, etc. /// **Tools:** Adobe Photoshop, Macromedia Flash, Macromedia Dreamweaver. /// **Cost:** 400 hours.

SHOOTSTUDIO

CANADA

www.shootstudio.ca

2002

Concept

Our website acts as an interactive medium for clients and prospects, to produce and deliver striped portfolios, similar to that of a contact sheet. //// Notre site Web est un média interactif destiné à nos clients et prospects et visant à produire et fournir des portfolios ressemblant à des bandes-témoin. //// Unsere Webseite dient als interaktives Medium für bestehende und potentielle Kunden, sowie zur Produktion und Repräsentation von Kontaktbögen ähnlichen Portfolios.

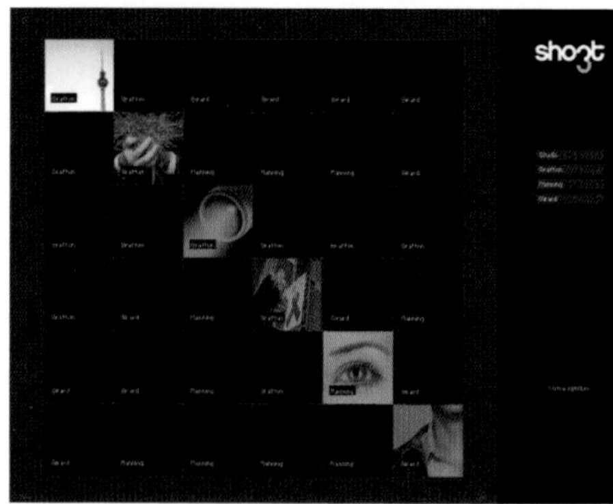

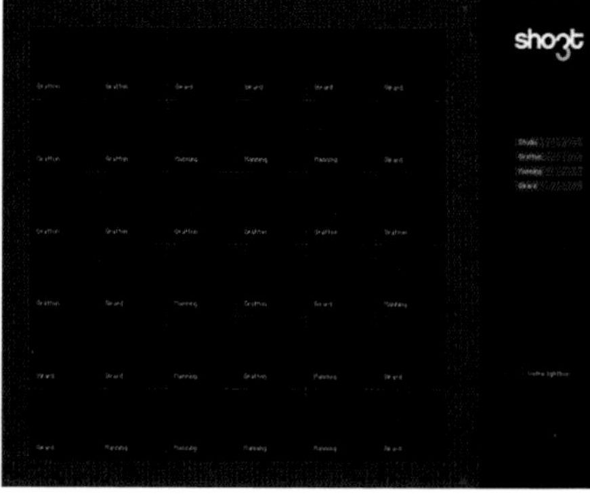

Infos

Design: JF Mayrand and JC Yacono (Epoxy) <www.epoxy.ca>. /// **Programming:** François Arbour, Serge Grenier and Julien Fondère. /// **Tools:** html, Macromedia Flash, php. /// **Cost:** 80 hours.

SIMON CHAPUT PHOTOGRAPHS FRANCE

www.simonchaput.com 2004

Concept

The play with shadows justifies the black underground, as well as the minimalist structure, so that the eyes can keep the focus on the poetry of the photography. //// Le jeu constant des ombres et des lumières dicta le choix d'un fond noir ainsi que d'une structure graphique minimaliste pour que l'oeil soit captif de la poésie des photos. //// Das kontinuierliche Licht- und Schattenspiel bestimmt sowohl die Wahl des schwarzen Hintergrundes als auch eine minimalistische grafische Struktur, da sonst das Auge nicht im Stande ist, die Poesie der Fotografie wahrzunehmen.

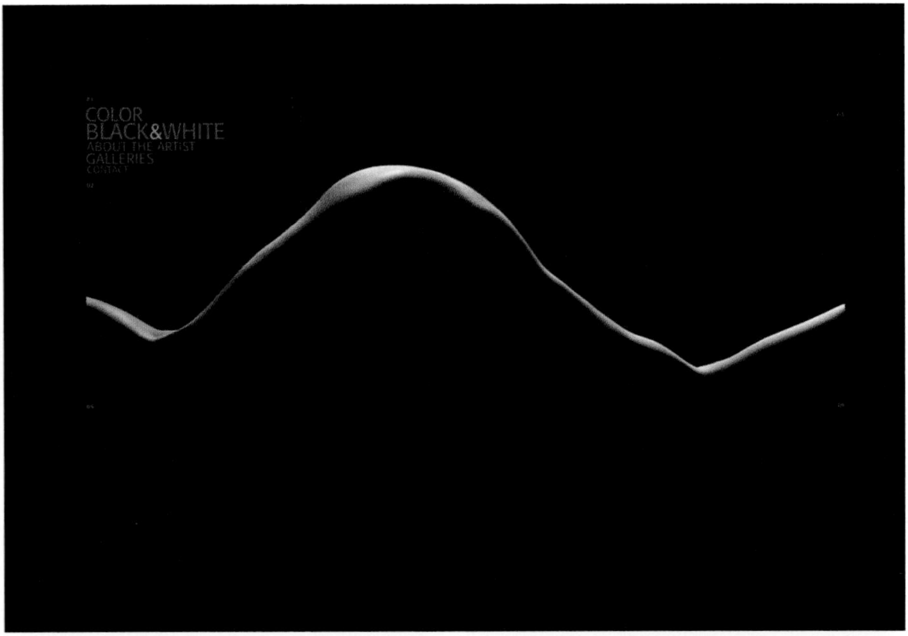

Infos

Design and Programming: UZIK <www.uzik.com>. /// **Tools:** Macromedia Flash, html, php. /// **Cost:** 1 month.

SKIN

NORWAY

www.skin.no

2003

Concept

Playful, dedicated and solid. The site changes randomly each time you visit. //// Ludique, engagé et compact. le site évolue au hasard de vos visites. //// Verspielt, engagiert und solide. Die Seite wechselt bei jedem Besuch nach dem Zufallsprinzip.

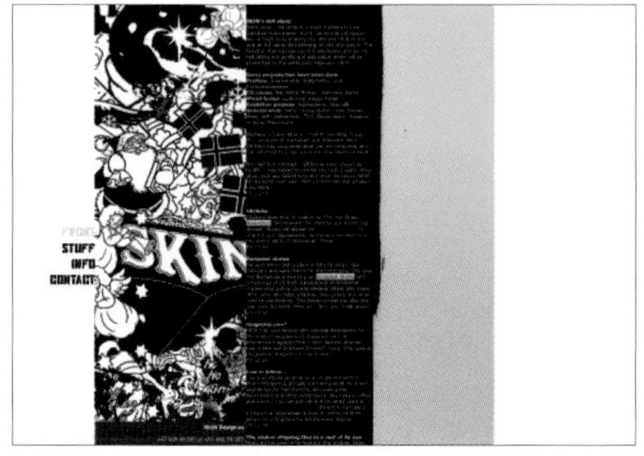

Infos

DESIGN AND PROGRAMMING: SKIN. /// TOOLS: html. /// COST: 15 hours. /// MAINTENANCE: 3 hours per month.

SKWAKCOLORS

FRANCE

www.skwak.com

2003

Concept

Just a happy mess quite mad. //// Un joyeux melting-pot complètement fou. //// Ganz einfach ein lustiges und verrücktes Durcheinander.

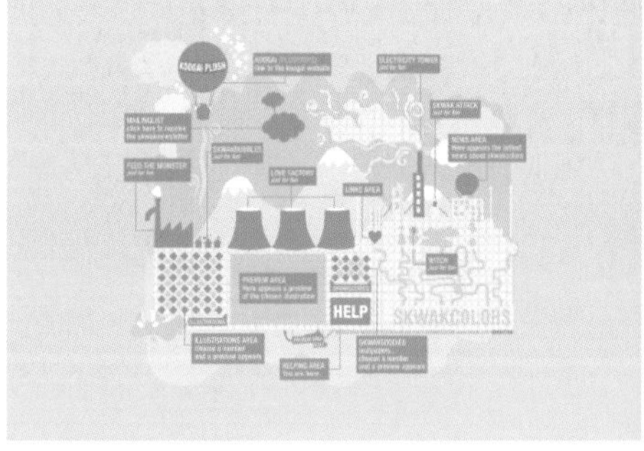

Infos

DESIGN AND PROGRAMMING: SKWAKCOLORS. /// TOOLS: html, Macromedia Flash. /// COST: 40 hours. /// MAINTENANCE: 10-20 hours per month.

SEAN KENNEDY SANTOS PHOTO USA

www.sksantos.com 2003

Concept

Image-based content to be accentuated by minimalist approach to design - all menu items had to be on 1 page - expedient loading time for 2 platforms. //// Du contenu d'image accentué par une approche minimaliste du design (tous les éléments de menu devaient tenir sur une seule page). Temps de chargement pour deux plate-formes. //// Auf Bildern basierender Inhalt, der durch minimalistische Annäherung an Design hervorgehoben wird - alle Elemente des Menüs befinden sich auf einer Seite mit einer angemessenen Ladezeit für zwei Plattformen.

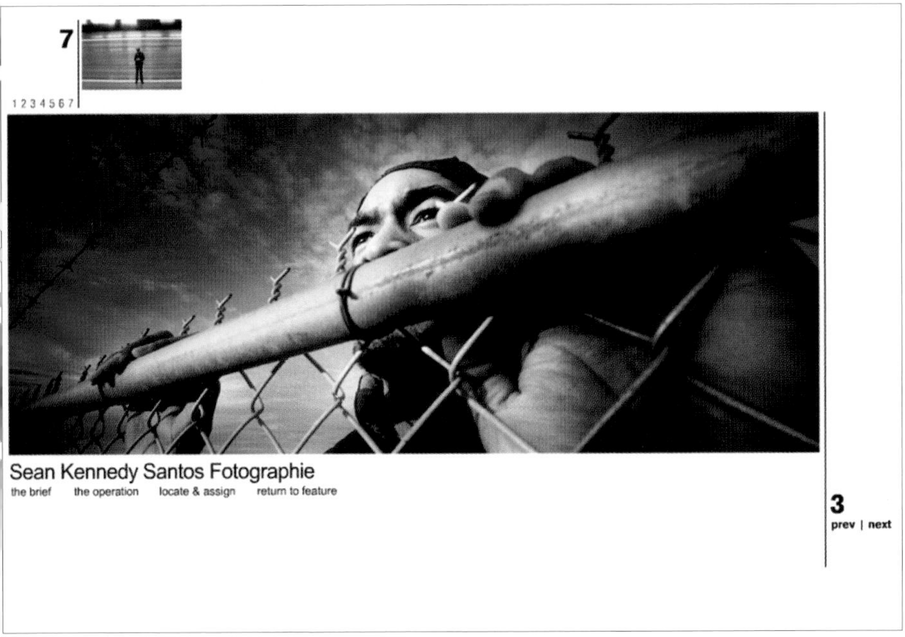

7

1 2 3 4 5 6 7

Sean Kennedy Santos Fotographie

the brief the operation locate & assign return to feature

3

prev | next

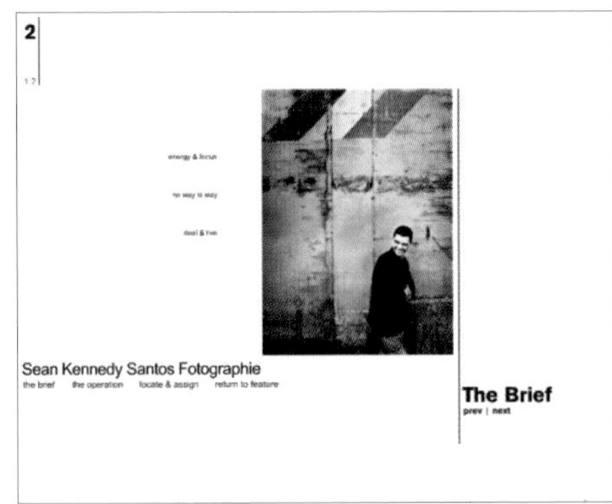

Infos

DESIGN: Eight x Ten. /// **PROGRAMMING:** Code & Theory <www.codeandtheory.com>. /// **AWARDS:** One Show, PDN Annual Best Site. /// **TOOLS:** Macromedia Flash. /// **COST:** 2 weeks.

SOPPCOLLECTIVE

AUSTRALIA

www.soppcollective.com

2002

Concept The mushroom-forest and the little creatures (the team) inhabiting it are supposed to link back to our identity, work as a fun element and are to reflect the loose nature of our collective. //// La forêt de champignons et les petites créatures (l'équipe) qui l'habitent renvoient à notre identité, fonctionnent en tant qu'éléments amusants et doivent traduire la nature décontractée de notre collectif. //// Der Pilzwald und die dort wohnenden kleinen Kreaturen (das Team) stellen den Link zu uns dar, ein lustiges Element, welches die entspannte Natürlichkeit unserer Gruppe wiederspiegelt.

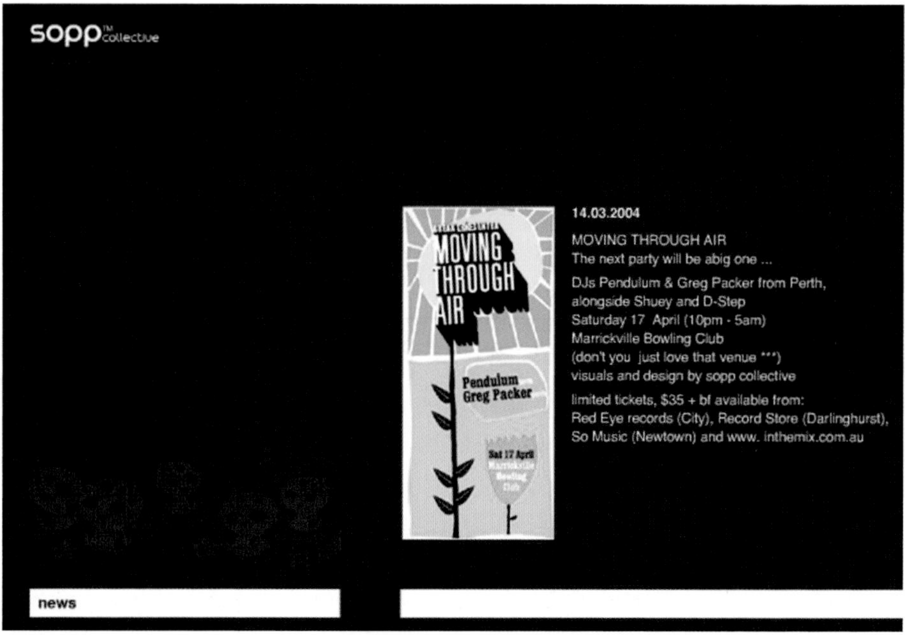

sopp™ collective
MOVING THROUGH AIR
Pendulum Greg Packer
Sat 17 April
14.03.2004
MOVING THROUGH AIR
The next party will be abig one ...
DJs Pendulum & Greg Packer from Perth,
alongside Shuey and D-Step
Saturday 17 April (10pm - 5am)
Marrickville Bowling Club
(don't you just love that venue ***)
visuals and design by sopp collective
limited tickets, $35 + bf available from:
Red Eye records (City), Record Store (Darlinghurst),
So Music (Newtown) and www. inthemix.com.au
news

posters/flyers _Home bar

sole
print _'Rossi Boots' catalogue

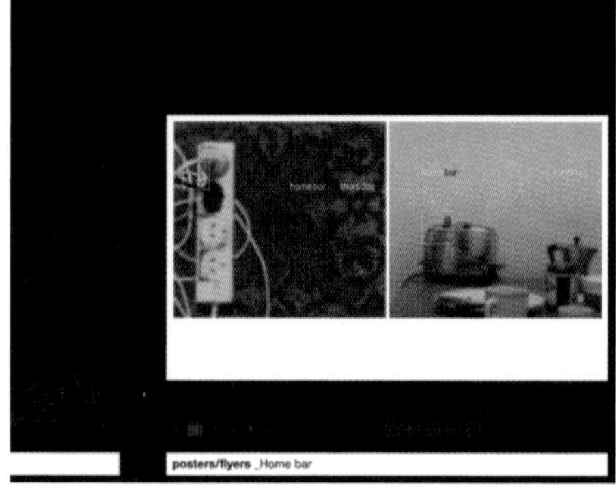

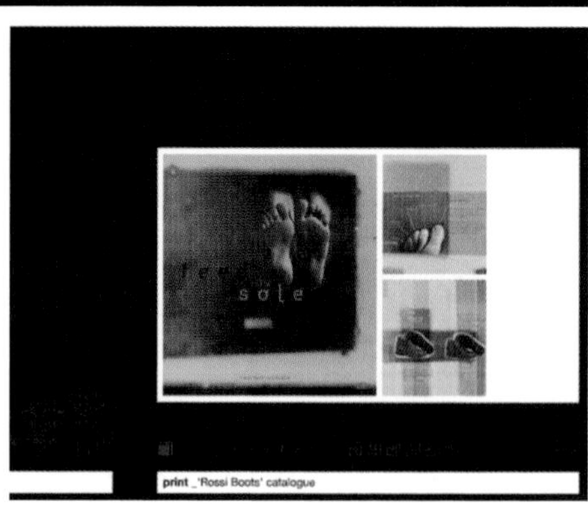

Infos DESIGN AND PROGRAMMING: Soppcollective. /// AWARDS: Guinness Young Contemporary Art, Output (Silver). /// TOOLS: html, Macromedia Flash. /// COST: we wish we'd remember. /// MAINTENANCE: 2 hours per month.

STEPHEN BLISS

USA

www.stephenbliss.com

2003

Concept

To entertain and inform. //// Pour divertir et informer. //// Zur Unterhaltung und Information.

Infos

Design and Programming: Futaba Hayashi <www.futabita.com>. /// **Awards:** NewWebPick (Site of the Day), FWA (Site of the Day), e-Creative (Site of the Day). /// **Tools:** html, Macromedia Flash. /// **Cost:** 9 months. /// **Maintenance:** 5 hours per month.

STRATO CUCINE

ITALY

www.stratocucine.com

2003

Concept

The visitor should just sit back, relax and... start dreaming. //// Le visiteur n'a qu'à se renverser sur sa chaise, se détendre et... rêver. //// Der Besucher sollte sich ganz einfach zurücklehnen, relaxen und... anfangen, zu träumen.

Infos

Design and Programming: group94 <www.group94.com>. /// **Awards:** Bombshock, BestFlashAnimationSite.com (Site of the Week), FWA (Site of the Day). /// **Tools:** Macromedia Flash, php. /// **Cost:** 6 weeks. /// **Maintenance:** 2 days every year.

STREETERS

UK

www.streeters.com

2004

Glamour and Function. //// Glamour et fonctionnel. //// Glamour und Funktionalität.

Design: Underwaterpistol <www.underwaterpistol.com>. /// **Programming:** Gary Carruthers and Gary Belton. /// **Tools:** html, Macromedia Flash, php, MySQL. /// **Cost:** 270 hours. /// **Maintenance:** 4 hours per month.

BREAKFAST DESIGN STUD

www.studiobreakfast.com

Concept

The idea was to make a simple website to improve the visibility of the works, with a nice and fluid naviga
//// L'idée était de créer un site Web simple afin d'améliorer la visibilité des travaux, et de le doter d'une navig
constitue l'aspect principal de ce portfolio. //// Die Idee war es, eine einfache Webseite mit verbesserter F
Und das Ganze mit einer reibungslosen Navigation - eines der Hauptanliegen unseres Portfolios.

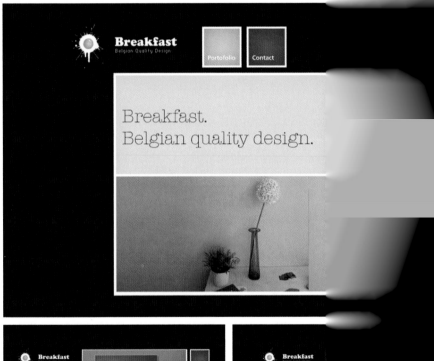

Breakfast
Belgian Quality Design
Portofolio
Contact
Breakfast.
Belgian quality design.

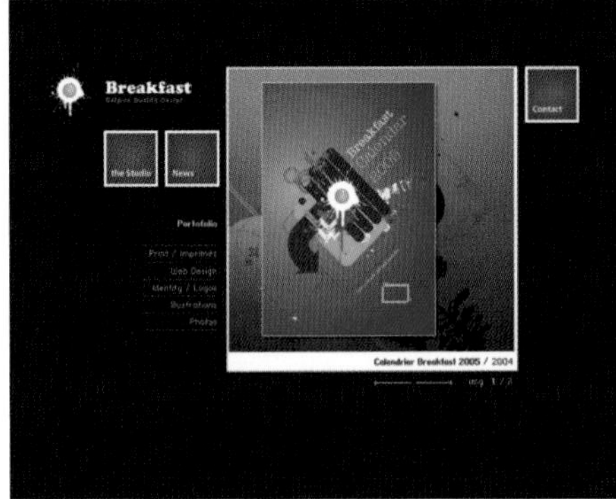

Infos

Design and Programming: Martin Dellicour (Breakfast). /// **Awards:** Styleboost, Linkdup, Newstoday, etc. /// T
script. /// **Cost:** 40 hours to create the actual site. /// **Maintenance:** 2-3 hours per month.

STUDIO SOI

GERMANY

www.studiosoi.com

2003

Your friendly animation studio. //// Votre studio d'animation. //// Ihr freundliches Animationsstudio.

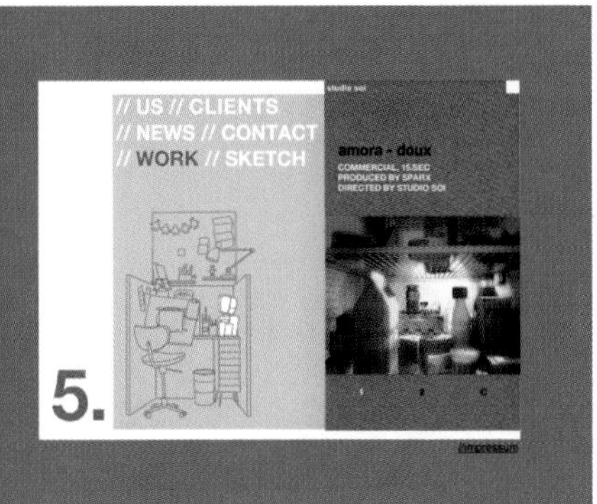

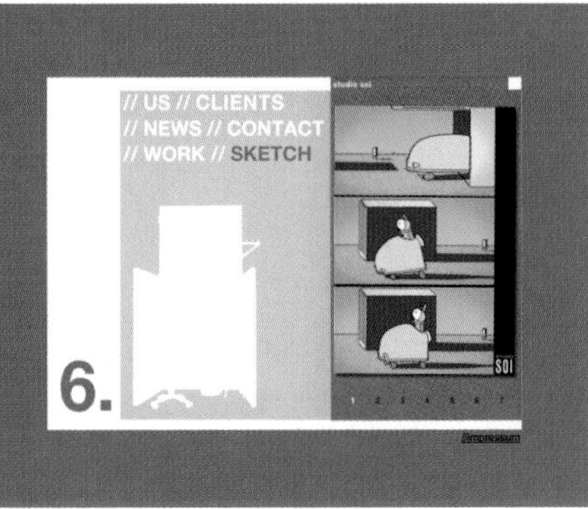

DESIGN: Jakob Schuh and Saschka Unseld (Studio Soi). /// **PROGRAMMING:** Saschka Unseld, Anna Kubik and Sandra Jakisch. /// **TOOLS:** html, Macromedia Flash, film. /// **COST:** 2 weeks. /// **MAINTENANCE:** 15 minutes per month.

SUPER 8

UK

www.super8.co.uk

2003

Concept

To create the opposite of the obvious involving theories from the philosophy of randomness and nonsense. //// Pour créer l'opposé de l'évidence en impliquant des théories relatives à la philosophie du hasard et de l'absurde. //// Genau das Gegenteil des Absehbaren kreieren, einschliesslich philosophischer Theorien des Zufalls und der Sinnlosigkeit.

Infos

Design and Programming: Andrew Cross (Super 8). /// **Tools:** Macromedia Flash, html, GIFs, MP3. /// **Maintenance:** 48 hours a month.

TESIS

BRAZIL

www.tesisweb.com.br

2004

Concept

Our challenges: to present Tesis audio production portfolio to create a distinctive web site that revealed a bit of the company's personality to make it an enjoyable experience. //// Nos défis : présenter efficacement l'incroyable portfolio de production audio de Tesis, créer un site Web différent révélant un peu de la personnalité de l'entreprise et faire de la visite de ce site une expérience amusante. //// Unsere Herausforderung: Auf effektivem Wege ein Portfolio mit Audioproduktion auf einer ganz besonderen Webseite zu kreieren, die ausserdem die Persönlichkeit unserer Firma reflektiert. Alles in allem, eine rundum positive Erfahrung.

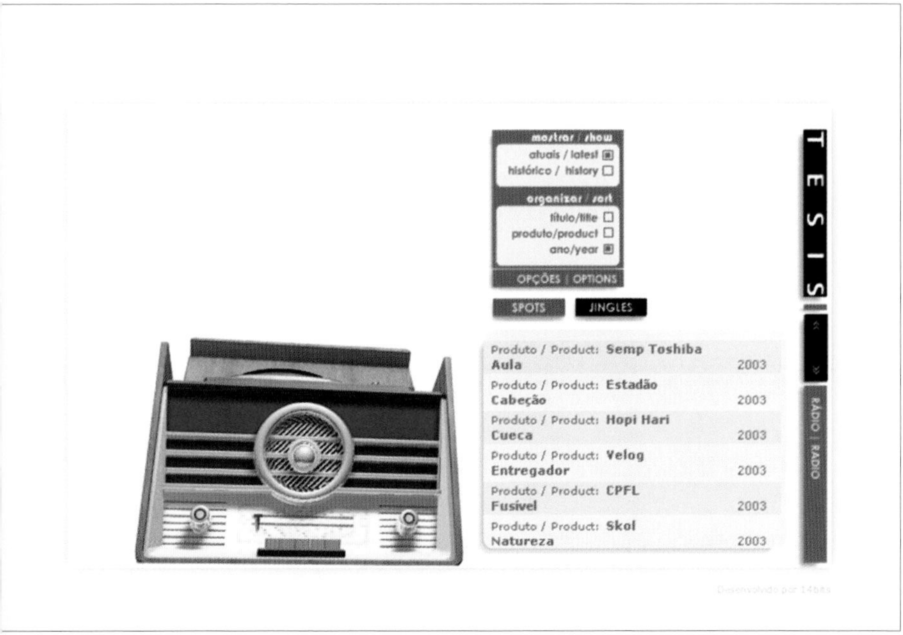

mostrar / show
atuais / latest
histórico / history
organizar / sort
título/title
produto/product
ano/year
OPÇÕES | OPTIONS
SPOTS
JINGLES
Produto / Product: Semp Toshiba Aula 2003
Produto / Product: Estadão Cabeção 2003
Produto / Product: Hopi Hari Cueca 2003
Produto / Product: Velog Entregador 2003
Produto / Product: CPFL Fusível 2003
Produto / Product: Skol Natureza 2003
TESIS
RÁDIO | RADIO

Infos

Design and Programming: 14bits Produções <www.14bits.com.br>. /// **Tools:** Macromedia Flash, 3D, php, pencil, video, film, music. /// **Cost:** 500 hours from briefing to publishing. /// **Maintenance:** there is no maintenance costs because Tesis updates the entire site via a content management system.

TETSOO PRODUCTION

SWITZERLAND

www.tetsoo.com

2004

Concept

I wanted a very clean, practical interface enhanced with 3D animations integrated to the general navigation. //// J'ai voulu une interface très claire et pratique mise en valeur par des animations en 3D intégrées dans la navigation générale. //// Ich wollte ein ganz reines und praktisches Interface, mit zusätzlich integrierter 3D-Animation im allgemeinen Navigationssystem.

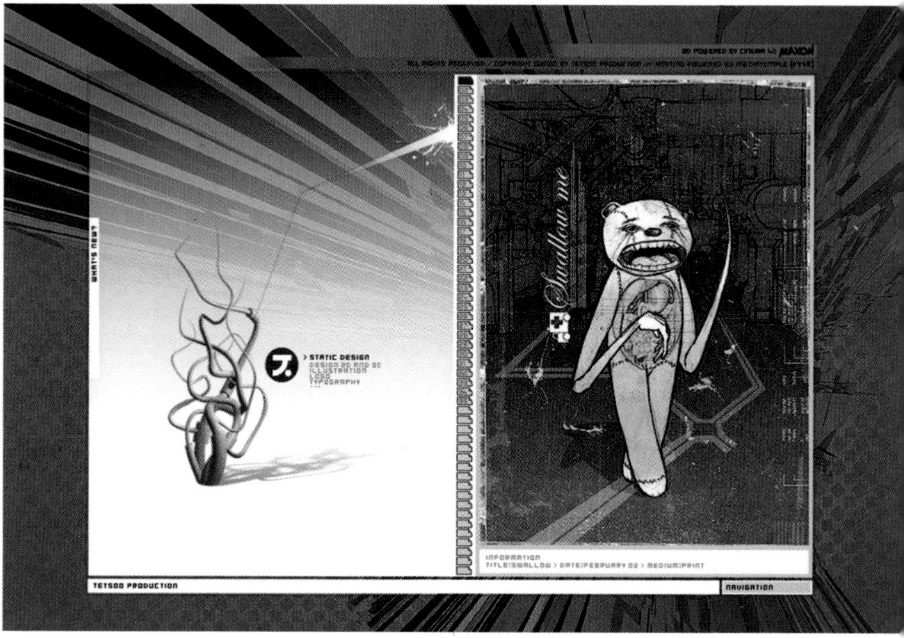

Infos

DESIGN AND PROGRAMMING: Grégoire Poget (Tetsoo). /// AWARDS: Bombshock, FWA, e-Creative. /// TOOLS: Macromedia Flash, Adobe Photoshop, Adobe Illustrator, Cinema 4D, Adobe AfterEffects, Reason. /// COST: 2-3 weeks. /// MAINTENANCE: almost zero.

ARS THANEA

www.thanea.com

POLAND

2003

Concept

Pure simplicity. //// Une simplicité pure. //// **Einfachheit pur.**

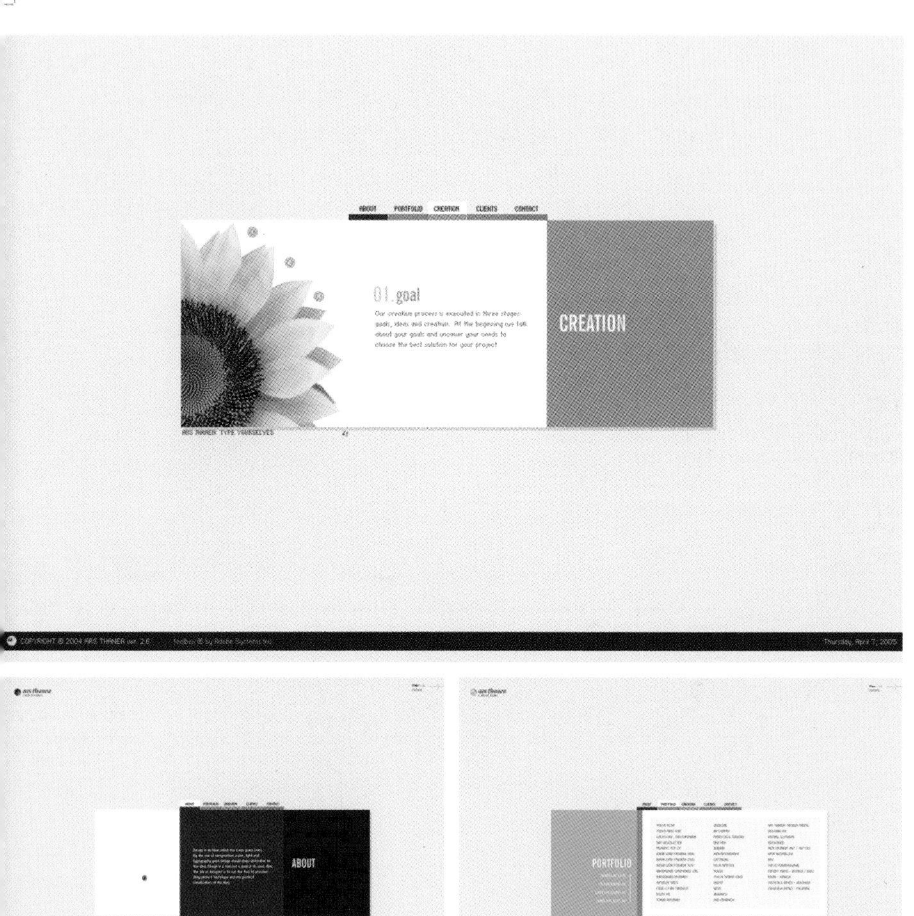

Infos

Design and Programming: Bartłomiej Rozbicki. /// **Awards:** fcukstar.com, Netdiver, FWA, BombShok, NewWebPick, TAXI, 4EFX, TINY, Flash Kit, Plasticpilots, American Design Award, etc. /// **Tools:** Macromedia Flash, xml, html, music /// **Cost:** it's hard to say.

THE LINEAR

SINGAPORE

www.thelinear.com

2003

Concept

A site to reflect the fact that the Linear is the longest condominium in Singapore. The navigation features an unbroken experience where each section 'flows' into the next. //// Le site du Linear, l'immeuble le plus long de Singapour. La navigation est ininterrompue, chaque section se fond dans la suivante. //// Eine Seite, die linear die längste Eigentumswohnanlage Singapurs darstellt. Das Navigationssystem demonstriert einen fliessenden Übergang von einem Bereich in den nächsten.

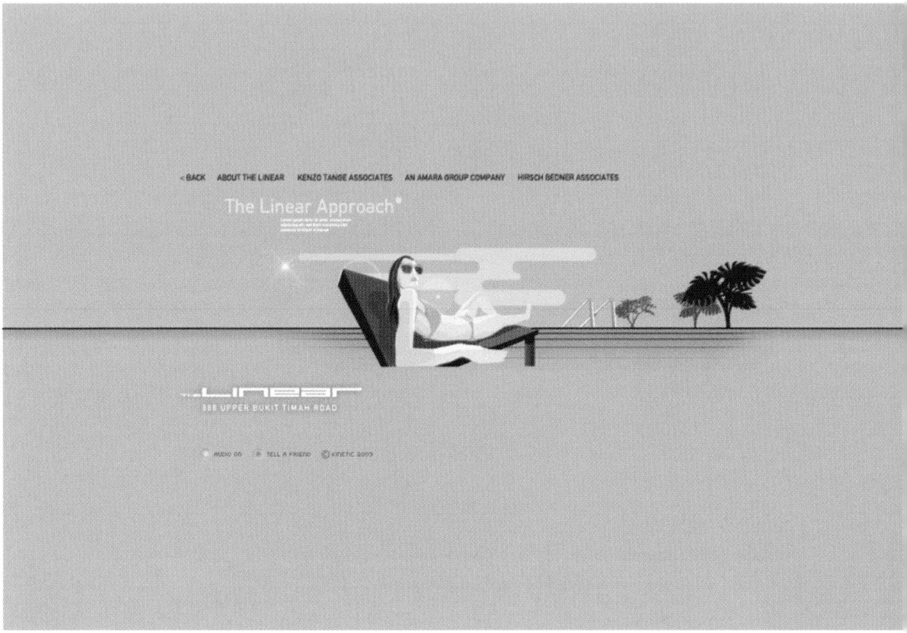

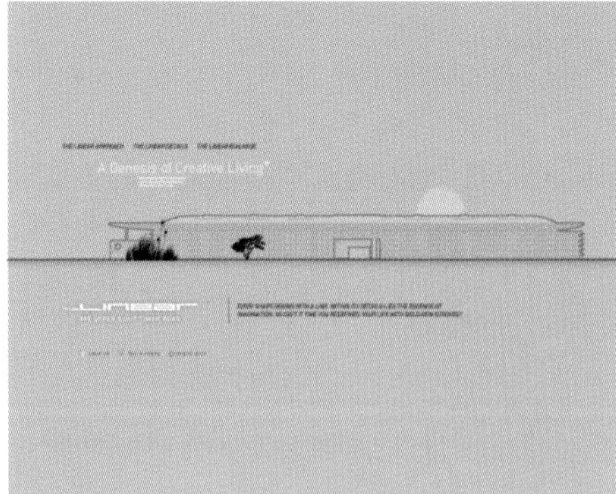

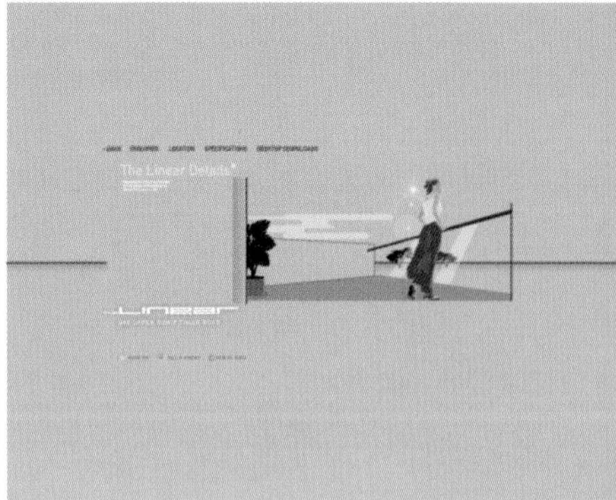

Infos

Design: Kinetic Interactive <www.kinetic.com.sg>. /// **Programming:** Benjy Choo. /// **Awards:** Young Guns, Singapore Creative Circle. /// **Tools:** html, Macromedia Flash, php. /// **Cost:** 120 hours. /// **Maintenance:** none.

ULI OESTERLE

GERMANY

www.the-oesterle.com

2004

Concept

The objective was to have a both entertaining and clean page so that one could navigate quickly and without complications. //// Le but était de créer une page à la fois divertissante et claire où l'on pourrait naviguer rapidement et sans problèmes. //// Das Ziel war eine unterhaltsame, aber aufgeräumte Seite zu kreieren, in der man unkompliziert und schnell navigieren kann.

Infos

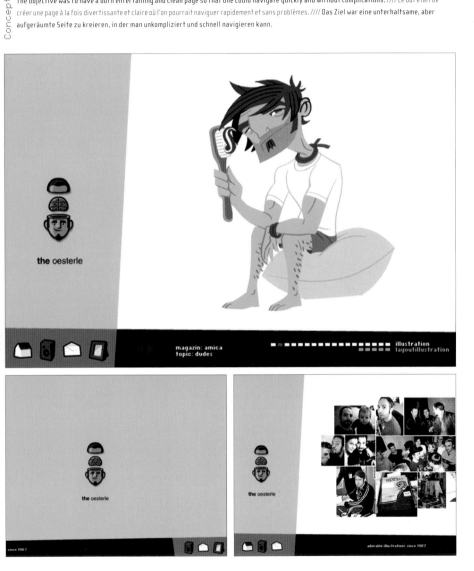

DESIGN: Uli Oesterle. /// **PROGRAMMING:** Matthis Herrmann. /// **AWARDS:** FWA, Turkey Awards. /// **TOOLS:** Adobe Photoshop, Adobe Illustrator, Macromedia Flash. /// **COST:** 110 hours. /// **MAINTENANCE:** 4-20 hours per month.

THE PHARMACY

THE NETHERLANDS

www.thepharmacy-media.com

2002

Concept

Explorer, mix and watch to experience thepharmacy. //// Explorateurs, mélangez et observez pour découvrir thepharmacy. //// **Entdecke, probiere aus und beobachte, mach dir ein Bild von The Pharmacy.**

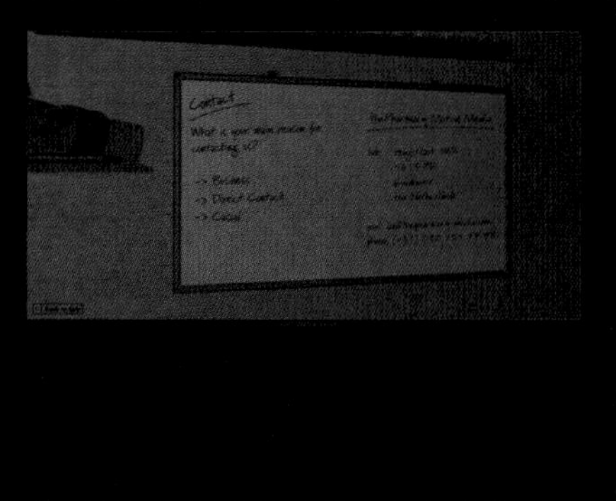

Infos

DESIGN: thePharmacy. /// **PROGRAMMING:** F. Litjens and J. Kessels. /// **AWARDS:** FWA. /// **TOOLS:** Macromedia Flash, Discreet 3D Studio Max, Adobe Photoshop. /// **COST:** 100 hours divided over 2 months. /// **MAINTENANCE:** if ever, 2 hours per month.

THE VILLAGE

www.thevillage.nl

THE NETHERLANDS

2004

Concept

Stunning graphics with subtle animation. Triggering the show-reel. Start playing right from entering the site. Flexible (random) 4:3 and 16:9 formats. Easy updating. //// Des graphismes époustouflants associés à une animation subtile. Déclenchement de la bande démo. Vous commencez à jouer dès que vous entrez sur le site. Formats 4 :3 et 16 :9 flexibles (aléatoires). Mise à jour facile. //// Beeindruckende Grafiken mit subtiler Animation. Die Vorführung beginnt. Schon auf der ersten Seite beginnt das Spiel. Flexible und willkürliche 4x3 und 16x9 Formate. Einfache Updates.

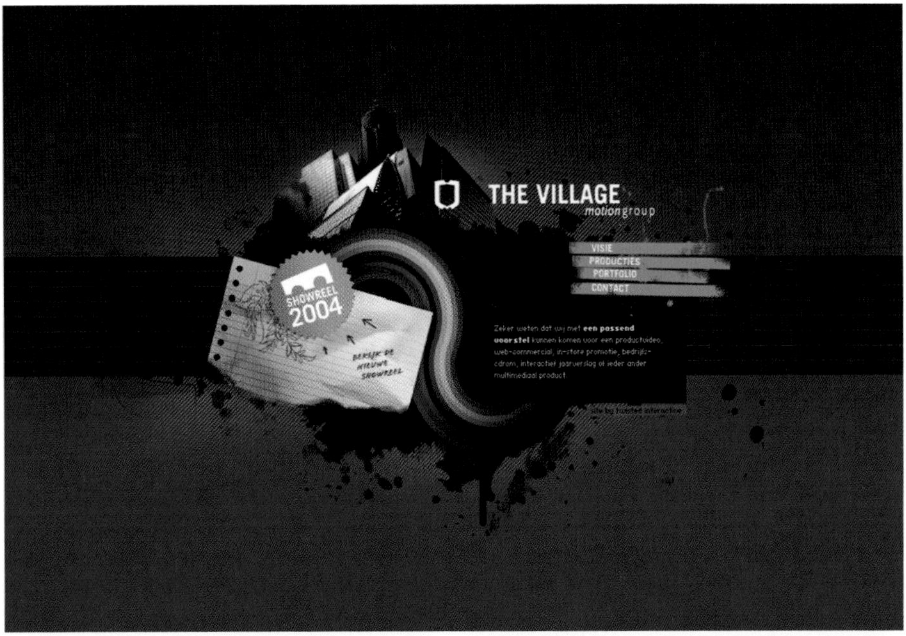

Infos

Design: Twisted Interactive <www.twisted.nl>. /// **Programming:** Dennis Danen. /// **Awards:** Linkdup, Styleboost, Uailab (Site of the Month), and various other notifications. /// **Tools:** Macromedia Flash, xml, php, video. /// **Cost:** 3 weeks. /// **Maintenance:** Depending on the amount of video- or animationprojects developed by The Village. Clips are uploaded via CMS.

T-MICHAEL.COM

NORWAY

www.t-michael.com

2004

Concept

Playful source of fashion inspiration. //// Une source d'inspiration fashion ludique. //// **Spielerisches Angebot an modischer Inspiration.**

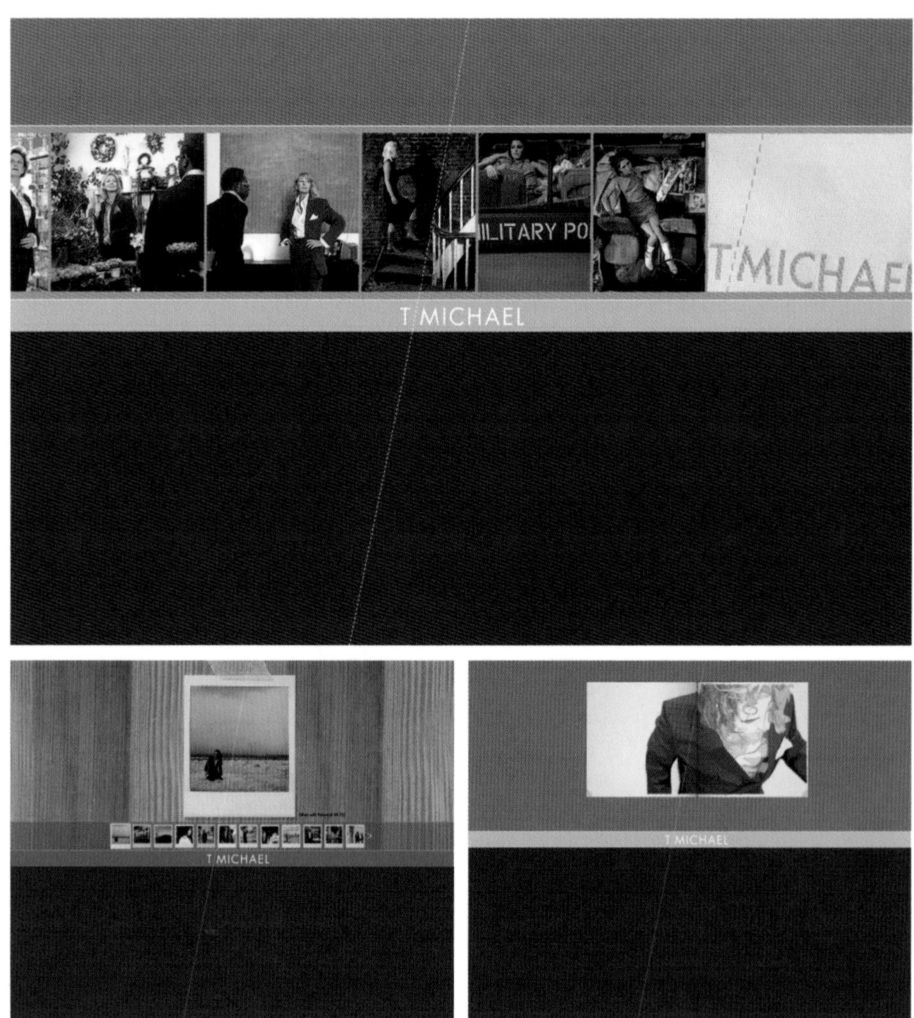

Infos

Design and Programming: Are Bu Vindenes <www.arervindenes.com>. /// **Tools:** Macromedia Flash, html. /// **Cost:** 100 hours.

TIM MITCHELL

USA

www.t-mitchell.com

2004

Concept

To present the Agent's photographers in a classic, clear way with a distinctive design that separates it from it's peers. //// Pour présenter les photographes de cet agent de façon classique et claire et avec un design caractéristique qui le distingue de ses pairs. //// Die Fotografen dieser Agentur werden auf eine klare, klassische Art und Weise präsentiert, wobei jeder Fotograf mit einem unterschiedlichen Design vorgestellt wird und sich somit von seinesgleichen unterscheidet.

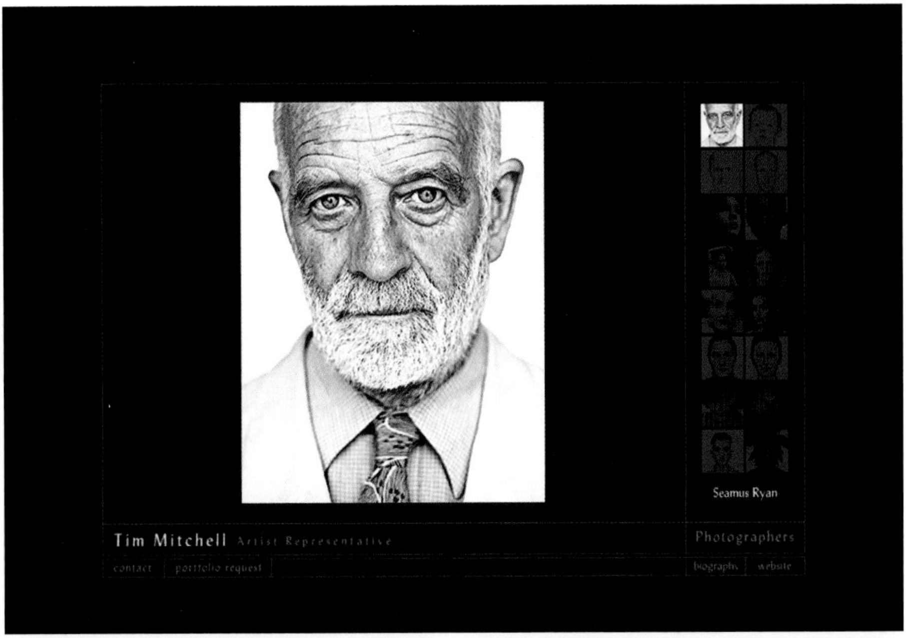

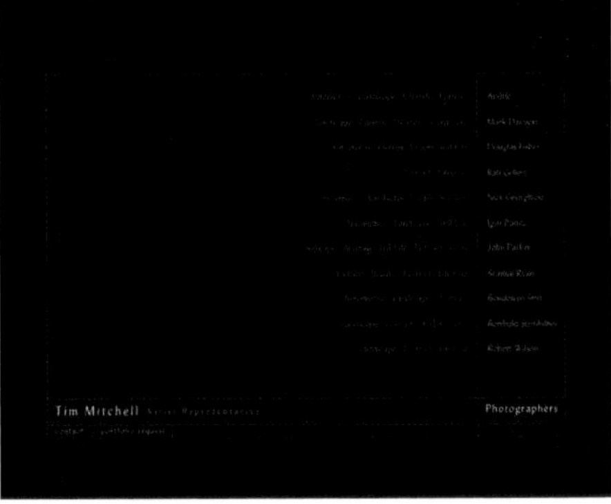

Infos

Design: Chris Christodoulou (Saddington & Baynes) <www.sb-showcase.com>. /// **Programming:** Duncan Hart. /// **Tools:** html, Macromedia Flash.

TOKIDOKI

ITALY

www.tokidoki.it

2002

Concept

Tokidoki started as my personal artistic diary , a place to display the art and soul, a house where the characters live. Now it's a brand. //// Tokidoki a commencé comme mon journal intime artistique, un endroit où je montrais mon art et mon âme, comme une maison où vivaient mes personnages. Maintenant c'est une marque. //// Tokidoki begann als mein ganz persönliches, künstlerisches Tagebuch, ein Platz zur Wiederspieglung von Kunst und Seele, ein Haus, in dem die Buchstaben lebendig sind. Nun ist es ein Markenprodukt.

Infos

DESIGN: Simone Legno (TOKIDOKI). /// **PROGRAMMING:** Emanuele Petrungaro and Simone Legno. /// **AWARDS:** Flash Film Festival New York, Flash Film Festival San Francisco, SXSW Interactive in Austin, FWA. /// **TOOLS:** Adobe Illustrator, Macromedia Flash, xml, php, html, music. /// **COST:** continuous update. /// **MAINTENANCE:** doesn't need maintenance, exept adding news or eventual little updates.

TRAGET SORGE

GERMANY

www.geraldmoll.de

2004

Concept

Not too long loading periods, not too complicated navigation but still fun surfing and finding good content. //// J'ai voulu concilier temps de chargement raisonnables et navigation aisée avec le plaisir de surfer pour chercher du contenu de qualité. //// **Keine zu langen Ladezeiten, keine zu komplizierte Navigation und dennoch viel Spass beim Surfen und Entdecken interessanter Themenbereiche.**

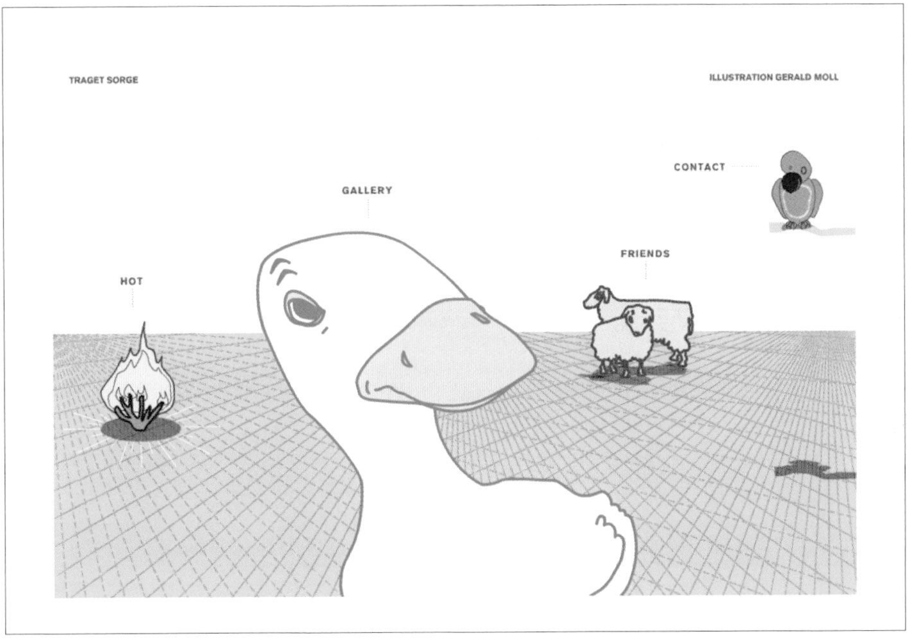

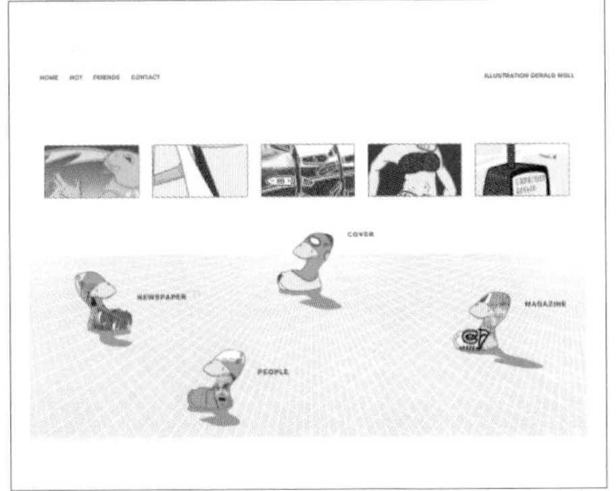

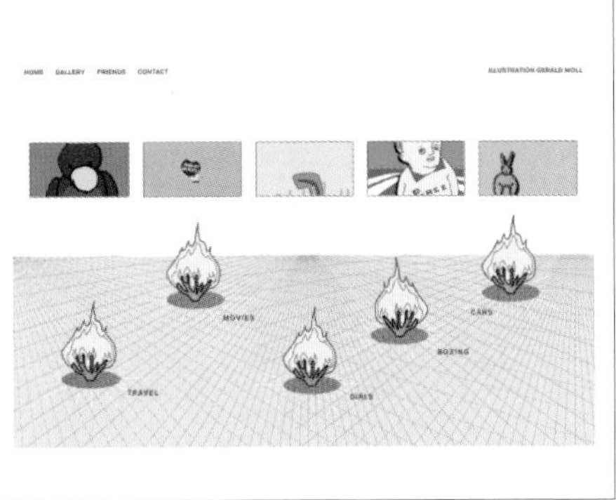

Infos

DESIGN: Gerald Moll (Traget Sorge). /// **PROGRAMMING:** Ralf Boller <ww.platzhalter.com >. /// **TOOLS:** Macromedia Flash, music, Adobe Image Ready, movies. /// **COST:** 111 hours, and a bar of cigarettes. /// **MAINTENANCE:** never counted them.

TRAUT FOTOGRAFEN

GERMANY

www.trautfotografen.com

2004

Concept

Create a quick site for 15 photographers. //// Créer un site rapide pour 15 photographes. //// **Eine schnelle Seite wird mit 15 Fotografen kreiert.**

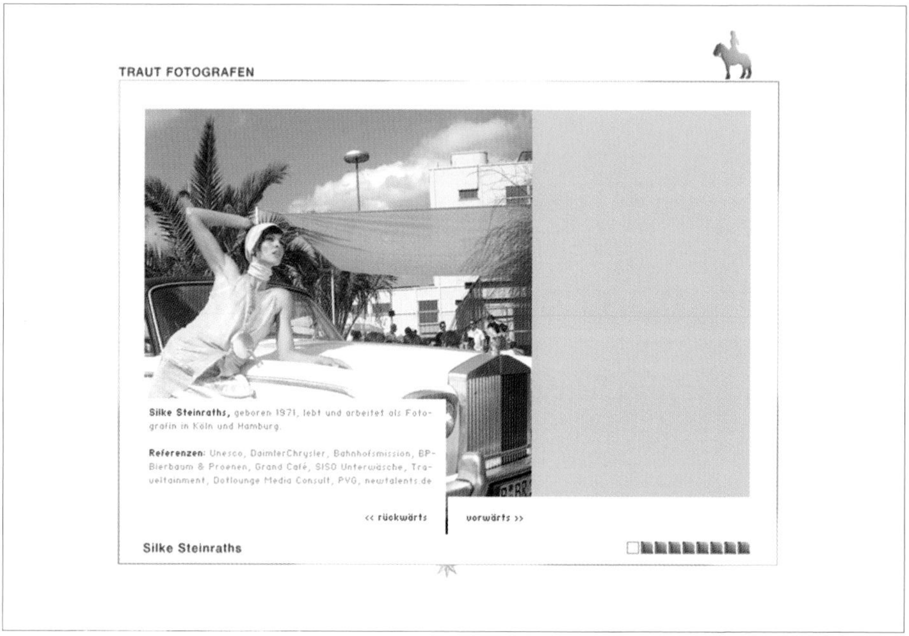

TRAUT FOTOGRAFEN
Silke Steinraths, geboren 1971, lebt und arbeitet als Fotografin in Köln und Hamburg.
Referenzen: Unesco, DaimlerChrysler, Bahnhofsmission, BP-Bierbaum & Proenen, Grand Café, SISO Unterwäsche, Traveltainment, Dotlounge Media Consult, PVG, newtalents.de
<< rückwärts
vorwärts >>
Silke Steinraths

TRAUT FOTOGRAFEN
WILLKOMMEN
FOTOGRAFEN-AUSWAHL

TRAUT FOTOGRAFEN
Dietmar Theis

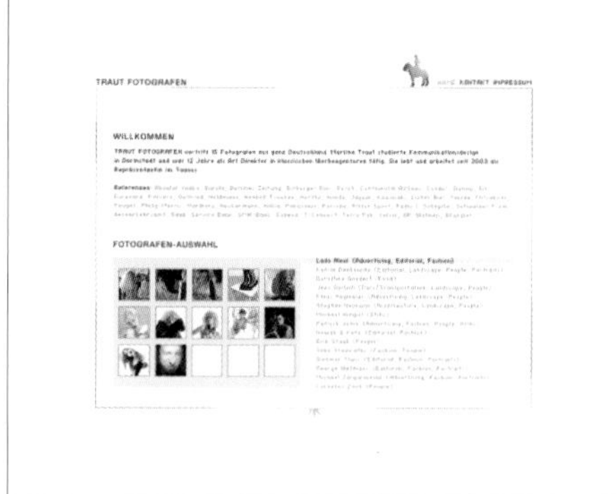

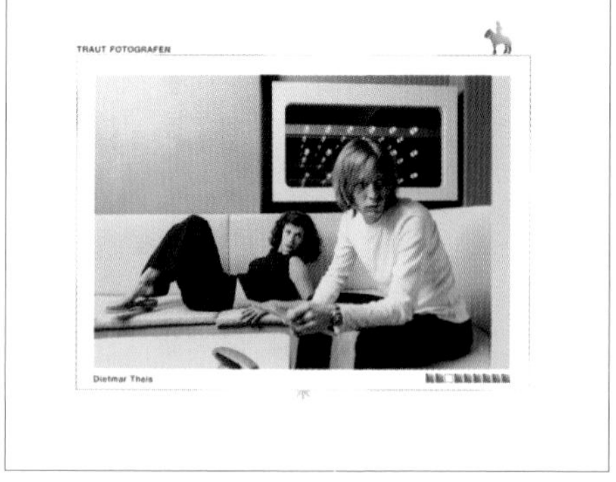

Infos

DESIGN: Struktour <www.struktour.de>. /// **PROGRAMMING:** Katharina Moelle. /// **TOOLS:** Macromedia Flash. /// **COST:** 65 hours /// **MAINTENANCE:** 2 hours per month.

UNREAL

UK

www.unreal-uk.com

2003

Concept

Focusing on the reason the viewer came to the site: to see what we do/say and how to get hold of us. It therefore becomes a simple and accessible platform to achieve this. //// Nous avons essayé de nous concentrer sur la raison qui a amené le visiteur à se rendre sur le site : pour voir ce que nous faisons ou disons et pour nous contacter. Le site est donc devenu une plate-forme simple et accessible. //// Den Fokus auf das Interesse des Besuchers richten: Er möchte wissen, was wir tun und sagen und wie er mit uns in Kontakt treten kann. Genau dies erreichen Sie auf unserer Seite.

Infos

DESIGN: Brian Eagle and Matt Barnes (Unreal). /// **PROGRAMMING:** Matt Barnes. /// **TOOLS:** Macromedia Flash, dhtml. /// **COST:** 20 hours. /// **MAINTENANCE:** 2 hours.

VIAGRAFIK

GERMANY

www.viagrafik.com

2003

Concept

Variety. //// Variété. //// Vielseitigkeit.

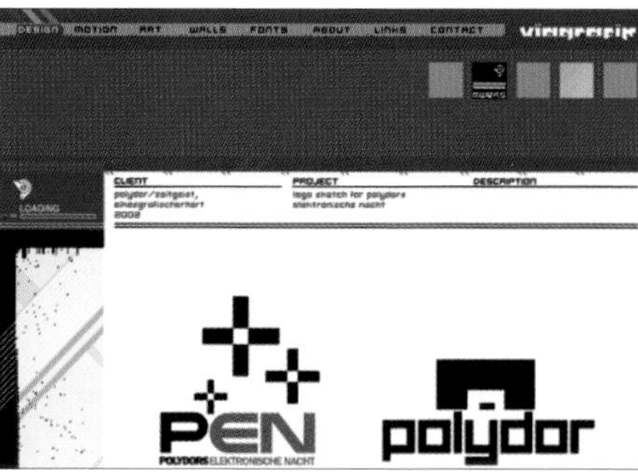

Infos

DESIGN AND PROGRAMMING: Viagrafik. /// **TOOLS:** Macromedia Flash, html, php, JavaScript, music, film. /// **COST:** 120 hours. /// **MAINTENANCE:** 5 hours per month.

URBANSOLDIERZ

SPAIN

www.urbansoldierz.com

2004

Concept

It was inspired by urban designs. //// Ce site a été inspiré par les peintures urbaines. //// **Inspiriert durch urbanes Design.**

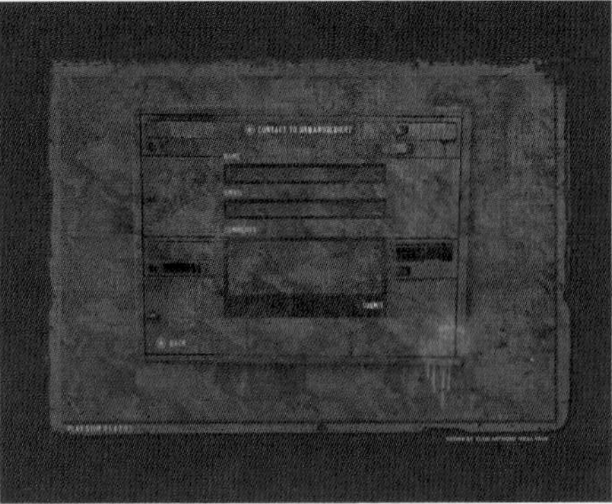

Infos

DESIGN AND PROGRAMMING: Jordi Oró Solé (Medusateam) <www.medusateam.com>. /// **AWARDS:** Plasticpilots. /// **TOOLS:** html, Macromedia Flash, Adobe Photoshop. /// **COST:** 3 months. /// **MAINTENANCE:** 3-5 days per month.

VERNE PHOTOGRAPHY

BELGIUM

www.verne.be

2000

Concept

The navigation system cleverly leads a little online taste while enveloped by a soothing blend of citar/yoga music. //// Le système de navigation véhicule intelligemment un petit goût online tout en étant enveloppé par un mélange apaisant de cithare et de musique de yoga. //// **Das Navigationssystem liefert Ihnen eine intelligente Online-Darbeitung, mit Zitter und Yogamusik unterlegt.**

Infos

DESIGN AND PROGRAMMING: group94 <www.group94.com>. /// **TOOLS:** Macromedia Flash, php. /// **COST:** 3 weeks. /// **MAINTENANCE:** 1-2 days every year.

VIADUCT

UK

www.viaduct.co.uk

2004

Concept

Filtering the users' request down from designers to materials, each search creates a collection of products that can be scrolled as if moving the canvas within the screen. //// En filtrant la requête des utilisateurs parmi les designers, les matériaux, mobilier et les fabricants, chaque recherche aboutit à une gamme de produits que l'on peut dérouler comme si l'on déplaçait le canevas dans l'écran. //// Den Anfragen des Nutzers, von Designern über Materialien, wird durch eine Auswahl an Produkten entgegengekommen, die auf dem Bildschirm wie auf einer Leinwand betrachtet und verschoben werden können.

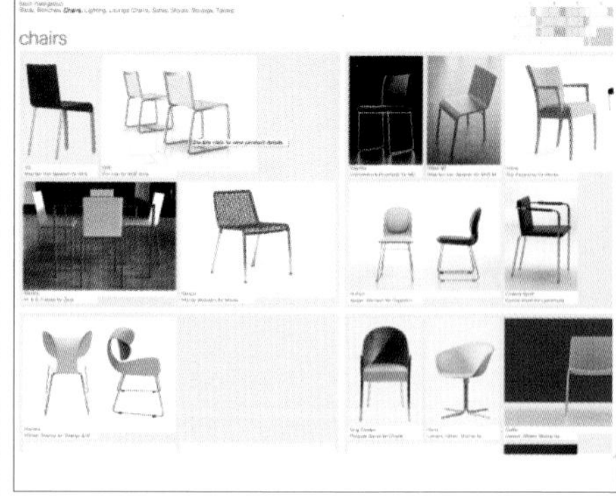

Infos

DESIGN AND PROGRAMMING: de-construct <www.de-construct.com>. /// TOOLS: Macromedia Flash, xml, music. /// COST: 7 weeks.

VIK MUNIZ

USA

www.vikmuniz.net

2004

Concept

The idea was to create a flow of information including texts and images arranged chronologically. This information was intended to be accessible and direct. //// L'idée principale a été de créer un flux d'informations incluant des textes et des images disposés de façon chronologique. Ces informations visaient à être facilement accessibles et directes. //// Das Interesse ist die Darstellung eines Informationflusses sowie chronologischen Bildwerkes. Es soll direkt zugänglich sein.

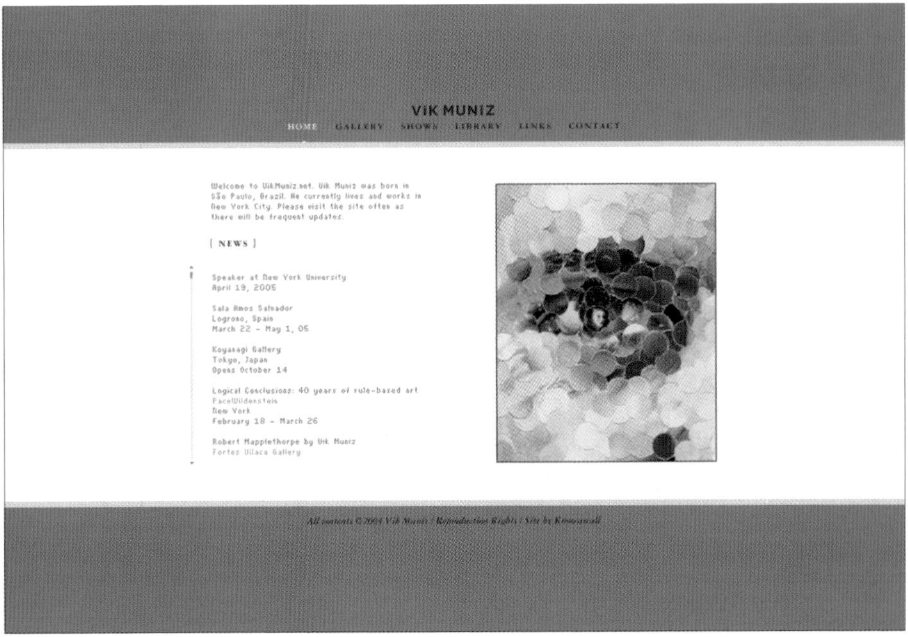

VIK MUNIZ
HOME GALLERY SHOWS LIBRARY LINKS CONTACT
Welcome to VikMuniz.net. Vik Muniz was born in São Paulo, Brazil. He currently lives and works in New York City. Please visit the site often as there will be frequent updates.
[NEWS]
Speaker at New York University
April 19, 2005
Sala Amos Salvador
Logrono, Spain
March 22 - May 1, 05
Koyanagi Gallery
Tokyo, Japan
Opens October 14
Logical Conclusions: 40 years of rule-based art
PaceWildenstein
New York
February 18 - March 26
Robert Mapplethorpe by Vik Muniz
Fortes Vilaca Gallery

VIK MUNIZ
1995
2000
2005
2010

VIK MUNIZ

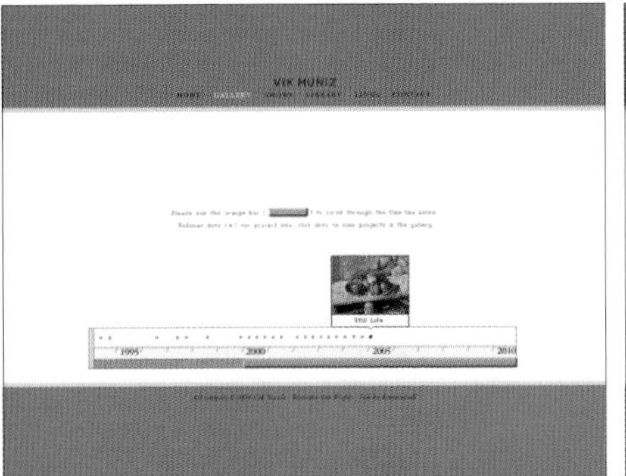

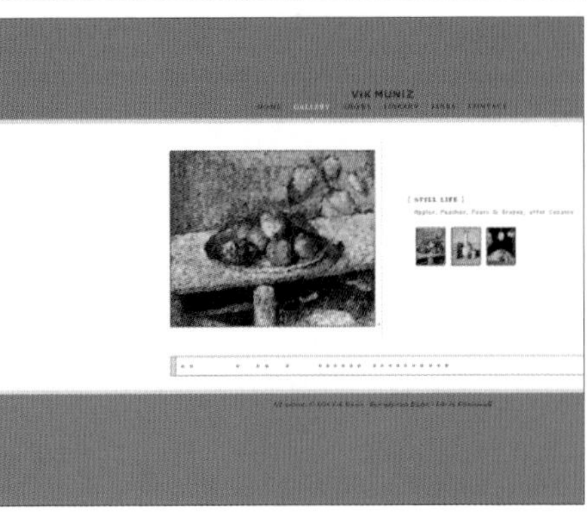

Infos

Design and Programming: Knowawall Design <www.knowawall.com>. /// **Tools:** Macromedia Flash, html. /// **Cost:** 90 hours. /// **Maintenance:** 5 hours per month.

VILLA EUGÉNIE

BELGIUM

www.villaeugenie.com

2003

Concept

Dynamic slideshows and customized multimedia shows are the core of this innovative website. //// Au cœur de ce site Web innovant, vous trouverez des diaporamas dynamiques et des show multimédias personnalisés. //// Diashows voller Dynamik und massgeschneiderte Multimedia-Präsentationen sind das Herzstück dieser Webseite.

villa eugénie

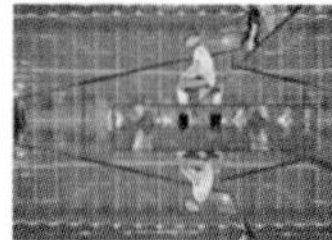

Enter

villa eugénie

Infos

DESIGN: Basedesign <www.basedesign.com>, Tentwelve <www.tentwelve.com> and Villa Eugénie. /// PROGRAMMING: Tentwelve. ///
TOOLS: Macromedia Flash, php, html, MySQL. /// COST: sorry, no idea. /// MAINTENANCE: programmer side: 1 hour per month; client: 50 hours.

VITOR VILELA

BRAZIL

www.vitorvilela.com.br

2004

Concept

Be cool, be funny, be smoothly. //// Soyez cool, soyez drôle. //// Sei cool, sei lustig und ohne Kanten.

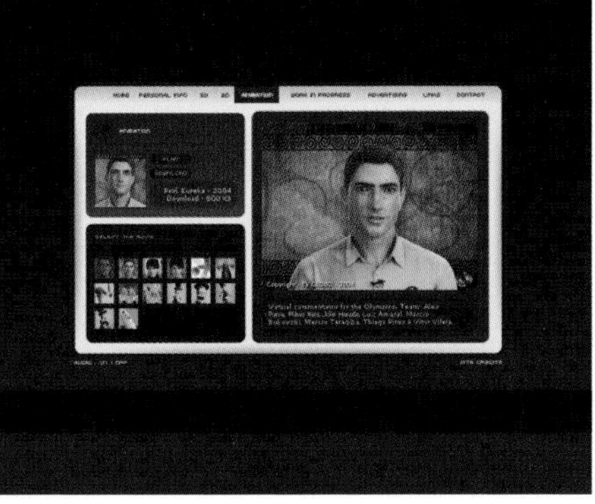

Infos

DESIGN: Vitor Vilela and Marcus Silva (GiantHouse Broadband Team). /// **PROGRAMMING:** Marcus Silva. /// **AWARDS:** FWA (Site of the Day), 4EFX (Site of the Month), Bombshock, Gold Site (Best Animation Flash), Netdiver, TAXI, XsiBase, TINY, and many others. /// **TOOLS:** html, Macromedia Flash, Quicktime, JavaScript. /// **COST:** 4 weeks.

BEN VULKERS PHOTO THE NETHERLANDS

www.vulkersfotografie.nl 2002

Concept

A straightforward navigation, and (minimal) graphic appearance leading to focal point of the pictures. Contents completely manageable by the photographer himself. //// Une navigation simple et un aspect graphique (minimal) menant au cœur des images. Le contenu doit être complètement gérable par le photographe lui-même. //// Die klare Navigation und das reduzierte grafische Erscheinungsbild richten das Augenmerk auf die Bilder. Der Inhalt ist für den Fotografen selbst leicht anzuwenden.

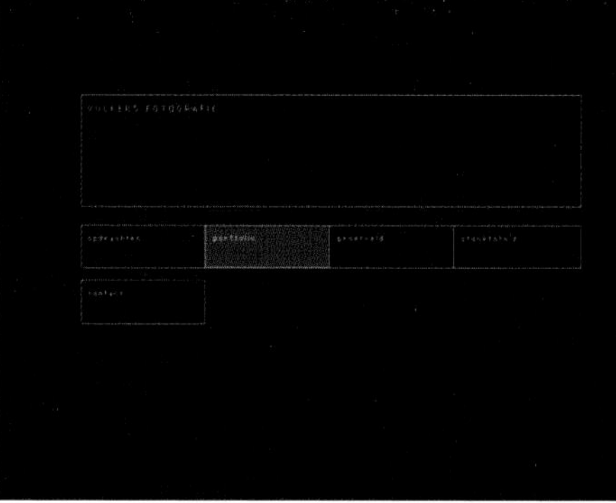

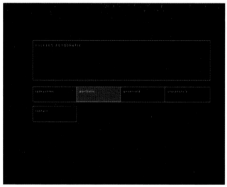

Infos

Design and Programming: Henk Gruppen (Gruppen Grafische Vormgeving). /// **Tools:** Macromedia Flash, plain FTP-based CMS. /// **Cost:** 20-30 hours. /// **Maintenance:** 2 hours per month.

WARREN HEISE ILLUSTRATION CANADA

www.warrenheise.com 2003

Concept

The design is like a collage, with paper scraps, stickers and typewritten text. Neutral colours and subtle animation were used to accentuate the work. //// Ce site est conçu comme un collage de bouts de papier, d'autocollants et de texte imprimé. Des couleurs neutres et une animation subtile ont été employées pour mettre en valeur les travaux. //// Das Design kommt einer Kollage gleich, mit Papierfetzen, Aufklebern und Schreibmaschinentexten versehen. Neutrale Farben und subtile Animation, um der Arbeit zu betonen.

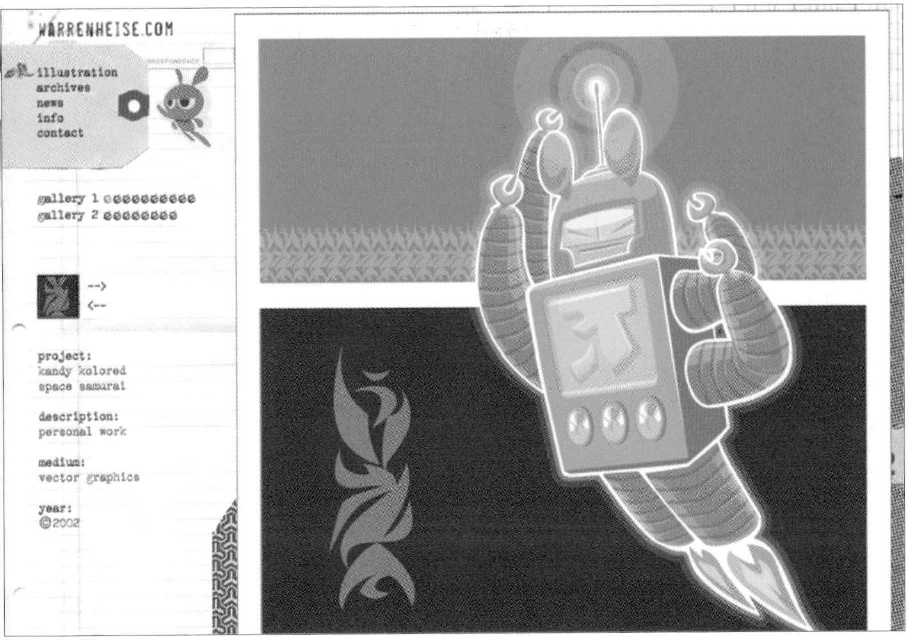

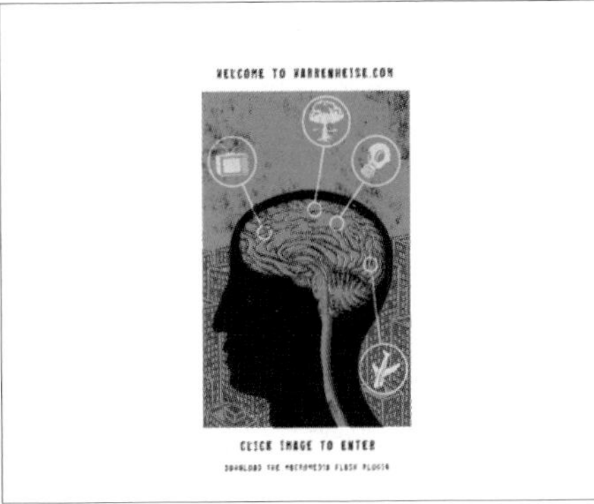

Infos

Design and Programming: Warren Heise. /// **Awards:** Netdiver Design Forte, VisualOrgasmus (Artist of the Month). /// **Tools:** html, Macromedia Flash. /// **Cost:** 150 hours. /// **Maintenance:** 4 hours per month.

WINTHERS WONDER WORLD

FRANCE

www.wintherswonderworld.com

2003

Concept

An interactive site, which invites the viewer to explore Winther's Winderworld. //// Un site interactif qui invite le visiteur à explorer le monde merveilleux de Winther. //// Eine interaktive Seite, die den Besucher dazu einlädt, Winther's Wonderworld zu entdecken.

Infos

Design: Pierre Winther. /// **Programming:** Malthe Sigurdsson. /// **Tools:** Macromedia Flash. /// **Cost:** 180-200 hours. /// **Maintenance:** 10 hours per month.

WISHART DESIGN

AUSTRALIA

www.wishartdesign.com

2002

Concept

Simple, functional and easy-to-navigate. //// Simple, fonctionnel et facile à naviguer. //// Einfach, funktional und mit leichter Navigation.

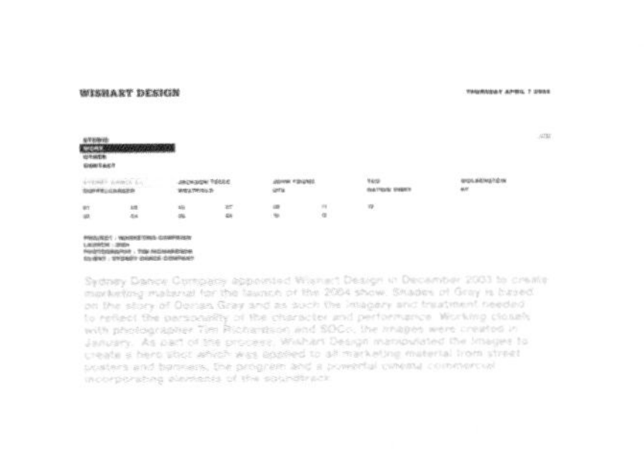

Infos

DESIGN: Zoe Wishart and Dan Ellis (Wishart Design). /// **PROGRAMMING:** Jason Stevenson. /// **TOOLS:** Macromedia Flash. /// **COST:** 3 weeks. /// **MAINTENANCE:** 4 hours per month.

YRMIS

USA

www.yrmis.com

2004

Concept

The clothes are the interface, the interface is the clothes. //// Les vêtements sont l'interface, l'interface est les vêtements. //// Kleidung ist Interface, Interface ist Kleidung.

Infos

DESIGN AND PROGRAMMING: Knowawall Design <www.knowawall.com>. /// **AWARDS:** TINY. /// **TOOLS:** Macromedia Flash, html. /// **COST:** 90 hours. /// **MAINTENANCE:** 2 hours per month.

DEAN ZILLWOOD PHOTO

NEW ZEALAND

www.zillwood.co.nz

2003

Concept

To avoid the sterility that some minimal websites have, we've brought some kiwi music to the site which gives it more flavor and personality. //// Pour éviter la stérilité dont souffrent certains sites Web minimalistes, nous avons agrémenté le site d'un peu de musique kiwi afin de lui donner davantage de saveur et de personnalité. //// Zur Vermeidung einer gewissen Sterilität, die einige minimalistisch gehaltenen Webseiten aufweisen, haben wir dieser Seite eine Art „Kiwimusik" hinzugefügt, eine Möglichkeit, der Website ein Stück weit Persönlichkeit und Geschmack zu vermitteln.

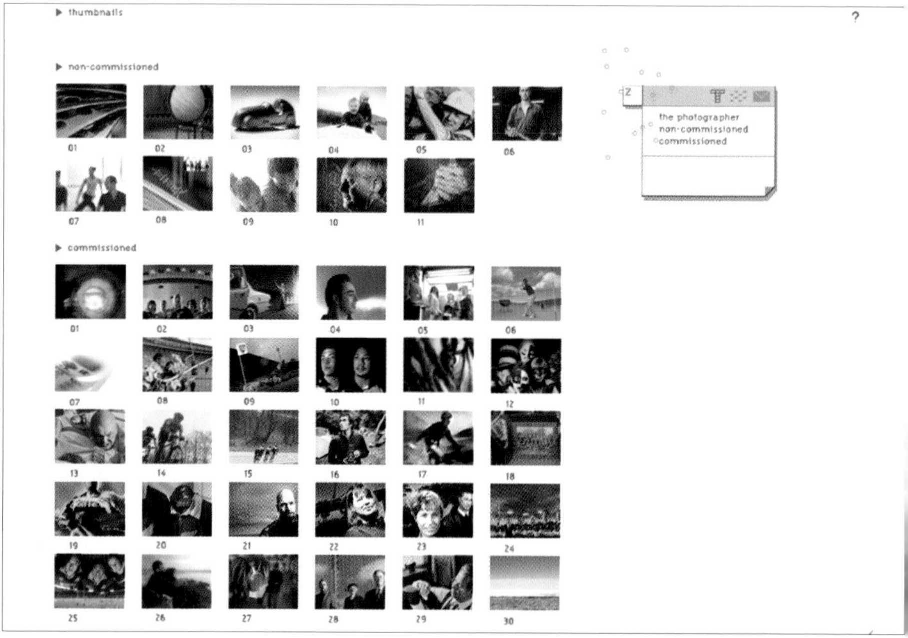

▶ thumbnails

?

▶ non-commissioned

01 02 03 04 05 06

07 08 09 10 11

▶ commissioned

01 02 03 04 05 06

07 08 09 10 11 12

13 14 15 16 17 18

19 20 21 22 23 24

25 26 27 28 29 30

Z

the photographer
non-commissioned
commissioned

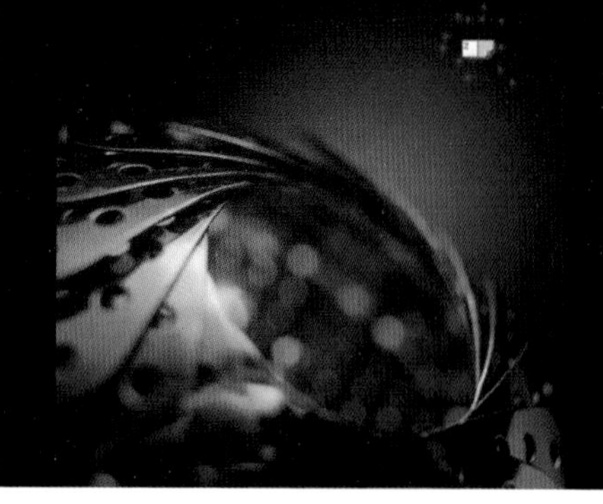

Infos

DESIGN: Native <www.nativehome.com>. /// **PROGRAMMING:** Spencer Levine and Toshi Endo. /// **TOOLS:** Macromedia Flash, html. /// **COST:** 20 hours. /// **MAINTENANCE:** 1 hour per month.

ZTAMPZ

www.ztampz.com

HONG KONG

2004

Concept

"ztamping". //// Complètement timbré ! //// "ztamping" (prägend).

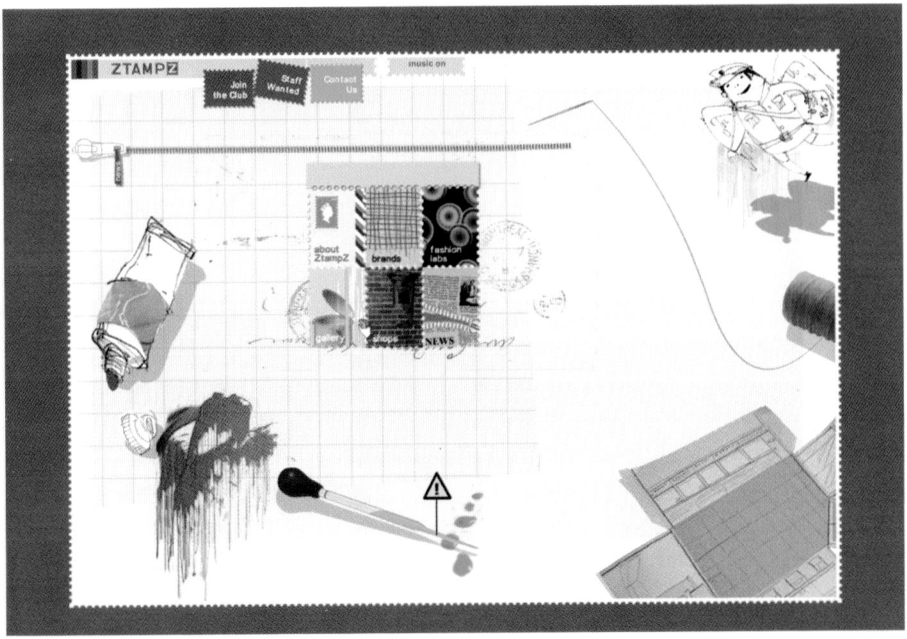

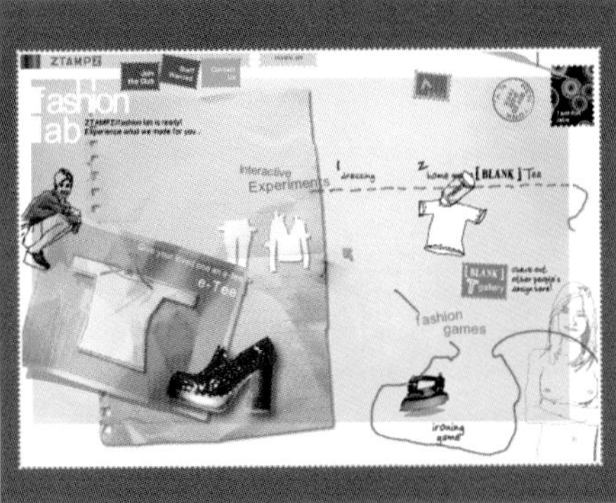

Infos

Design and Programming: rice 5 <www.rice5.com>. /// **Tools:** html, Macromedia Flash, xml. /// **Cost:** 1 month.

CREDITS

TASCHEN is not responsible when web addresses cannot be reached if they are offline or can be viewed just with plug-ins.

I would like to thank all studios and professionals participating in the book, as well all people involved, for their contribution and effort to provide the materials and information that enriched this publication. Also Daniel Siciliano Bretas for his tireless work contacting all the offices we wanted to include in this book and for his work designing and layouting the book. His work has been fundamental to make this a great inspirational series. Moreover, Stefan Klatte for guiding us always in the technical details and helping us making a better job every day.

IMPRINT

Web Design: Portfolios

To stay informed about upcoming **TASCHEN** titles, please request our magazine at **www.taschen.com** or write to **TASCHEN**, Hohenzollernring 53, D–50672 Cologne, Germany, Fax: +49-221-254919. We will be happy to send you a free copy of our magazine which is filled with information about all of our books.

Hohenzollernring 53, D-50672 Köln
www.taschen.com

Design: **Daniel Siciliano Brêtas**
Layout: **Daniel Siciliano Brêtas & Julius Wiedemann**
Production: **Stefan Klatte**

Editor: **Julius Wiedemann**
Assitant-editor: **Daniel Siciliano Brêtas**
French Translation: **Anna Guillerm**
German Translation: **Heike Lohneis**
Spanish Translation: **Raquel Valle**
Italian Translation: **Olivia Papili**
Portuguese Translation: **Ricardo Esteves Correia**

Printed in Italy
ISBN-13: 978-3-8228-4043-6
ISBN-10: 3-8228-4043-2

ICONS